# THE DEAD SEA SCROLLS
# AND THE NEW TESTAMENT

# THE DEAD SEA SCROLLS AND THE NEW TESTAMENT

by

WILLIAM SANFORD LaSOR

WILLIAM B. EERDMANS PUBLISHING COMPANY
GRAND RAPIDS, MICHIGAN

To my wife
BETSY

who has heard more lectures
on the Dead Sea Scrolls
than should be expected
of anyone

this work is lovingly dedicated

אשת־חיל מי ימצא
ורחק מפנינים מכרה

(Proverbs 31:10)

# PREFACE

As I write these words — nearly twenty-five years after the first discovery of the Dead Sea Scrolls — word comes that a sensational book is "sweeping Germany and western Europe." The book, now available in English translation, is *Rabbi J.* by Johannes Lehmann (New York: Stein and Day, 1971). After some delay I was able to get a copy of the book and read it.

It was not necessary to tear up my manuscript, or even to rewrite it. *Rabbi J.* is but the latest in a succession of books that have been written, the authors of which take the Dead Sea Scrolls as their springboard to attempt to show that Jesus Christ was not the originator of Christianity. *Rabbi J.* contains nothing new, in spite of its fanciful claims. There are numerous factual errors, some glaring. The author appears to depend upon about a half-dozen other writers. He attempts to make Zealots out of Essenes. Doubtless he has already convinced thousands of readers, most of whom have read nothing else on the Dead Sea Scrolls and haven't the foggiest notion that many of the claims made by Lehmann were already old in the nineteenth century.

The controversy continues, even though the discovery of the Dead Sea Scrolls is no longer "news." One of the most prolific writers has been Professor André Dupont-Sommer, whose published works on the subject go back to 1949. Many other writers have based their polemical works on his writings, usually without the depth of scholarship that he so richly and clearly displays. In the course of the "battle of the Scrolls," some ungentlemanly charges have been hurled. New Testament scholars have been accused of "boycotting" the Scrolls. Christian and Jewish scholars alike have been accused of refusing to face the facts that the Scrolls have revealed for fear that religious tenets they hold dear will have to be discarded.

5

As a matter of fact, the very scholars who have been thus maligned are the ones who have published books and articles in which comparisons between the Qumran writings and those of the Old and New Testaments have been very carefully and fully explored. The sensationalists have in almost every case been forced to draw their material from the works of scholars whom they accuse of religious bias.

My own studies in the Scrolls go back to about 1952. In the course of my research I accumulated an almost complete list of publications on the Scrolls which I extended to cover the first ten years of Qumraniana (1948-1957). Thereafter I served for five years as the editor of bibliography of *Revue de Qumrân*. As a result, I became very well aware of what was being written on various aspects of the Dead Sea Scrolls. It was obvious that one of the most important areas of study was the relationship between the Dead Sea Scrolls and the New Testament.

Lectureships at the University of Southern California; at the Japan Summer School of Theology near Tokyo; at the Israel-American Institute in Jerusalem, Israel; at Bethel Theological Seminary, St. Paul, Minnesota; and shorter series or single lectures at many other institutions, gave me the opportunity to develop the material which now appears in this book. I wish to express my gratitude to all who by their gracious invitations encouraged me to pursue this research, or who by their penetrating questions helped me to clarify my own thinking on the many subjects that must necessarily be included. The American Association of Theological Schools, by a Sealantic Fellowship, made it possible for me to spend a year in Israel in concentrated study, and I would here record my deep appreciation for this privilege.

In my translations, I have used the standard signs: parentheses to indicate explanatory words (explanation); square brackets to indicate restorations in broken texts [restoration] or unrestored gaps [ . . . ]; angular brackets or carets to indicate that something seems to have fallen out of the text and needs to be supplied <scribal omission>; SMALL CAPS to indicate consonantal text; *italics* to indicate the text as normally vocalized in modern scholarship.

It is no longer possible for me to mention by name all who contributed to this study. I have lost track of the number of times the manuscript has been revised and retyped; I know that the following secretaries typed substantial portions or entire manuscripts: Louise Hoffman, Madrene Bierma, Delores Loeding, Winnie Ladd, Grace Atwood, Charmian Pugh, and Janice Tuttle. My very cordial thanks — and forgive me if I have omitted someone! Proofreading was done and the indexes were prepared by Richard J. Saley, D. Dale Gerard, and Gerald J. Sheppard, faithful students who have become co-workers. Many others have read chapters, criticized statements, raised objections, and interacted with my observations in the ways that are necessary if we are to examine our positions with any kind of objectivity.

Not long after the first Scrolls were published, when addressed with a query that suggested impatience with the progress of Scrolls research, I replied that it would be twenty-five years before we had a clear understanding of the Scrolls. This year marks the twenty-fifth anniversary of their discovery — and I am convinced that there is still much to be done. Friends in France and England tell me that publishers in those lands consider the Dead Sea Scrolls to be a "dead issue." This is not so — as *Rabbi J.* reminds us. Jesus still attracts the attention of men and women, and even if only by time and place, the Dead Sea Scrolls are juxtaposed with the New Testament accounts of Jesus and His followers. Men and women are still asking, "What have the Dead Sea Scrolls done to Jesus and the New Testament?" As long as they ask the question, the subject will be a live issue.

I would like to help answer such questions.

WILLIAM SANFORD LaSOR
*Fuller Theological Seminary*

*Good Friday 1972*

# CONTENTS

## CHAPTER ONE

# WHAT IT'S ALL ABOUT

In late 1947 and early 1948 the Dead Sea Scrolls came to the attention of the scholarly world. Several bundles of what appeared to be dirty rags or decomposed leather, in the hands of an Arab merchant and later in those of an archbishop, created at first more skepticism than excitement. But in a short time all was changed. Scholars who are usually reticent in making sensational statements issued announcements that startled the rest of the scholarly world:

William F. Albright, the dean of American archeologists, called it "the greatest manuscript discovery of modern times."[1] He ventured that it would bid fair "to revolutionize our approach to the beginnings of Christianity,"[2] and that it would "be necessary to rewrite all our New Testament background material."[3]

The French savant, Professor André Dupont-Sommer, wrote, "It is not a single revolution in the study of biblical exegesis . . .; it is . . . a whole cascade of revolutions."[4]

From there on, the statements become more and more startling. Scholars permitted themselves to publish their convictions as settled conclusions and their feelings as established facts. Journalists and sensationalists got into the act, and by quoting extreme statements of some scholars they gave

[1] In the *Biblical Archaeologist* 11 (1948), p. 55.
[2] In W. H. Brownlee, *The Dead Sea Manual of Discipline* (*BASOR Supplementary Studies 10-12*) (New Haven: American Schools of Oriental Research, 1951), p. 58.
[3] From a review in the *New York Herald Tribune* book supplement, July 18, 1954.
[4] A. Dupont-Sommer, *The Dead Sea Scrolls* (Oxford: Blackwell, 1952), p. 96.

an air of authority to writings that should have been dismissed without being taken seriously. Terms such as "the battle of the Scrolls" were used. Charges were hurled. Scholars who were hardly accustomed to such ways of "scholarship" began to exchange opinions in newspaper columns — perhaps it was quicker than waiting for scholarly publications, which sometimes take a year to two before getting around to printing an article. Actually there was little venom in such exchanges of opinion, and I have seen scholars cheerfully chatting, perhaps hand on shoulder, even while their articles or broadcast statements were controverting each other in detached scholarly — or sometimes subscholarly — objectivity.

## The Big Question

"Of all the questions raised by the study of the Dead Sea Scrolls," wrote Professor H. H. Rowley of Manchester University in England, "the most controversial is that of the influence of the Qumran community on the Early Church, and the significance of the Scrolls for the understanding of Christian origins."[5]

It is precisely in this area that the most extreme statements appeared. Dupont-Sommer, who for the first fifteen years was the most prolific writer on the Dead Sea Scrolls, wrote as follows:

> Everything in the Jewish New Covenant heralds and prepares the way for the Christian New Covenant. The Galilean Master, as He is presented to us in the writings of the New Testament, appears in many respects as an astonishing reincarnation of the Teacher of Righteousness. Like the latter, He preached penitence, poverty, humility, love of one's neighbour, chastity. Like him, He prescribed the observance of the Law of Moses, the whole Law, but the Law finished and perfected, thanks to His own revelations. Like him, He was the Elect and the Messiah of God, the Messiah redeemer of the world. Like him, He was the object of the hostility of the priests, the party of the Sadducees. Like him, He was condemned and put to death. Like him, He pronounced judgement on Jerusalem, which was taken and destroyed by the Romans for having put Him to death. Like him, at the end of time, He will be the supreme judge. Like him, He founded a Church whose adher-

---

[5] H. H. Rowley, "The Qumran Sect and Christian Origins," *Bulletin of the John Rylands Library* 44 (1961), p. 119.

ents fervently awaited His glorious return. In the Christian Church, just as in the Essene Church, the essential rite is the sacred meal, whose ministers are the priests. Here and there, at the head of each community, there is the overseer, the "bishop." And the ideal of both Churches is essentially that of unity, communion in love — even going so far as the sharing of common property.

All these similarities — and here I only touch upon the subject — taken together, constitute a very impressive whole.[6]

This view, first expressed in the French edition in 1950, is essentially the same as that which is expressed in his most comprehensive work on the Scrolls:

At the outset of Christianity, there was therefore a new Prophet, a new Messiah, whose existence or originality I, for one, have never dreamt of denying. But, this point established, the documents from Qumran make it plain that the primitive Christian Church was rooted in the Jewish sect of the New Covenant, the Essene sect, to a degree none would have suspected, and that it borrowed from it a large part of its organization, rites, doctrines, "patterns of thought" and its mystical and ethical ideals.[7]

## America Discovers the Scrolls

The American continent, as is often the case in scholarly matters, was slow in discovering the Dead Sea Scrolls. In *The New Yorker* of May, 1955, the gifted journalist and author Edmund Wilson published an article on the Dead Sea Scrolls. *The New Yorker* is not the place one normally looks for scholarly announcements — but the article was sufficiently accurate (and substantiated by some big names), and sufficiently sensational, that America suddenly became aware that something big was happening. In a short time Wilson had revised and enlarged the article and it was published as a book by a major publishing house.[8]

Wilson reported the more sensational statements of Dupont-Sommer and Professor David Flusser of Hebrew University in Jerusalem. This, of course, is good newswriting, but it

6 Dupont-Sommer, *The Dead Sea Scrolls*, p. 99.

7 A. Dupont-Sommer, *The Essene Writings from Qumran* (Oxford: Blackwell, 1961), p. 373.

8 E. Wilson, *The Scrolls from the Dead Sea* (New York: Oxford, 1955; 121 pp.).

is not sound scholarship. In addition, Wilson protested against the fact that many of the men working on the Scrolls had "taken Christian orders or been trained in the rabbinical tradition," and he felt that they may have therefore been "somewhat inhibited in dealing with" the problems which in Wilson's opinion they had ignored.[9] This partial truth overlooks the complementary fact that scholars who have no religious faith are often committed to an antireligious *a priori* which can be at least as effective as a religious *a priori* in reducing objectivity. It also overlooks the fact that by far the overwhelming majority of scholars trained to handle materials such as the Dead Sea Scrolls have gone into the pertinent areas of scholarship because of an interest in the Scriptures or some closely related field. Where was Wilson going to get five hundred — or even fifty — equally well-qualified scholars who had no religious convictions?

Incidentally, when Wilson got around to specifying the men with "prejudices and preconceptions" he named only Professors Solomon Zeitlin and Joseph Reider, of Dropsie College, Philadelphia, and Professor G. R. Driver of Oxford University — and with all due respect to these men and their splendid scholarship, it must be said that they were not representative of the direction in which Dead Sea scholarship was moving even when Wilson wrote his book.

But Wilson's most serious blunder — one that was echoed by others who were not as well versed in the subject or as well trained in journalism as he was — arose from his famous "boycott" charge. "New Testament scholars, it seems," wrote Wilson, "have almost without exception boycotted the whole matter of the scrolls."[10] "These new documents have thus loomed as a menace to a variety of rooted assumptions, from matters of tradition and dogma to hypotheses that are exploits of scholarship."[11]

These were serious charges. They not only attacked scholarly ability or accuracy, they also attacked scholarly integrity. But far worse — they were grossly untrue.

Even when Wilson was gathering the materials for his first draft New Testament scholars had already published many

9 *Ibid.*, p. 98.
10 *Ibid.*, p. 99.
11 *Ibid.*, p. 100.

articles on the very subjects that Wilson thought were being "boycotted." A hasty check of my *Bibliography of the Dead Sea Scrolls 1948-1957* will reveal that through 1954, at least forty-three scholars had published articles on various questions concerning the originality of Jesus Christ, the early Church, doctrinal and organizational points of comparison, and many related subjects. These articles had appeared in French, German, Dutch, Danish, Swedish, Spanish, Italian, Latin, and even a few in English. Many other scholars were at the same time collecting the material, doing the necessary checking and rechecking, and preparing articles and books for publication—articles and books that appeared in 1955 and 1956, when the ink on Wilson's book was not yet dry.

Of course we cannot expect a news reporter to have access to the details of scholarly activities scattered through a dozen and more countries. And we can suppose that to some extent Wilson was only reporting — probably with the necessary amount of distortion or exaggeration that inevitably gets into any account — what others were saying.[12]

Still the fact remains, that when a writer with the stature of Edmund Wilson makes a blanket statement, and when a publisher of established reputation publishes it, there are tens of thousands who will accept what is said as final truth, and no amount of explanation by scholars can alter these convictions. The arena was being filled for the Battle of the Scrolls.

## Enter the Sensationalists

At this point the pulp writers took up their pens to enter the contest. A. Powell Davies published a paperback book that gave the appearance of some degree of respectability.[13]

12 In 1969 Edmund Wilson brought out an updated work, *The Dead Sea Scrolls 1947-1969* (London: W. H. Allen, 1969; 320 pp.). The first 120 pages of this book are "a slightly revised reprinting" of his earlier work (Preface, page not numbered). In the remainder of the work Wilson has at times interacted with statements that had been published concerning his views. There is no willingness, whatever, to retract any of his extreme statements. If anything, his position is even more intransigent — at times notably hostile to scholars who have ventured to differ with his groundless statements. At such points he is neither the objective reporter nor the qualified scholar.

13 A. Powell Davies, *The Meaning of the Dead Sea Scrolls* (New York: New American Library, 1956; 144 pp.).

Charles Francis Potter not long thereafter put out one that from front cover to last word was clearly sensationalism.[14] Davies' work sounded as though his research had consisted of Wilson and perhaps Dupont-Sommer; Potter's book sounded as though he had depended mostly on Davies. Both of them were writing with one obvious purpose: to attack historic Christianity. Neither of them could claim the slightest degree of Qumran scholarship. Under normal circumstances, their publications would not rate the paragraph just devoted to them.

But those of us who were invited to speak at various college and university campuses soon found that the students were learning about the Dead Sea Scrolls only from these paperbacks. I was a member of a panel on which sat also the dean of a prominent law school and an author of historical fiction of world renown; and in the course of the discussion, the only source that these men referred to was Powell Davies' book which lay on the table in front of the moderator of the panel. Up until that moment I had not known of its existence — and I had already published a book on the Scrolls and collected over 1,000 titles for my Bibliography! It was obvious that at the college level, at least, more people were reading Powell Davies than Millar Burrows.

Davies echoed Wilson in stating that "until recently, the Dead Sea Scrolls have been largely ignored by the majority of New Testament scholars."[15] He must have used the same source when he mentioned Zeitlin and Driver as though they were representative of the bulk of scholarship on the date of the Scrolls, and then said, "There were many who hoped that they [the Scrolls] did not go back before the beginnings of Christianity."[16] But he went far beyond Wilson, and may have exceeded the limits of gentlemanly behavior, when he attacked scholars for something bordering on hypocrisy:

> When theological scholars say, as they have recently been saying, that the discovery of the Scrolls has brought them no information that obliges them to revise their view of Christian beginnings . . . it can be *for them* the truth. But they should go on to tell the laity in what sense it is the

[14] C. F. Potter, *The Lost Years of Jesus Revealed* (Greenwich, Conn.: Fawcett, 1958; 128 pp.).
[15] A. P. Davies, *The Meaning of the Dead Sea Scrolls*, p. 23.
[16] *Ibid.*, p. 92.

truth. What they mean, if they would express it more in-formatively is *that they have known for a long time that the traditional view of Christian origins is not supported by history so much as by theology.*[17]

It could easily be pointed out that the scholars he refers to have not published in hieroglyphics or secret writing. Any layman who is interested can find all sorts of publications setting forth in plain language the whole range of scholarly opinion concerning Christian origins. And surely Powell Davies had heard of the long and bitter Fundamentalist-Modernist controversy, one result of which was to let the layman know full well what scholars were saying about Christian origins.

It could also be pointed out that a scholar of recognized stature and unquestionable integrity has written these words:

> It is quite true that as a liberal Protestant I do not share all the beliefs of my more conservative brethren. It is my considered conclusion, however, that if one will go through any of the historic statements of the Christian faith he will find nothing that has been or can be disproved by the Dead Sea Scrolls.[18]

Even today I frequently am asked about statements made by Davies. It is not my purpose, however, to enter the contest with Davies or any other individual who has written on the Scrolls. Davies, Wilson, Dupont-Sommer, and others who write with varying degrees of sensationalism, have served to turn the attention of many, in a way that those of us who plod more weary ways could never have done, to the Dead Sea Scrolls and the problems that have been raised by their discovery. We intend to address ourselves to these problems.

## John Marco Allegro

A different kind of sensationalist is John Marco Allegro. At the time of the first important studies of the Scrolls, Allegro was a young scholar studying under Professor Rowley. Allegro was fortunate enough to have the time and opportunity to serve on the international team of scholars who worked on the scrolls and fragments from the Qumran caves, and his scholarly ability was quickly apparent.

[17] *Ibid.*, p. 84; italics his.
[18] Millar Burrows, *More Light on the Dead Sea Scrolls* (New York: Viking, 1958), p. 39.

Early in 1956, Allegro broadcast some fantastic claims over BBC to the effect that the crucifixion of the Teacher of Righteousness was reported in a fragment of the Scrolls. The five remaining members of the international team immediately repudiated his claim in a letter which was published in the March 16, 1956, issue of the London *Times*. The letter was signed by R. de Vaux, J. T. Milik, P. Skehan, J. Starcky, and J. Strugnell — all prominent scholars whose names are well known to everyone working with the Dead Sea Scrolls. Even Allegro's former teacher denied Allegro's claims.[19]

Allegro, however, was not silenced by these scholarly rebukes. He went on to greater sensationalism. Violating an agreement which gave first publication rights for the Copper Scroll (cu3Q15) to another scholar, Allegro rushed his own "first edition" into print. He was again rebuked. It is possible that he lost some of his privileges at that time; at any event, he made claims that there was an attempt to hold back certain publications. (I have never heard any other scholars speak of any restraint imposed on them in working on the Scrolls.) That Volume V of *Discoveries in the Judaean Desert of Jordan*[20] was published under his name would seem to belie his claim.

In the August, 1966, issue of *Harper's Magazine*, Allegro spun a story of falsifications, distortions, and innuendoes, the total effect of which was to belittle Jesus Christ, to discredit the New Testament, and to charge nearly all who have published anything on the Dead Sea Scrolls with being so biased that their works are not reliable. He said, "Scholars are afraid of what the scrolls reveal," and claimed that "the main message of the scrolls remains hidden nearly twenty years after their discovery." Echoing Edmund Wilson, he maintained that New Testament scholars boycotted the Scrolls, and complained that most of the scholars working on the Scrolls had "taken Christian orders or been trained in the rabbinical tradition." In effect suggesting that he alone was capable of giving an unbiased report, since he had no religious commitment, he made a plea for money, so that "a new generation of uncommitted scholars" might have "the means of probing the signifi-

[19] H. H. Rowley, *The Dead Sea Scrolls and the New Testament* (London: S.P.C.K., 1957), p. 6.

[20] *Qumran Cave 4, I*, ed. John M. Allegro (Oxford: Clarendon, 1968; 186 pp.).

cance [of the Scrolls] without fear or favor, undeterred by religious or academic pressure."[21]

A number of scholars, including myself, immediately protested to *Harper's Magazine* for publishing such a completely distorted and unscholarly article. The magazine refused to print all but one of these statements.

Allegro went on to more fantastic theories, including his work on the "sacred mushroom" which seeks to propound the common denominator of all religions.[22]

We shall make no effort to guess the motivation of this young scholar. Certainly he was a scholar. Certainly he was aware that he had set himself in opposition to all but a very, very few of the nearly 1,000 scholars who have published on the Scrolls. Most of these men did (and do) have a religious commitment, as he claimed. But by what logic can Allegro maintain that a man "without commitment" is a more objective scholar than a man with commitment to a religious vocation? It is a popular fallacy today, but false nevertheless, that a professor who has rejected a religious commitment is more reliable and "objective" in religious matters than one who has religious faith. G. R. Driver rightly speaks of this as a "strange delusion," which he further describes in these words:

> . . . that agnosticism *per se* confers a lack of bias, an absolute impartiality unattainable by other men, and that "only an independent scholar, not committed to any religion" can be trusted to give an unbiased and independent opinion where questions of religion are involved. . . . Those who hold such views are apparently unaware that unbelief is as much a *praejudicium* as belief, that suspended judgment may be due to nothing else than sloth, and that the *tabula rasa* of a mind which they admire as a guarantee of disinterested scholarship can hardly exist in a normal man. . . .[23]

21 J. M. Allegro, "The Untold Story of the Dead Sea Scrolls," *Harper's Magazine* (August 1966), pp. 46-54.

22 J. M. Allegro, *The Sacred Mushroom and the Cross. A Study of the Nature and Origins of Christianity Within the Fertility Cults of the Ancient Near East* (Garden City, N.Y.: Doubleday, 1970; 349 pp.). This work is an almost unbelievable mixture of fantasy and scholarship, built on linguistic "equivalents" that deny all scientific philological rules and pervaded by an emphasis on the sex organs that borders on the neurotic. For a calmly written review, see W. H. C. Frend, "Worshipping the Red Mushroom," *The New York Review of Books* 15,11 (Dec. 17, 1970), pp. 12-14.

23 G. R. Driver, *The Judaean Scrolls. The Problem and a Solution* (Oxford: Blackwell, 1965), p. 3.

## What We Want to Do, and How

Scholars sometimes arrive at different results or conclusions even though they have used exactly the same materials. This does not mean that someone has falsified his work. And it certainly does not mean that he is less competent in his field of specialization. Often it is simply a matter of method, for the method a man uses may possibly provide the result he desires.

If, for example, I wish to demonstrate a close similarity between the Dead Sea Scrolls and the New Testament, I can go through both bodies of literature and select the statements that are most similar. The results will be impressive.

On the other hand, if I wish to demonstrate that there is really no similarity between these two religious writings, then I can list all of the striking differences. Again the results will be impressive.

Of course, it is not quite so simple. No true scholar sets out to prove a theory. Rather, he sets out in search of truth. But in the course of the search he develops a theory, and then he attempts to test that theory. In so doing he inclines to select material that proves the theory, and only by extraordinary effort will he impose the controls that are necessary to keep the results from being one-sided. Seldom are we human beings so completely objective that we can give as much weight to that which opposes our theory as we give to that which supports it.

To complicate the matter still further, no scholar comes to a new area of research with a completely blank mind. He has a number of unsolved problems lying around; he has accumulated a heterogeneous mass of material in the course of study; and he always has a few matters that he could solve if he could only find one or two more facts. Along comes a fantastic discovery such as the Dead Sea Scrolls, and the scholar pokes around the material hoping to find parts that will piece out the unfinished jigsaw puzzles in his mind.

This is, of course, legitimate scholarship. Someone once pointed out to me that it is not vast knowledge of a single field that produces original scholarship: it is great knowledge of two or more fields. One scholar combines Zoroastrianism and Qumranism; another Gnosticism and Qumranism; another Rabbinical Literature and Qumran Literature. From such scholars come brilliant ideas. But once again, the necessity for rigid controls must be emphasized; otherwise we get a "proof-text" methodology that simply looks for statements to prove a theory. At the same time, those of us who are not expert in the areas under discussion may be swept off our feet by the brilliance of ideas that we are not qualified to test.

A few years ago a "world-shaking" book appeared. Its scholarship was beyond comprehension, and it "solved" most of the problems that others had been unable to solve in many years. It received extravagant reviews. Then geologists could be overheard saying, "This man has colossal knowledge of many fields; but, of course, he doesn't seem to know much about geology." Assyriologists were commenting on his tremendous grasp of knowledge, while confessing that he was disappointing in Assyriology. Astronomers felt the same way about his astronomy. And finally, when his publishers refused to allow their name to be used on his book any longer, it became obvious that the problems were still around to be solved.

Sometimes we look at the staggering mass of scholarship that has been produced since the Dead Sea Scrolls were discovered, and we begin to wonder how anyone can have sufficient knowledge to evaluate objectively all the claims and counter-claims that have been made.

The matter of methodology, therefore, becomes increasingly important. It is absolutely essential that the material be presented in such a way that theories will have a minimum of distorting effect. How can this best be done?

The best method, in my opinion, is *not* that of listing similarities and differences. There is already an anterior step hidden in that method, namely, the selection of the points under comparison.

Rather, it is better to go through the two bodies of material — the Dead Sea Scrolls and the New Testament — and set down as much of the relevant material as possible concerning the two movements.

First, then, I shall attempt to describe in detail, from the sources, the Qumran Community, its beliefs, and its Teacher of Righteousness. Whenever it seems advisable, in order to use the context as a control, I shall quote extensively from the sources, rather than merely giving the reference or quoting a few words. I shall then attempt to do same with the New

Testament. After that I shall attempt to point up comparisons and differences — but I shall try to leave the reader to form his own opinions from what I hope will be a reasonable and reliable basis.

It is admitted that there is still an element of subjectivity. After all, I am not merely reprinting the Dead Sea Scrolls and the New Testament; rather, I am doing editorial work, arranging, classifying, selecting, etc. Moreover, I am offering my own translations of the portions quoted — for such extensive quotation from other authors would involve all sorts of copyright problems — and translators, too, are only human. But with these handicaps, it is still my conviction that there is less subjectivity in this methodology than in any other I have been able to devise.

The objection might be made that by using this methodology I have deliberately obscured some of the similarities that have been pointed out by other scholars. I shall therefore attempt to give all such points of comparison that have not already been noted in the method we are following, after we have gone through the two bodies of material.

Another basic point of methodology should be stated. To do this, I shall quote from Dupont-Sommer, with whose conclusions I may frequently be in disagreement. He says:

> The golden rule for the interpretation of these Essene texts must undoubtedly be the following: read the texts exactly as they stand; feel no surprise at any of their revelations; do not try to align them with doctrines current in Judaism . . .
> History is essentially constructed upon texts.[24]

It is my opinion that there has been entirely too much disregard of the texts as they stand. Philo, Josephus, and Pliny the Elder are being "interpreted" or "corrected" in the light of the Qumran materials. The Qumran materials are being interpreted in the light of Josephus and others, and also in the light of the New Testament. The New Testament is being reinterpreted in the light of the Qumran materials. And so it goes, around the circle.

Now, I have no objection to critical study of texts. Moreover, our ultimate goal certainly is to be able to understand

24 Dupont-Sommer, *The Essene Writings from Qumran*, pp. 15, 42.

each of these bodies of material better in the light of the others. But the trouble is that sometimes the interpreting has come first, and then the comparison is made on the basis of the reworked product.

Let me give an example, chosen because it is much more obvious than some of the subtle ones of the same nature. Powell Davies, speaking of the meals of the Qumran sect, says (with no textual basis whatever) that the priest may have said, when blessing the bread, "This is my body." Then Davies says that the members of the sect may have thought of the wine as the blood of the Messiah. Then he concludes, "This, then, was the Essenic sacred meal, so close as to be almost identical with the sacred meal of the early Christians."[25] But notice that he first read into Qumran what he found in the New Testament, and then he found that the Qumran document resembled the New Testament. This is circular logic of the most flagrant sort.

Or take another example of this type of methodology. Dupont-Sommer is examining the thesis that the Wicked Priest was Hyrcanus II and the Teacher of Righteousness was Onias the Just. The theory, he points out, has some difficulties inasmuch as "the place and method of execution of this Onias the Just, as reported by Josephus, do not correspond to the information which the biblical *Commentaries* from Qumran seem to give of the tragic end of the Teacher of Righteousness." (It should be added at this point that most scholars do not agree that the information concerning the tragic end of the Teacher is clear either as to place or as to method.) Then Dupont-Sommer leaps to this fantastic statement: "Is it possible that the Josephus account refers to a partly legendary tradition substituted for the historically more exact tradition reflected in the Qumran documents?"[26]

There is practically no historical material in the Qumran documents so far published: no names beyond dispute, no places beyond dispute, no dates except those based on hypothecated identifications of persons. In fact, there is nothing in the Qumran documents that even resembles historical writing. Josephus, for all his faults, was a historian and he did a reasonably good job. On the basis of Josephus, Dupont-Sommer

[25] A. P. Davies, *The Meaning of the Dead Sea Scrolls*, pp. 100f.
[26] Dupont-Sommer, *The Essene Writings from Qumran*, p. 359 n. 3.

would have us arrive at a possible identification of the Wicked Priest and the Teacher of Righteousness in the Dead Sea Scrolls. Then, on the basis of the Scrolls as interpreted by Josephus we are to relegate Josephus' account to the realm of "partly legendary tradition" and replace it with the Qumran material as reconstructed by Dupont-Sommer. By no stretch of definition can this be called historical method!

There is only one historical method, and Dupont-Sommer has himself defined it: "History is essentially constructed upon texts." "Read the texts exactly as they stand."

I shall therefore set down the Qumran materials, without first interpreting them in the light of Josephus, or the New Testament, or any other non-Qumran materials. To avoid the criticism that I have ignored what is written of the Essenes, I shall present the pertinent material from Philo, Josephus, and Pliny the Elder. I shall then present the material from the New Testament, as it stands in the text.

Due allowance will be given to critical methodology so far as texts are concerned, but I rule out as a violation of the historical method any prior alteration of texts based on non-textual hypotheses.

When we have worked through this material, I shall attempt to gather together the remaining points that have not been included. Conclusions will be held to a minimum, for our purpose is to present the evidence. False conclusions based on faulty logic or improper handling of the text will be pointed out, not in order to coerce the reader, but to try to clarify the problems.

Pointed difference of opinion and criticism is of course not to be looked upon as personal. Professor Dupont-Sommer, for example, I consider to be an honored colleague, a gifted scholar, and a friend of some years. I shall have occasion more than once to disagree with him quite markedly. He will doubtless disagree with me quite as positively. That is scholarship, and if any of us is not willing to have his methods and conclusions challenged and disputed, then he should not publish. I mention this not for the sake of scholars, who thoroughly understand the principle; I mention it because the layman often fails to understand what is going on. Sometimes he refers to this type of discussion as "argument." He thinks that scholars with "liberal" or "radical" views must have hidden motives. Our problem is not with hidden motives, but with *a priori* convictions — and we all have them. Or else we have hypotheses that we have lived with for so long that we have come to think of them as established facts. It is the task of scholarship to discover such things, to challenge them, and so far as possible to correct them.

## Where Does It Lead Us?

It should be understood that we wish to go wherever the facts lead us. We have nothing to fear from truth; only ignorance can hurt us.

We have already read a long passage from Dupont-Sommer comparing Qumran and Christianity. Supposing everything he says is true, where does that lead us? Strack and Billerbeck were able to fill four huge volumes with parallels between the Gospels and the Talmud and Midrash. Christianity was not thereby destroyed; rather it was enriched. The alleged parallels between the Dead Sea Scrolls and the entire New Testament fill only one rather modest-size volume — and even then only with considerable repetition and wandering into by-paths.

We may have some difficulties with our convictions and interpretations. New truths always challenge old opinions. But new truths never destroy old truths; they merely separate truth from falsehood.

We are interested only in following truth. But we are not willing to accept a statement as true simply because it is novel. There is no virtue in being clever, if by being clever we are merely being wrong. Some years ago a scholar, who had just published a very controversial theory, said to me, "It's either an awfully good theory, or an awfully bad one." The sages long ago learned that truth is generally somewhere near the golden mean. Yet even the golden mean can sometimes be misleading: it is better to listen to the time signals than to take an average reading of the clocks in your house. But however we accomplish it, we desire to find the truth.

With this as our purpose, and with the methodology we have outlined, we turn to our subject.

CHAPTER TWO

# WHAT ARE THE DEAD SEA SCROLLS?

Before we go further with our discussion it is necessary to set down the facts about the Dead Sea Scrolls, their discovery, their contents, and other descriptive data. The story has been told many times, and there is a temptation to dismiss it by referring the reader to any of several good books and articles. However, to make this book as complete as possible within the limits of its declared purpose, and for the sake of those who have not previously read the story, we shall include the essential facts.

## The First Dead Sea Scrolls

The first "Dead Sea Scrolls" were brought to the attention of prospective buyers in 1947. Presumably they were found early that year, although there is a vague story, unconfirmed, that they were found as early as 1945. The details differ in various accounts. Two shepherds of the Ta'âmira tribe — Muḥammad eḏ-Ḏi'b and Aḥmad Muḥammed — sought shelter in a cave, or threw a stone into a cave to chase out a straying goat, or — but what does it matter? The story has been told and retold so many times that there is little hope of getting absolute accuracy at this late date. Essential details of the story are not denied by variations in the unessential parts: this is a basic law of testimony. The Bedouin shepherds found a number of clay jars, and in or near the jars a number of bundles of what appeared to be rags but turned out to be manuscripts.

The Bedouin attempted to sell their find. The scrolls passed into the hands of a merchant, Khalîl Iskandar Shahîn, familiarly known as Kando. Other intermediaries were doubtless in the transaction, but at last the scrolls came into the possession of Mar Athanasius Y. Samuel, then-Metropolitan of St. Mark's Syrian Orthodox Convent in Jerusalem, who in turn attempted to sell the scrolls to scholars. An occasional writer will confess that he saw one or more of the scrolls and declined to purchase out of fear of fraud. At last, some of the scrolls were bought by Eleazar L. Sukenik of the Hebrew University on November 29, 1947. Others were photographed by John C. Trever at the American School of Oriental Research in Jerusalem, after he had seen them on February 18, 1948. This second group ultimately came into the possession of the Hebrew University in 1954, hence all of the original find of Scrolls (to the best of our knowledge — rumors of a missing scroll or scrolls are heard from time to time) are in the Shrine of the Book in the Hebrew University, Jerusalem.[1]

The original Scrolls were promptly published and numerous editions and translations are available, in English and in several other languages. The list, with a brief description of each, is as follows:

The *St. Mark's Monastery Isaiah Scroll* (1QIs[a]).[2] This is a complete copy of Isaiah, consisting of fifty-four columns of writing on seventeen sheets of leather sewn into a scroll approximately 24 feet long, and varying in width from about $9\frac{1}{2}$ to $10\frac{1}{2}$ inches. The writing is placed on the scroll with the long dimension of the scroll horizontal, as is customary, and the

[1] For first-hand accounts, see John C. Trever, *The Untold Story of Qumran* (Westwood, N.J.: Revell, 1965); Mar Athanasius Yeshue Samuel, *Treasure of Qumran: My Story of the Dead Sea Scrolls* (Philadelphia: Westminster, 1966); and Yigael Yadin, *The Message of the Scrolls* (New York: Simon and Schuster, 1957) — the last named contains some details of the part played by Yadin's father, E. L. Sukenik. For a nearly complete list of the early reports, see W. S. LaSor, *Bibliography of the Dead Sea Scrolls 1948-1957* (Pasadena, Calif.: Fuller Theological Seminary Library, 1958), §§1000-1159, 1650-1688, particularly those entries marked with asterisks.

[2] The system of *sigla* used to identify the Scrolls is as follows: first, the provenance (1Q = Cave 1 Qumran, 2Q = Cave 2 Qumran, C = Cairo, etc.); second, the document (Is=Isaiah; S=*sérek;* pHab=*pésher* [commentary] on Habakkuk, etc.); third, the exemplar (a = first copy found, b = second, etc.). This system has been adopted all but universally by scholars working in the area of study.

sheets have been scribed (or ruled) horizontally with the writing hanging from the lines. Writing in Hebrew is from right to left, hence the columns have straight right-hand margins. The number of lines per column varies from 28 to 32, and the number of columns per sheet of leather varies from two to four. The scribe made numerous errors, some of which he himself corrected, some of which were corrected in other handwriting. Paragraph divisions correspond almost exactly to those in the modern Hebrew Bible. There is no noticeable separation between chapter 39 and chapter 40 (the division between "First Isaiah" and "Second Isaiah"), but there is a noticeable space between chapters 33 and 34.

The *Hebrew University Isaiah Scroll* (1QIs^b). The second scroll is a poorly preserved copy of Isaiah containing portions of chapters 10, 13, 16, 19-30, and 35-66. The text of this manuscript is nearer to the Masoretic text — the traditional Hebrew text in use today — than is the first Isaiah scroll from Qumran; this is particularly so in spelling.

The *Habakkuk Commentary* (1QpHab). This scroll contains the text of chapters 1 and 2 of Habakkuk with interspersed "interpretations" — actually the word *pésher* means something like "interpretation, application, and commentary."[3] The scroll was made of two strips of leather sewn end to end, probably about five feet long (some of the beginning is now missing) and $7\frac{1}{4}$ inches wide (from one to two inches irregularly is missing along the bottom edge), and is ruled both horizontally (lines) and vertically (columns). The writing is very neat and legible, and the divine name, YHWH ("Jehovah"), is always written in the ancient "Phoenician" script. The comments are important for historical purposes, although the language is enigmatic, and for religious purposes, showing how the Sect handled the Scriptures.

The *Manual of Discipline* (1QS; S = *sérek,* "rule, order"). One of the most important of all the discoveries, this scroll was originally longer; at present, eleven columns remain, about $6\frac{1}{2}$ feet long and ten inches wide, formed by sewing together five pieces of leather. The writing shows many corrections, erasures, and additions, and seems to have had much use — which is in keeping with its contents, for this scroll is in the nature of a book of rules, describing admission into and life

---

[3] Yigael Yadin, *The Message of the Scrolls,* p. 90.

in the Community. From it we are able to reconstruct much of what we know about the Qumran Sect.

The *Thanksgiving Hymns* (1QH; H = *hôdāyôt*, "thanksgivings"). These "hymns" or liturgical compositions, much in the style of the Biblical Psalms, were doubtless the devotional hymns of the Community. Originally there were two parts, one consisting of three pieces of leather, each of four columns of writing and about 39 lines per column, the other consisting of about seventy fragments of varying sizes. It is estimated that the original scroll was at least ten feet long and about 12 inches wide. Two scribes can be distinguished, one who wrote the first ten and a half columns in beautiful script, and a second who wrote the balance in a markedly inferior kind of handwriting. The Hymns reveal rich insights into the religious and spiritual life of the Community.

The *Order of Warfare* (1QM; M = *milḥāmā*, "war"), also known as the *War of the Sons of Light against the Sons of Darkness*, and the *War Scroll*. This work is unlike anything ever found in Jewish or Christian writings. It describes a war, real or spiritual, between the tribes of Levi, Judah, and Benjamin, on the one hand, and the Ammonites, Moabites, Edomites, and others, on the other hand. The scroll consists of five sheets of leather, nearly ten feet in length and six inches wide, containing twenty columns of text, averaging about twenty lines to a page. The bottom edge of the scroll had decomposed. The columns were ruled both horizontally and vertically, and the scribe wrote beautifully, hanging his letters, as was the custom, from the line.[4] The contents are important for at least two reasons: from this document we learn much of military life in the Jewish armies of the period; from it we also learn some of the details of the great and final war which ends the dominion of "Belial" and brings victory to the Sons of Light.

The *Genesis Apocryphon* (1QApGen). This scroll was badly decomposed and at first could not be unrolled. On the

---

[4] Because the *right* margins are straight, whereas we are accustomed to straight left-hand margins, and also because the writing hangs from the line, whereas we are accustomed to writing above the line, the illustrations of the Dead Sea Scrolls are sometimes printed upside down in modern books. I have found publishers reluctant to believe that they could be mistaken, even though any student of Hebrew script can readily recognize that the writing is upside down.

basis of a detached fragment it was tentatively called the *Lamech Scroll,* and the earlier writings refer to it as such. The scroll was subsequently unrolled with great difficulty, and although much of it was almost useless, the innermost portion was well preserved. Written in Aramaic, it tells in an apocryphal manner the story of the birth of Noah, and the story of Abraham and Sarah from Genesis 12—15. Much legendary material, some of it fantastic, has been added to the Biblical account, and the style is reminiscent of Jubilees and Enoch. In addition to the legends which are preserved in the scroll, several details of geography have been recorded in the account of the battle of the kings (Gen. 14). From a linguistic point of view, the scroll is of great significance inasmuch as it preserves a specimen of Aramaic from Palestine from approximately the time of the beginning of the Christian era.

These seven scrolls constituted the original "Dead Sea Scrolls." Three of them, the *Hebrew University Isaiah Scroll,* the *Thanksgiving Hymns,* and the *Order of Warfare,* were purchased by Professor Sukenik and subsequently published by him. The others (except the "Lamech Scroll") were photographed by Trever and subsequently published by the American Schools of Oriental Research, edited by Millar Burrows, assisted by William H. Brownlee and John C. Trever.[5]

## The Damascus Document or Zadokite Fragments

One of the most important Qumran documents was not discovered at Qumran but in Cairo, and not in 1947 but in 1897. It was published in 1910 under the title, the *Zadokite*

---

[5] Published editions of these scrolls, plus translations and commentaries, will be found listed in my *Bibliography of the Dead Sea Scrolls 1948-1957,* §§ 2020-2026 and under the particular scrolls in the sections that follow. A convenient volume containing the text, plus vowel points, has been edited by A. M. Habermann, *mᵉgillôt midbar yᵉhûdā* (Tel Aviv: Machbaroth Lesifruth, 1959; 213 pp. text and notes; 175 pp. concordance; 20 plates; XVI pp. English summary). This includes 1QpHab, 1QS, CD, 1QM, 1QH, and many of the significant fragments from later discoveries. Habermann does not always indicate the extent of his editorial work. Somewhat more complete is Eduard Lohse, *Die Texte aus Qumran, Hebräisch und Deutsch, mit masoretischer Punktation, Übersetzung, Einführung und Anmerkungen* (München: Kösel, 1964, xii + 294 pp.).

*Fragments,*[6] but today it is more widely known as the *Damascus Document.*

The *Damascus Document* (CD for Cairo exemplar; 6QD, etc. for Qumran fragments of same work). The "Zadokite Fragments" were discovered in a Genizah in Cairo among a thousand manuscripts that were too worn to use and too sacred to destroy. The "Fragments" originally were not scrolls, but rather in codex or book form, and came from the tenth and eleventh centuries A.D. There were two exemplars: Manuscript "A" from the 10th century A.D. consisting of eight leaves of parchment (sixteen pages), and Manuscript "B" from the 11th or 12th century consisting of one leaf or two pages. When edited, Manuscript B was arbitrarily numbered columns 19 and 20, columns 17 and 18 being omitted. Manuscript B (i.e., columns 19 and 20) is a different recension of columns 7 and 8 of Manuscript A, and in some editions is integrated with the text of Manuscript A accordingly.[7]

The Damascus Document contains two parts, so different that some scholars think they originally were two distinct compositions: the first part is in the nature of an exhortation, with some historical background, some hints as to the origin of the Sect, and a sketch of the obligations of membership and the punishments for unfaithfulness; the second part is a code of laws governing many details of the life of the membership. As soon as the work was published, it aroused the interest of scholars, and a stream of articles began to appear and continued right down to the time of the Qumran discoveries. The discussions in many ways were of the same type and concerned the same problems as the discussions of the Dead Sea Scrolls.

[6] Solomon Schechter, ed., *Documents of Jewish Sectaries, Vol. I, Fragments of a Zadokite Work* (Cambridge: University Press, 1910; lxiv + 20 pp.). For bibliography up to the time of the Qumran discoveries, see L. Rost, *Die Damaskusschrift* (Berlin: Töpelmann, 1933; 324 pp.); and H. H. Rowley, *The Zadokite Fragments and the Dead Sea Scrolls* (Oxford: Blackwell, 1952; 133 pp.).

[7] The various systems of numbering are most confusing. Dupont-Sommer makes a good case for using "B-1" and "B-2" instead of 19 and 20; but the other numbers are too thoroughly a part of the vast literature to be altered easily. Habermann has integrated the A and B texts with no indication whatever, and his numbering of column 8 therefore does not coincide with any other system of numbering. Rabin has integrated the two manuscripts, but gives both sets of numbering in the margin — a commendable system but bulky to use in quotation. The system ultimately to be used for the Qumran fragments can become positively frightening!

The scholarly world was able to immerse itself so quickly and so deeply in the problems of the Dead Sea Scrolls because the lines were staked out, the research was already done or well under way, and the interest was already developed by the Damascus Document.

When the Dead Sea Scrolls were discovered, particularly the Manual of Discipline, scholars recognized at once a relationship between the new discoveries and the Damascus Document, and interest in the manuscripts that had been found in the Cairo Genizah became even more keen.[8] Many were willing to say that the Damascus Document must have come from Qumran, because of the similarities in language, idea, and several specific details. A few, however, questioned the identification.

Any remaining doubt that the Damascus Document came originally from Qumran was dispelled when fragments of the Damascus Document were found in Cave Four and Cave Six. The Cave Four discoveries represent seven different manuscripts, which have not yet been published. The Cave Six fragments which have been published correspond to CD 4:19-21; 5:13-14, 18; 6:2, 20; 7:1.

The name "Damascus Document" was given to the composition because it mentions a withdrawal of the members of the Covenant to Damascus (CD 6:5, 19; 7:19; 8:21 = 19:34; 20:12). Whether the word Damascus is to be interpreted literally or figuratively is a matter of scholarly debate. The name "Zadokite Fragments" had been used because the members of the Sect referred to themselves as "the sons of Zadok" (CD 4:3). Neither name is particularly appropriate.

## Exploration of the Caves

When articles began to appear, a controversy over the age and the place of the discovery developed. There was nothing scholarly or scientific in a report that valuable manuscripts had been found in a cave by Bedouin, turned over to a merchant, sold to an archbishop, bought through a barbed-wire fence from an intermediary, or photographed while in temporary custody of a research fellow. Then fragments of similar ma-

---

[8] See my *Bibliography of the Dead Sea Scrolls 1948-1957*, §§2650-2667 and cross-references listed there.

terial began to appear on the market, and it was apparent that systematic exploration was necessary.

The first cave, "Cave One," was excavated in 1949. Broken pieces of jars, pieces of cloth, and fragments of manuscripts were found, but because others who were not capable of doing scientific excavation had gotten there first and considerably disturbed the floor of the cave, the results were not acceptable to some critics and certainly not satisfactory to anyone. It was clear, however, that the scrolls were of the same type of documents as the fragments found in the caves: the writing, the material, and the contents were unquestionably similar.

More and more fragments of scrolls were appearing on the market, and it was urgent that the source be discovered promptly. An all-out campaign to explore the region resulted in the finding of more than 200 caves, of which twenty-five contained pottery similar to that found in Cave One, and eleven contained fragments of manuscripts similar to the Dead Sea Scrolls. The term "Dead Sea Scrolls" therefore was expanded to include all the documentary materials found in the same vicinity. The term is not good, since only a small part of the finds were actually scrolls, and also since they were not recovered from the Dead Sea. Other terms have been used, such as "the Scrolls from the Judean Caves," "the 'Ain Feshkha Scrolls," "the Hidden Scrolls," and "Discoveries in the Judean Desert." Perhaps the best term is "Qumran Literature," or "the Ancient Library of Qumran." But the term "Dead Sea Scrolls" is now part of our language, and probably will continue to be the term used for the discovery.

## Location of the Caves

At this point, a bit of geographical description may be helpful. The Dead Sea is a body of salt water whose surface is 1,292 feet below sea level. Its northern end (N. Lat. 31°46′) lies 16 miles due east of Jerusalem. Jerusalem is situated about 2,600 feet above sea level, and the territory east of Jerusalem, called the Wilderness of Judea, is a rolling, arid region cut by numerous valleys and wadis (a wadi is a dry valley or a seasonal river, often dry). The elevation of the wilderness drops gradually to about 300 feet below sea level, and then ends abruptly in a line of cliffs running almost north-and-south near the western shore of the Dead Sea. At this point the elevation drops precipitously to the shore, which then slopes gradually to the level of the sea. The cliffs are of marl, and in the face of the cliffs are numerous caves, almost entirely natural, so completely obscured by the rugged terrain that they cannot readily be seen except by climbing the cliffs — which is one reason why the contents of the caves had remained undiscovered for so many centuries.

From a point about six miles south of the northern end of the Dead Sea, the western shoreline makes a sweeping curve northeastward. The cliffs reach the water's edge at the point mentioned, which is known as Ras Feshkha ("Cape of Feshkha"), and about a mile north there is a freshwater spring bubbling from the ground, known as 'Ain Feshkha ("the spring of Feshkha"). The cliffs are unbroken except for two places: approximately opposite the northern end of the sea a valley leads westward to Jerusalem; and at a distance of about three miles north of Ras Feshkha, a very noticeable wadi known as Wadi Qumrân slices its way through the cliffs.

During the pluvial period at the end of the last Ice Age the waters of Wadi Qumrân eroded the region above the cliffs, cut their way through the cliffs, and formed a plateau with the deposit. On the eastern part of this plateau, located nearly a mile from the shore of the sea, about 200 feet above the surface of the sea, are the ruins of a building compound, known by the Arabic name Khirbet Qumrân ("the ruins of Qumrân"). This was the building used by the people of the Dead Sea Scrolls, whom we call, for want of a better name, the Qumranians. In the cliffs behind Khirbet Qumrân, and also in the sides of a gorge which Wadi Qumrân has subsequently cut through the plateau, are the caves of the Dead Sea Scrolls. Jericho is eight miles due north.

## The Discoveries

In Cave One were found the seven scrolls which we have already described in detail, plus numerous fragments of Biblical and non-Biblical works. The more significant include: fragments of two works that were thought to have been part of the Manual of Discipline, the *Order of the Congregation*

(1QSa or 1Q28a),[9] and the *Benedictions* (1QSb or 1Q28b); fragments of commentaries on Micah, Psalm 37, and Psalm 68; and fragments of the *Book of Mysteries* (1QMyst or 1Q27), the *Sayings of Moses* (1QDM or 1Q22), and the portion of Daniel where the language changes from Hebrew to Aramaic (Dan. 2:4; 1QDan[a]).

Cave Two, discovered in February, 1951, yielded a small quantity of fragments of Biblical and non-Biblical works. Cave Three, discovered in March, 1952, yielded, in addition to the customary fragments, two copper scrolls listing a fabulous amount of hidden treasure (3QInv or 3Q15).

Caves Four, Five, and Six were discovered in September, 1952. By far the most important of the three, and perhaps the most important of all the caves, is Cave Four, which yielded tens of thousands of fragments. An international team of experts worked for several years putting together this gigantic puzzle, and reports that 382 manuscripts are represented, about 100 of them being Biblical manuscripts which include every book of the Old Testament with the exception of Esther. Fragments of Daniel where the language changes from Aramaic to Hebrew (Dan. 7:28—8:1; 4QDan[a, b]) are of particular interest. The significance of these Biblical manuscripts for Old Testament Textual Criticism can hardly be overestimated.

Among the non-Biblical documents recovered from Cave Four, the following are of special significance: a *Florilegium* or collection of messianic promises (4QFlor); a portion of Genesis 49 with commentary, known as the *Patriarchal Blessings* (4QPatrBless); a document which sheds some light on the messianic beliefs of the Qumran sectarians, known as the *Testimonia* (4QTest); a *Commentary on Psalm 37* (4QpPs37); fragments of seven manuscripts of the Damascus Document (4QD[a–g]); and fragments of the War Scroll (4QM).

Among the significant discoveries from Cave Six might be mentioned fragments of the Damascus Document (6QD).

Caves Seven, Eight, Nine, and Ten, excavated in the spring of 1955, yielded only a few fragments.

Cave Eleven was discovered early in 1956, but detailed work

---

[9] The *siglum* 1QSa indicates that it is a supplement to 1QS (similarly 1QSb). Many fragments were identified by numbers, particularly when the titles or appropriate descriptive names were not available; later, as titles have been suggested, the numbers have sometimes been retained to aid in identifying the work as used in earlier publications.

on the materials did not begin until the fall of 1961. The contents are of importance comparable to the discoveries of Caves One and Four. Cave Eleven is located in the cliff more than a mile north of Khirbet Qumran, only a short distance south of Cave Three (which is the most distant from the Community buildings). A scroll of Ezekiel (11QEz), three scrolls of Psalms (11QPs[a], 11QPs[b], possibly 11QPs[e]), an Aramaic Targum of Job (11QtgJob), and several other works were found. In some respects, the most important — and surprising — was the large Psalms Scroll (11QPs[a]), which includes thirty-six canonical Psalms, Psalm 151 (previously known from the Septuagint, but not in the Hebrew Bible), and eight other Psalms not otherwise known.[10]

During the Six-Day War, a very large scroll was found in the possession of an unauthorized dealer. When opened, it proved to be the largest scroll yet found among the Qumran discoveries, over twenty-eight feet in length. Part of the beginning is missing, but a blank sheet at the end proves that that portion is intact. Parts of sixty-six columns have been preserved. Professor Yadin, who published the first reports, has provisionally named the manuscript the *Temple Scroll*. It is believed that the scroll may have come from Cave Eleven. A large part of the contents describe how the Temple is to be built, in the style of the description of the Tabernacle in Exodus 35–38.[11]

Discoveries at Wadi Murabba'ât, Wadi en-Nâr (Khirbet Mird), and Naḥal Davîd (En Gedi) have not been included in this account since they do not belong to the Qumran Community and have no place in our present study.

The question is often asked, "Why were no New Testament documents found at Qumran?"[11a] The answer is clear. First, the Qumran sectarians were not Christian, as we shall see in

[10] See J. A. Sanders, "Cave 11 Surprises and the Question of Canon," in *New Directions in Biblical Archaeology*, ed. D. N. Freedman and J. C. Greenfield (Garden City, N.Y.: Doubleday, 1971), pp. 113-130.

[11] Y. Yadin, "The Temple Scroll," in *New Directions in Biblical Archaeology*, pp. 156-166. Since both the provenance and the complete contents are unknown, no *siglum* has been assigned, to the best of my knowledge. I shall provisionally indicate it as 11QTemple.

[11a] After this statement was in type, news came that New Testament fragments from Cave 7 had been identified. Cf. Jose O'Callaghan, "¿Papiros neotestamentarios en la cueva 7 de Qumran?" *Biblica* 53 (1972), pp. 91-100. It is too early to evaluate the suggestion. I have pointed out one possible weakness of the theory in a brief article to appear in the July 1972 issue of *Eternity*.

our study of the two bodies of literature, and there is no reason why Christian documents should have reached Qumran. Second, the Qumran Community was destroyed in A.D. 68, probably by the advancing Roman Tenth Legion in its historic march on Jerusalem.[12] The earliest writings of the New Testament — letters addressed to churches in the West (at Thessalonica and Galatia) and possibly written sources of the Gospels — were probably not written before A.D. 50. They were certainly written in Greek, with perhaps the exception of a hypothetical Aramaic original of Matthew. This leaves little time for the works to be translated into Hebrew or Aramaic and find their way back to Jerusalem or Qumran.

## The Ruins of the "Monastery" (Khirbet Qumrân)

The ruins on the plateau by Wadi Qumrân had long been known but were never excavated — which probably was fortuitous, for the excavation would have meant far less without the manuscripts to assist in interpreting the ruins. With the discovery of the Scrolls excavation of the ruins became advisable, and the site was explored in 1949, and excavated in 1951, 1953, 1954, 1955, and 1956.[13]

There was one large structure, approximately 100 by 122 feet, with other buildings at the northwest, west, and south. Part of the compound was a two-story structure, and at the northwest corner was a massive tower. The building had been destroyed twice and rebuilt twice; in other words, there were three levels of occupation. The lowest and the second levels gave signs of occupation by the same group or by similar groups of persons. The presence of kitchen facilities and a pantry with the remains of nearly 1,100 plates and bowls, indicated that a large group met for eating. There was no provision for sleeping, suggesting that the group found lodging either in tents or in the nearby caves. Remains of a pottery factory indicated that the group provided for its own needs in this respect.

The remains of a plastered brick structure when reconstructed in the Archaeological Museum formed a low, narrow table, over sixteen feet long and about 20 inches high. It was

---

12 See Josephus *War of the Jews* 5.1-2 §§1-97.

13 The authoritative account is by Roland de Vaux, *L'Archéologie et les manuscrits de la Mer Morte* (London: Oxford, 1961). For other titles see my *Bibliography of the Dead Sea Scrolls 1948-1957*, §§1770-1803.

too far distant from the kitchen to be a dining-room table, and the presence of inkwells in the same room led to the suggestion that the room in which it was found was the *scriptorium* in which the scrolls were copied or composed.

The discovery of a complex of tanks, cisterns, and aqueducts led to a scholarly discussion of the purpose of this equipment. Père Roland de Vaux, the principal authority on the archeology of Qumran, was convinced that two of the tanks were for ritual bathing — one at the extreme northwest, one at the southeast — and that the others were for water storage. The system is connected by an aqueduct with the *Buqêʻah*, or region above the cliffs, where the water was gathered during the rainy season.

An earthquake fault runs through the eastern end of the building, approximately in a north-and-south line. There is evidence that the building was vacated either at the time of the earthquake or a few years earlier, and that it was rebuilt some years later and used for the same purposes.

A layer of ash separating the middle from the upper level of occupation indicated that the building had been destroyed by fire at the end of its second period of occupation. Weapons in the ash further suggested that the fire was the result of military action. The third occupation was obviously of an entirely different kind.

At this point, the results of the analysis of several hundred coins found in the ruins will help us interpret the occupation levels. The coins in the lowest level can be dated from 136 B.C. to 37 B.C.; the coins in the middle level can be dated from 4 B.C. to A.D. 67 or 68; most of the coins in the third level belong to the time of the Second Revolt, A.D. 132-135, although there were a few from the period of the capture of Judea and the destruction of Jerusalem, or between A.D. 68 and A.D. 70.

The first period of occupation, then, extended from about 136 B.C. to the reign of Herod the Great. According to Josephus, a great earthquake occurred in 31 B.C. killing 10,000 or 30,000 persons.[14] It would seem that this was the earthquake that destroyed the building at Qumran, and may have brought to an end the first occupation.

The second period of occupation extended from some time

---

[14] Cf. Josephus *Antiquities* 15.5.2 §121 and *War of the Jews* 1.19.3 §370. Josephus gives both figures.

either toward the end of the reign of Herod the Great or just after that (i.e., 4 B.C.), to the invasion by the Romans in their march on Jerusalem, A.D. 68. The Scrolls were probably hidden for safety when it became obvious that the Romans were preparing to march; the Community was probably destroyed by the Roman legion and the building burned in the action that followed.

Afterwards it seems that the building was repaired and used as a Roman outpost for a short time. It was used again for a brief period in the days of Bar Cochba's rebellion, A.D. 132-135.

East of the building compound is a large cemetery with more than 1,000 graves. A number of graves were excavated, and the skeletons identified by competent scholarship. Several were female.

The number of plates and bowls found in the ruins, and the number of graves found in the cemetery, suggest that the number of persons living in the Qumran Community at any one time was probably between two and four hundred.

## The Date of the Dead Sea Scrolls

When the Scrolls were first described to the world, they were dated, on the basis of paleography (the study of ancient writing) and pottery chronology, to the second or first century B.C. Scholars who lack confidence in these methods of dating were openly critical of the dates obtained.

Fragments of cloth obtained in Cave One were tested for residual radioactive carbon ("Carbon-14"). According to the established norms at that time, the results were announced as A.D. 33 ± 200 years; the half-life of Carbon-14 has since been revised, altering the date obtained to 20 B.C. ± 200 (220 B.C. to A.D. 180). Samples of palmwood from the ruins at Qumran have been tested by the same process, yielding a date between 7 B.C. and A.D. 18, with an average date of A.D. 8 ± 40 years (32 B.C. to A.D. 48).

Linguistic studies of the Hebrew and the Aramaic of the Scrolls have led certain scholars to date the language of the Scrolls in the first centuries B.C.-A.D.

The coins found at Khirbet Qumrân likewise indicate a date between 140 B.C. and A.D. 68.

It can therefore be stated that five independent lines of

evidence (pottery chronology, paleography, Carbon-14, linguistic analysis, and coins) lead to a common conclusion: The Community was occupied and the Scrolls were produced during the last century and a half B.C. and the first part of the first century A.D.

The extremely small number of scholars who refuse to accept this evidence — probably not more than one percent — have presented no comparable evidence to support their claims. Rather, they have been openly critical of all "scientific" methodology, and have insisted that internal evidence and logic alone are valid criteria — and internal evidence has largely been dominated by their *a priori* hypotheses.[15]

## What Has Been Done with the Qumran Discoveries?

The publication of the Dead Sea Scrolls proceeded with what in the scholarly world is amazing rapidity. All of the materials of Caves One, Two, Three, Five, Six, Seven, Eight, Nine, and Ten have been published. One volume of the fragments found in Cave Four has been published, but it is estimated that there will be eight or nine volumes on Cave Four when all the fragments have been published. One volume on Cave Eleven has been published, and several other works are devoted to items from that cave which are not included in that volume.[16]

All of this work has required great technical skill in opening or unrolling scrolls, in cleaning fragments, in photographing with ultraviolet and infrared light, and in many other areas. It has required great patience in identifying fragments, often as small as the nail on your little finger, and in locating

---

[15] An exception to this general statement is G. R. Driver, *The Judaean Scrolls*. This work is a tightly packed historical study, which by proposed identifications of persons and movements, seeks to identify the Qumranians with the "fourth of the philosophies" (Josephus *Antiquities* 18.1.6 §23), set up by Judas the Galilean (pp. 252-259). Driver also traces relationships with the Zadokites and Boethusians (pp. 226-237), the Zealots, Assassins and Brigands (pp. 237-251), and with the Sadduceans (who are to be distinguished from the New Testament Sadducees) (pp. 259-266). However, he completely sets aside the evidence of paleography, of the coins found at Qumran, of the Carbon-14 tests — in a word, all archeological evidence.

[16] For a convenient reference-work to the principal publications of these materials, see J. A. Sanders, "Palestinian Manuscripts 1947-1967," in *Journal of Biblical Literature* 86 (1967), pp. 431-440. See also C. Burchard, *Bibliographie zu den Handschriften vom Toten Meer, II* (Berlin: Töpelmann, 1965), pp. 321-344.

passages of Biblical or non-Biblical writings. It has required great scholarship in translation and interpretation of the portions that have been found intact or that have been pieced together. It has required great amounts of money to buy the materials from the finders (the rate for a while was $2.80 per square centimeter, or about $18.00 per square inch), to maintain the staff of experts working on the Scrolls, and to underwrite the cost of publication. Above all, it has required a vast amount of time. Hundreds of scholars have invested thousands of days and hours in the work. And there still remains much to be done.

Some idea of the enormous amount of scholarly production can be gained, perhaps, from the following facts. My *Bibliography of the Dead Sea Scrolls 1948-1957* contains well over 2,000 titles of books and articles on the Dead Sea Scrolls that were published in the first ten years. In the international periodical *Revue de Qumrân,* where this bibliographical effort continues, over one hundred titles are listed in each issue. In the second volume of Burchard's *Bibliographie zu den Handschriften vom Toten Meer, II,* which brings the list down to 1962, 2,903 additional titles are listed. H. Stegemann in *Zeitschrift des Deutches Palästinavereins* 83 (1967), pp. 95-101, adds many additional titles. It can be safely estimated that the total of all items, including books, articles, reviews, and brief notices, is around 6,000, written by about 1,000 scholars, in 25 or more languages.

## Summary

The Dead Sea Scrolls are the literary remains of a Community that lived at Qumran from c. 135 B.C. to A.D. 67 or 68. They include scrolls or fragments of scrolls of several hundred manuscripts, including Biblical and non-Biblical writings. The non-Biblical writings include documents that were produced by the Community, some of which were previously known, some of which are completely new to us.

From these Scrolls we are able to reconstruct something of the life of the Community, something of its religious beliefs, and something of its religious rites and practices. To describe this reconstruction, and to compare it with the life and teachings of Jesus and with the belief and life of the early Church, is our task in this work.

## CHAPTER THREE

# QUMRAN—
# "THE COMMUNITY OF GOD"

How shall we reconstruct a community that has been extinct for 1900 years? From its written records we can learn many details of its life: admission to the group, beliefs, practices, attitudes toward nonmembers, etc. From the archeological remains we can add other details: the kind of buildings used, the water cisterns, the materials of daily life (dishes, ovens, etc.), an estimate of the size of the community, and other data of significance. From external written sources, if any, we can add other points or fill in additional facts in the areas already mentioned. With the help of a gifted imagination we can clothe this skeleton with flesh and blood and bring the community to life.

The order given is significant. The primary sources are the written materials; everything else must be controlled by documentary records. Archeological evidence is certainly to be put ahead of subjective reconstruction (or controlled imagination) — although it must be recognized that the interpretation of archeological evidence, unless controlled by written sources, is frequently subjective. External documentary material, i.e. written material from outside the community, can be used with confidence only if the relationship to the group in question is clearly established. Finally, imagination that is not rigidly disciplined by these other items in the order given can produce only fantasy.

In the case of the Qumran Community we have both written documents and archeological evidence. It may be that we also have external source material concerning the Sect in the writings of Philo, Josephus, Pliny the Elder, *et al.*, concerning the Essenes. This, however, depends on two other questions: Were the Qumranians Essenes? and, if so, were the Essenes as described in the sources mentioned exactly the group at Qumran? Most scholars working in the area of Qumran studies are convinced that the Qumran sect was Essene, and these scholars use the material from Qumran and from external sources interchangeably. However, the complete identity of the two movements has not been established. There are important differences between what is written in the Qumran Literature about the Qumran movement and what is written in the sources mentioned concerning the Essenes. Good methodology requires separating the two bodies of material.[1]

## The Origin of the Qumran Sect

It is not yet possible to trace in detail the historical rise and development of the Qumran movement, nor is this necessary for our study. Some minimal idea can be gained from the following passage in the Damascus Document.

> For in their disloyalty, when they left Him, He hid His face from Israel and from His Temple, and He gave them to the sword. Then when He remembered the covenant of the Patriarchs, He left a remnant to Israel and He did not give them up to annihilation. And in the end-time of anger 390 years after He gave them into the hand of Nebuchadrezzar king of Babylon — He visited them, and He caused to sprout from Israel and from Aaron a root of planting to possess His land and to grow fat in the goodness of His earth.
>
> Then they understood their iniquity, and they knew that they were guilty men. But they were like blind men, like men groping their way, for twenty years. And God considered their deeds, that they sought Him with a whole heart, and He raised up for them a teacher of righteousness to guide them in the way of His heart, and He made known to the last generations what He did with the last generation, the congregation of traitors, those who had turned aside from the way. (CD 1:3-13)

The Qumranians, then, thought of themselves as a Jewish

[1]The external source material will be presented in Chapter Ten.

remnant, living in the "end-time of anger," a "root of plant-ing" who had recognized their sins, whom God had remem-bered and for whom He had raised up a "teacher of right-eousness." If we take the figures literally, 390 years from the fall of Jerusalem in 586 B.C. would bring us to 197 B.C. for God's "visitation," and 20 years later (177 B.C.) for the raising up of the Teacher of Righteousness. Such literalism, how-ever, should not be pressed.

Some development in official Judaism led to a schism, and the Qumran group withdrew to "Damascus."

> And God remembered the covenant of the Patriarchs, and He raised up from Aaron men of understanding, and from Israel men of wisdom, and He will hear them.
> And they dug the well: "The well which the princes dug, the nobles of the people dug it with a rod." The well is the Law, and those who dig it are the Penitents of Israel who go out from the Land of Judah, and they shall dwell in the land of Damascus, all of whom God called princes because they sought Him, and their honor was not returned (?) by the mouth of anyone. (CD 6:2-7)

Whether "Aaron" and "Israel" are to be taken as synonymous — in which case "men of understanding" and "men of wis-dom" would also be synonymous — or whether the terms here refer to the priests and the laity, need not for the moment concern us overmuch. This group, the "Penitents of Israel," withdrew from official Judaism. They went out from "the Land of Judah" to dwell "in the Land of Damascus." Wheth-er "Damascus" is to be understood literally is a point of schol-arly difference; some think it simply means the place we know as Qumran. This sectarian group of Jews may have called itself "the men who entered into the New Covenant in the Land of Damascus" (CD 6:19; 8:21; 19:33-34; cf. CD 20:2).

A further indication of their attitude toward themselves is given in the following passage:

> And God in His wonderful mysteries made atonement for their iniquity and took away their rebellion, and He built for them a firm house in Israel and there never was one like it until now. Those who hold fast to it are for perpetual life and all the glory of man shall be theirs, even as God estab-lished for them by Ezekiel the prophet, saying, "The priests, and the Levites, and the sons of Zadok who guarded the care

of My Temple when the sons of Israel went astray from Me in their treacheries, they shall offer to Me fat and blood."
The priests are the penitents of Israel who go out from the land of Judah, and <the Levites>[2] are those who join them, and the sons of Zadok are the chosen ones of Israel, those called by name, who stand in the latter days. (CD 3:18–4:4)

Their attitude toward the Jerusalem priesthood is illustrated by these words:

The priests of Jerusalem, who will heap up wealth and unjust gain from the plunder of the people. (1QpHab 9:4-5)

Of the Holy City, they said:

The city is Jerusalem in which the wicked priest did works of abominations and defiled the Temple of God. (1QpHab 12:7-9)

Works of this Wicked Priest are further described in the same commentary. Either the same person or some other — it makes no difference for the moment — was identified as "the man of the lie" (1QpHab 2:1f.), and perhaps the same person is called "the preacher of the lie" (1QpHab 10:9). In the Damascus Document we read that there arose in the days of the Teacher of Righteousness a "man of mockery" (CD 1:14) who led Israel astray with waters of falsehood.
During the time the sons of Zadok (i.e., the Qumranians) were in penitence in the desert, Belial was let loose on Israel (CD 4:13) to ensnare men in his nets. One of these nets is the profaning of the Temple (CD 4:18; 5:6-11). The men of mockery and the man of the lie are mentioned again in another passage (CD 20:11, 15). In the Manual of Discipline the same group, it would seem, is referred to as "the dominion of Belial" (1QS 1:18), the "men of Belial's lot" (1QS 2:4-5), "sons of perversion" (1QS 3:21), "men of the pit" (1QS 9:22), and other similar epithets. It would be easy to enlarge this list from other Qumran documents.

## The Names of the Qumran Sect

Names are often given to groups by those outside, and unless the Qumranians were the "Essenes" we do not know what

2Apparently the word dropped due to its similarity to the following word: <HLWYM> HNLWYM.

they were called. They did use certain descriptive names for themselves.

*The Community* (*hayyáḥad*). This term in its various forms occurs slightly over one hundred times in the texts, nearly always referring to the Sect. The basic meaning is "to be or have in common," and various forms can have a range of meanings such as "together," "union," "to commune with," "private," etc. The word occurs alone and in compound terms such as:

> The Community
> The Counsel of the Community (*‛ăṣat hayyáḥad*), used about 20 times in 1QS and 1QSa.
> The Counsel of the Men of the Community
> The Men of the Community, used about 12 times, all but once in CD
> The Community of His Council
> The Community of the Ages, or Eternal Community

*The Counsel* (*hā‛ēṣā*). The basic meaning of this word is "to advise." The word can be translated "advice," and is used as a common noun in this sense. Compound terms are found:

> The Counsel of the Community (see above)
> The Counsel of Holiness, or Holy Counsel
> The Counsel of Truth
> The Counsel of the Torah
> The Counsel of God
> The Counsel of His Righteousness
> The Counsel of the Ages, or Eternal Counsel
> The Counsel of the Fellowship of Israel; used mostly in 1QS

*The Congregation* (*hā‛ēdā*). The basic meaning of this word is "to appoint, designate," and a derived form has the meaning of "appointed time, meeting, assembly." The form used for the Sect is difficult to translate exactly; I shall use "Congregation." It is found in compound terms, and is used for those outside the Sect as well as for those of the membership:

> The Congregation of Israel
> The Holy Congregation
> The Congregation of the Men of the Name
> The Congregation of the Community
> The Congregation of God
> The Congregation of the Sons of Heaven

The Congregation of Belial
The Congregation of Men of Unrighteousness
The Congregation of Traitors
The Congregation of Nothing

*Assembly (qāhāl)*. This term is also translated "Congregation," but to avoid confusion I shall use "Assembly."[3] It is also used for nonmembers as well as for members:

The Assembly
The Assembly of God
The Assembly of the Wicked
The Assembly of the Gentiles

*Council (sôd)*. This word is difficult to translate; it also means "secret," hence "secret council" might be a satisfactory translation. Names used, both for members and for nonmembers, are:

The Council of the Community
The Council of Men
The Sons of an Eternal Council
A Council of Truth and Understanding (?) (1QH 2:10)
The Council of Violence
The Council of Nothing and the Congregation of Belial

Not all scholars translate these terms uniformly, nor is there agreement among scholars concerning the translation of any of the terms. Some scholars think certain terms may refer to subgroups within the larger group. For our purpose this is not a serious problem, but we should be aware of it.

## Aaron and Israel

In the Qumran Literature, the expression "Israel and Aaron" (CD 1:7) or "Aaron and Israel" (QS 9:11) seems to mean "the Community." As I understand the expression, it indicates that the Sect was composed of priests ("Aaron") and laymen ("Israel"). The members of the Sect were to be separated into "a house of holiness for Aaron . . . and a house of community for Israel" (1QS 9:6). Immediately following this statement we read:

3 This word does not occur in 1QS; it occurs 7x in 1QM, and 3x each in 1QSa, 1QH, and CD.

> Only the sons of Aaron shall rule in justice and in wealth,
> and according to their mouth shall go forth the lot for every
> regulation of the men of the Community. (1QS 9:7)

The members of the Community volunteered

> ... to be separated from the congregation of the men of un-
> righteousness to become a community in the Torah and in
> wealth, and being restored according to the authority of the
> sons of Zadok, the priests who keep the covenant, and ac-
> cording to the majority of the men of the Community who
> maintain the covenant. (1QS 5:1-3)

When new members came into the Community, the priests
and Levites pronounced the blessing (1QS 1:18-19). The Community is described as consisting of priests, Levites, and "all
the people" (1QS 2:19-21), or "Israel and Levi and Aaron"
(1QM 5:1), or priests, Levites, sons of Israel, and proselytes
(CD 14:3-6).

This seems to rule out the suggestion that the Community
looked upon itself as "an idealized priesthood."

## The Many

One possible name of the Sect, about which there is serious
difference of opinion, is *The Many* (*hārabbîm*).[4] The word,
a common noun in the plural, can simply mean "the many (in
number)," or it can also mean "the great ones, the chiefs." It
could therefore mean (a) the entire Community, or (b) the
majority in any given action, or (c) a ruling body in the Community. The word occurs about 56 times in the Qumran
documents, about 34 times in columns 6-8 of the Manual of
Discipline. In columns 13-15 of the Damascus Document there
is also significant use of the word. The following passage is
instructive:

> This is the order for the Session of the Many:
> Each man in his position: the priests shall sit first, and the
> elders second, and all the rest of the people shall sit, each in
> his position. In this manner they shall make request with
> regard to judgment and to every counsel and matter which

---

[4] C. Daniel thinks that Josephus refers to the Essenes (=Qumranians)
as "the Many" in *War* 2.8.9 §159; he also finds the same term in 2 Cor. 2:17,
and suggests it refers to the Essenes. Cf. "Mention Paulinienne des Esséniens de Qumrân," *Revue de Qumrân* 5,20 (July 1966), pp. 554f.

belongs to the Many, and each one shall reply (by giving) his knowledge to the counsel of the Community.

Let no one speak in the midst of the words of his fellow, before his brother has finished speaking. Likewise let him not speak before his position which is written before him. The man who is asked shall speak in his turn, and in the session of the Many let no man speak anything which is not at the wish of the Many.

And when the man who is the Examiner over the Many, or any man who has a matter to speak to the Many who is not in the standing of the man who is asking the counsel of the Community (has something to say), the man shall stand on his feet and say, "I have a matter to speak to the Many." If they shall say to him, "Let him speak," <then he may speak>.[5] (1QS 6:8-13)

## Order of Precedence

In the passage we have just read, we note an insistence on "position" or "turn" in the Community. The following passages indicate the order of precedence both regarding new members and also with reference to the entire Community.

And when he shall enter into the covenant to do according to all these statutes, to be united to the Congregation of Holiness, then they shall investigate his spirit in community between man and his fellow according to the measure of his prudence and his deeds in the Torah, according to the sons of Aaron who volunteer in community to raise up His covenant and to attend to all His statutes which He commanded (them) to do, and according to the majority of Israel who volunteer to return in community to His covenant; and to write them in order, each before his neighbor, according to the measure of his prudence and his deeds and the perfection of his way, so every man can be heard by his fellow, the small by the great; and to be mustering them, their spirit and their deeds, year by year, to elevate a man according to the measure of his prudence and perfection of way, or to retard him according to his perversity; to admonish each his neighbor in t[ruth] and humility and love of mercy for each. (1QS 5:20-25)

And the order of the session of all the camps:

They shall be mustered all of them by their names (= reputation?), the priests first, and the Levites second, and

5 I assume that a word was dropped: LW YDBR <WYDBR>. It makes sense, however, without emendation.

the sons of Israel third, and the stranger fourth. And they shall be written by their names, each after his brother, the priests first, and the Levites second, and the sons of Israel third, and the stranger fourth. And thus they shall sit, and thus they shall ask questions concerning everything. (CD 14:3-6)

A similar passage in the Manual of Discipline lists priests, Levites, and all the people, and continues:

. . . so every man of Israel will know each one the house (= place) of his standing in the Community of God for the Counsel of the Ages. And a man shall not go lower than the house of his standing, and he shall not rise above the place of his lot. (1QS 2:22-23)

This arrangement according to rank extended to the smallest meeting:

And in any place where there shall be ten men from the Counsel of the Community, let there not be lacking there a man, a priest; and each according to his position shall sit before him; and in this manner they shall ask for their counsel on any matter. (1QS 6:3-4)

It seems clear that rank or precedence represented a spiritual and moral position and was not merely social or hereditary. From the statements of Jesus in the Gospels we might come to the conclusion that there was a love of position and prominence among the religious men of His day.[6] The regulations at Qumran may have been an attempt at partially correcting this attitude by giving it a spiritual value — or they may have been merely an adaptation by the Qumranians of an existing custom.

## Admission to the Sect

Details of admission to the Qumran Community are spelled out in the Manual of Discipline.

And anyone who volunteers from Israel to be added to the Counsel of the Community, let the man who is appointed at the head of the Many examine him as to his understanding and his works. And if he comprehends the instruction, he (the official) shall bring him into the covenant to return to

6 Cf. Matt. 23:6; Luke 11:43; 20:46.

truth and to turn away from all unrighteousness, and he shall cause him to understand all the judgments of the Community.

And afterwards, when he comes to stand before the Many, they shall be asked everything about the affairs. And when the lot shall go forth according to the counsel of the Many, he shall draw near or he shall depart.

And when he draws near to the counsel of the Community, he shall not touch the Purity of the Many until they investigate him as to his spirit and his work, to the fulfilling of a complete year. Also he himself shall not mingle (his wealth) with the wealth of the Many.

And when he has fulfilled a year in the midst of the Community, the Many shall ask concerning his affairs according to the measure of his understanding and his works in the Torah. And if the lot shall go out to him to draw near to the secret council of the Community, according to the mouth of the priests and the majority of the men of their covenant, let them bring near also his wealth and his work into the hand of the man who is the Examiner. To the property of the Many he shall write it in the account in his own hand, but for the Many he shall not expend it.

Let him not touch the Drink of the Many until he has fulfilled a second year in the midst of the men of the Community.

And when he has fulfilled the second year, they shall muster him according to the mouth of the Many. And if the lot shall go forth to him to draw near to the Community, they shall write him in the order of his position in the midst of his brothers, for Torah, and for judgment, and for purity, and for mingling his wealth, and let his counsel belong to the Community and his judgment. (1QS 6:13-23)

The following provisions are found in the Rule of the Congregation, and seem to indicate certain restrictions on membership.

And any man (who is) simple, let him not enter into the lot to be stationed over the Congregation of Israel for co[ntention and judgm]ent[7] to take up the burden of the

<hr/>

[7] Additions in (parentheses) are simply for clarity. Additions in [square brackets], on the other hand, are translations based on restorations of broken texts. I have tried to indicate, by the number of letters *outside* the brackets, the position and amount of text remaining, hence "co[ntention and judgm]ent" indicates that the first two letters of the Hebrew word translated "contention" and the last three letters of the word translated "judgment" remain. Furthermore, I have tried to figure the amount to be restored by the available space in the manuscript.

> Congregation or to be stationed in the war to subdue the
> gentiles. (1QSa 1:19-21)

> And any man (who is) smitten in any one of the defile-
> ments of humanity let him not enter into the Assembly of
> God. And any man who is smitten with these so that he can-
> not hold a position (or standing) in the midst of the Con-
> gregation, and anyone smitten in his flesh, afflicted in the
> feet or hands, lame or blind or deaf or dumb, or smitten with
> a blemish in his flesh visible to the eyes, or a stumbling old
> man so that he cannot hold himself up in the midst of the
> Congregation, let these not en[ter] to be stationed [in] the
> midst of the Congregation of the Men of the Name, for holy
> angels are [in] their [congregatio]n. (1QSa 2:3-9)

It is of course possible that the "Assembly" and the "Congregation" are not identical, and that these restrictions are
for a select group within the Community. However, I have
been unable to discover any clear evidence to support such
a view.

## Organization of the Community

Details of organization can be pointed out, but the organizational structure is not entirely clear.

*The Priest.* Authority was committed to the priests (the
"sons of Zadok" or "the sons of Aaron"). One priest apparently was above the others, quite possibly the one who is referred to in the War Scroll as the "Chief Priest." In the
Damascus Document, a section headed "rule of the session of
all the camps" (CD 14:3) contains a description of the Priest,
followed by a description of the Examiner; the order is probably significant. The statement concerning the Priest is as
follows:

> And the priest who shall muster the Many (shall be) from
> thirty to fifty years of age, instructed in the Book of [the
> Hagû and] in all the judgments of the Law to speak them
> according to their judgment. (CD 14:6-8)

In the War Scroll, "[the] chief priest and his second (or alter-
nate, lieutenant)" are mentioned, and after them twelve "Chiefs
of the priests" (1QM 2:1-2). All other references in the War
Scroll simply describe the priestly duties of the Chief Priest
during the eschatological war (1QM 15:4; 16:13; 18:5; 19:11).

*The Examiner.* An individual of significance was the "Examiner" (*mᵉbaqqēr*), a word that can be translated also "supervisor, superintendent, overseer, visitor," etc. The word occurs fifteen times — twice in the Manual of Discipline, the rest of the occurrences in the Damascus Document — always in passages where the "Many" are under discussion.[8]

The qualifications of the Examiner are as follows:

> And the Examiner, who belongs to all the camps, shall be from thirty to fifty years old, possessed of every secret of men and of every language by their numbers. By his authority shall enter all who come into the Congregation, each in his turn. And to every matter which anyone shall have to speak about, to the Examiner he shall speak relevant to any controversy or judgment. (CD 14:7-11)

And this is the order for the Examiner for the camp:

> He shall instruct the Many in the works of God, and he shall cause them to understand His wonderful mighty acts, and he shall recount before them what was done in former times in —?—.[9]

> And he shall pity them as a father his sons, and he shall restore their wandering ones as a shepherd his flock. He shall loose all the bonds that bind them so th[ere will n]ot be any oppressed and broken in his Congregation.

> And everyone who is added to his Congregation he shall examine as [to his wo]rks, his understanding, his strength, his might, and his wealth, and he shall write him in his place according to the measure of his right in the lot of t[ruth].

> And no man from the sons of the camp shall have authority to bring a man into the Congregation [without] the authority of the Examiner who belongs to the camp.

> And of all who come into the covenant of God, no one shall give [to] the sons of the pit [ex]cept hand to hand. And no one shall do a thing to b[uy] or to s[e]ll [ex]cept [he has told] the Examiner who is in the camp and he has acted [in good fai]th. (CD 13:7-16)

---

8 Some distinguish between the "Examiner" and the "Examiner who is over all the camps."

9 Dupont-Sommer reads BPRTYH, "in Parthia" (*Essene Writings from Qumran*, p. 157 n.2), but this seems out of keeping with the rest of the document.

Other duties of the Examiner are: hearing witnesses in serious offenses (CD 9:16-22), advising the priest in case of disease in the camp (CD 13:5-6), arbitrating disputes between members (CD 14:10-11), and taking the oath of the Covenant (CD 15:7-18).

*The Twelve and the Three.* The following passage describes a body of men with important responsibilities. It is not certain whether the Counsel of the Community is the group of twelve or the entire Community.

> In the Counsel of the Community (there shall be) twelve men and priests three, perfect in all that which is revealed from all the Law to do truth and righteousness and judgment and love of mercy and modesty, each with his fellow, to guard faith on the earth with firm impulse and a broken spirit, and to make satisfaction for iniquity with deeds (?) of justice and the distress of refining, and to walk with all in the measure of truth and in the plan of the time.[10] (1QS 8:1-4)

*The Judges of the Congregation.* The body of Judges resembles the Twelve and the Three, and one may have developed from the other. The description is found in the Damascus Document.

> And this is [the] order for the Judges of the Congregation: Up to ten men selected from the Congregation by the measure of the time, four to the tribe of Levi and Aaron, and from Israel six, instructed in the Book of the Hagu and in the foundations of the covenant, from twenty-five to sixty years old. (CD 10:4-7)

In each case the number of laymen is greater than the number of priests.

The *Fathers of the Congregation* and the *Heads of the Courses.* In the War Scroll, fifty-two "Fathers of the Congregation" are mentioned (1QM 2:1), and twenty-six "Heads of the Courses," that is, priests who rotate in the service, are specified (1QM 2:2, 4). The Fathers of the Congregation chose the fighting men for the eschatological battle (1QM 2:7).

---

[10] This passage is not without difficulties. Some scholars believe that the "Twelve" included the "Three." Reicke finds difficulty in the fact that laymen seem to outnumber priests; cf. B. Reicke, in *The Scrolls and the New Testament*, ed. K. Stendahl (New York: Harper, 1957), p. 151.

The Heads of the Courses were to be responsible for the burnt offerings and sacrifices and other priestly functions (1QM 2:4-6). The "Heads of the Fathers of the Congregation" are mentioned in the Rule of the Congregation. They hold a place of honor and responsibility below the priests, the Messiah of Israel, and the heads of the tribes (cf. 1QSa 1:16, 23f., 25; 2:16). Other details are not given.

The *Prince of All the Congregation.* In a passage in the Damascus Document based on the star-and-sceptre prophecy (Num. 24:17), we read, "The sceptre is the Prince of all the Congregation, and when he arises he will destroy all the sons of Seth" (CD 7:20f.). The passage is in the nature of a prophecy, hence the Prince seems to belong to the future. The same title, the Prince of All the Congregation, occurs on the shield (?) of this person in the eschatological battle (1QM 5:1), and in the Benedictions (1QSb 5:20),[11] but in neither case is anything recorded concerning the Prince.

## Summary

The Qumran Community was a sectarian or schismatic movement of Judaism that developed, almost certainly, in the second century B.C., repudiating the Jerusalem priesthood and withdrawing from Jerusalem. It moved to the "desert" and "Damascus," which may designate the location at Qumran. The members believed they were the "Penitents," obedient to God's will and keeping His covenant. More details of this will be considered in the chapter following.

Admission to the group was a long process, covering two years and divided into two stages, with rigid examination at the beginning and also at the end of each stage. All property or wealth was handed over to the Community. Within the Sect there was an order of precedence or rank and each member had an assigned place. Annually there was an examination, and members were advanced or set back in precedence. Rigid discipline was maintained by an Examiner or Superintendent.

Organizational details are not entirely clear. The Sect was composed of both priests and laymen, and authority rested chiefly, but not exclusively, in the hands of the priests. The Chief Priest seems to have been the highest official, followed

11 In Habermann, *megillôt midbar yehûdā,* line 82 (p. 163).

by the Examiner. A body of fifteen men was responsible for the faith and life of the Community; whether this group was the same as the "Judges of the Congregation," mentioned in the Damascus Document, is not clear. The Community expected the Prince to arise at the end of days.

## CHAPTER FOUR

# DAILY LIFE IN QUMRAN— "THE PENITENTS OF ISRAEL"

From the manuscripts we know that the Qumranians had withdrawn from Jerusalem Judaism and established a sectarian community. From the archeological discoveries we know that this community, or at least one "camp," was located at Qumran. But do we know anything of their daily life? Were they a group of monks? Did they have a religious regimen? To answer these and similar questions we turn again to their literature.

## Separation from the World

Separation from evil and perverse men, we have seen,[1] was basic to the concept of the Community. The member was to continue to walk in the ways of the truth.

> And all who enter into the order of the Community shall pass over into the covenant before God, to do according to all which He commanded, and not to turn back from following Him because of any fear or terror or refining fire brought into being by the dominion of Belial. (1QS 1:16-18)

A strong sense of cultic separation pervades the following paragraph:

> . . . [to] do the good and the right before Him as He commanded by Moses and by all His servants the prophets; and to love all that He has chosen, and to hate all that He has rejected; to keep distant from all evil and to cling to all who

[1] Cf. 1QS 5:1-2, p. 50 above.

do good; to do truth and righteousness and justice in the earth, and not to walk any more in stubbornness of a guilty heart and eyes of fornication to do all evil; and to bring all who volunteer to do the statutes of God in the covenant of lovingkindness, to be united in the Counsel of God and to walk before Him perfectly (according to) all that which is revealed with reference to the appointed times of their testimonies; and to love all the sons of light, each according to his lot in the Counsel of God, and to hate all the sons of darkness each according to his guilt in the revenge of God. (1QS 1:2-11)

## Community of Goods

When a "volunteer" entered the Community, he turned over his wealth to the Sect (1QS 6:17, 22, p. 53 above). In another passage, knowledge, strength, and wealth all belonged to the Community:

And all the volunteers for His truth shall bring all their knowledge and their strength and their wealth into the Community of God, to purify their knowledge in the truth of the laws of God, and to regulate their strength according to the perfection of His ways, and all their wealth in the counsel of His righteousness. (1QS 1:11-13)

Community life extended to other activities, such as eating:

And they shall listen, the small to the great, with respect to work and to wealth; and together they shall eat and together they shall bless and together they shall be counselled. (1QS 6:2-3)

Some of these points, together with the isolated location of the Community, have led to the suggestion that the Qumran Sect was a monastic group, renouncing wealth, marriage, and other pleasures of the world.

## Poverty

For example, it is sometimes said that the Community referred to itself as "the Poor." Two words used in the texts require study in order to evaluate this statement.

The *Poor* (*'ebyôn*). This word occurs about fifteen times in the Qumran writings. In the Habakkuk Commentary it is used three times, and in each case seems to refer to the Sect

(1QpHab 12:3, 6, 10). It occurs in the Commentary on Psalm 37 in a form that appears to be a title, "Its interpretation, concerning the Congregation of the Poor . . ." (4QpPs37 2:10 [Habermann, *gimel* 29]). Once in the Thanksgiving Hymns, the term may refer to the Sect (1QH 5:22), where we read of "the poor ones of grace." The preceding lines, however, refer to the orphan and the needy, and the passage is therefore not convincing. In the War Scroll the word is used once (1QM 11:9) in a manner that may refer to the Sect, "the poor ones of Thy redemption." In all other cases it simply refers in general to those in poverty. Except for the usage in the Commentaries on Habakkuk and Psalm 37, then, there is no strong evidence that this was a name for the Sect.

The *Afflicted*, or humble ('*ānî*), or humility ('*ănāwā*). The former word is used six times only, each time referring in general to the needy or afflicted man, without any implied reference to the Sect.[2] The second word occurs eight times in the Manual of Discipline (never with reference to the Sect), three times in the Thanksgiving Hymns, and once in the War Scroll.[3] Two of these passages call for study.

In the Hymns, Dupont-Sommer finds an allusion to Isaiah 61:1-2 in the expression "the humble of spirit," and refers to Luke 4:16-22. The text is broken, but can be restored approximately as follows:

> to [be] according to Thy truth one preaching good news [   ]
> Thy goodness, to preach good news to the humble according
> to the multitude of Thy mercies . . . . (1QH 18:14)

There seems to be an overtone of the Isaiah prophecy, but the only verbal parallel is found in the words "to preach the good news to the humble." The context seems to be autobiographical and could refer to the Teacher of Righteousness. It does not necessarily follow that the name "humble" was used of the Community.

In the War Scroll, the words, "and by the humble ones of spirit [   ] heart of hardness . . ." (1QM 14:7), have been compared to the words of Jesus, "Blessed are the poor in Spirit" (Matt. 5:3). The phrase in the War Scroll is in the midst of a section that refers to "the melted heart," "the

[2] CD 6:16, 21; 14:14; 1QH 2:34; 5:13, 14.
[3] 1QS 2:24; 3:8 (2x); 4:3; 5:3, 25; 9:22; 11:1; 1QH 5:22; 18:14 and a fragment identified by Habermann as Frag. 18:4; 1QM 14:7.

mouth of the dumb," "weak [hands]," "shaken of knees," "the wounded of shoulder," and "the perfect of way." The context seems to relate to the Community, but it does not follow that any of these terms were used as names of the Community.

The Community was opposed to greed. Wealth was one of the three nets of Belial (CD 4:17). The Wicked Priest was denounced because he "stole the goods of the Poor" (1QpHab 12:10). Poverty and oppression were probably looked upon as signs of blessedness as they sometimes are in the Biblical Psalms. It is perhaps somewhat misleading, however, to speak of a vow of poverty, of "charismatic poverty," or of the readiness to accept poverty as "a state of grace"; these ideas seem rather to be read into Qumran from Christian monasticism.

## Celibacy and Marriage

The ruins at Qumran are often referred to as the "Monastery," and the Qumranians as the "monks of Qumran." The following passages, specifically the references to women and children, are relevant to the problem:

> When they enter they shall assemble all who are entering, from tiny tot to women, and they shall read in [their] e[ars] [a]ll the statutes of the covenant and to instruct them in all their judgments, lest they stray in [    ].
> This is the Order for all the hosts of the Congregation for every citizen in Israel:
> And from [his] yo[uth to tea]ch him in the Book of the Hagû, and as the measure of his days (i.e., according to age) to instruct him in the statutes of the covenant and to [receive] his [instructi]on in their judgments, ten years [from] entering with the tots (?). And at the age of twenty ye[ars he shall pass over among] the mustered ones to enter into the lot in the midst of his fam[il]y to be united in the Co[ngregation] of Holiness. And he shall not [approach] a woman to know her sexually un[le]ss there is fulfilled to him tw[ent]y years in the knowledge of [good] and evil. And then she shall receive (the privilege) of testifying against him the judgments of the Torah and to st[ati]on (herself) in the hearing of the judgments and in the fulfilling of them. (1QSa 1:4-12)
>
> And if (they live in) camps, they shall dwell according to the order of the earth, and they shall take women and they shall beget sons and they shall walk according to the Torah and according to the judgment of admonitions, according to the

order of the Torah even as He said, "Between a man and
his wife, and between a father and his daughter." (CD 7:6-9)

That the Qumranians condemned the sins of the flesh
there is no doubt: lust was the first of the three nets of Belial
(CD 4:17). But this imposes chastity, not celibacy. That the
location of Qumran was not well suited for normal family
life is clearly apparent, yet, as the presence of female skeletons in the cemetery testifies, there were some women at Qumran. There is therefore no objective basis for finding obligatory
celibacy as a condition of membership at Qumran.

## The Study of the Law

The withdrawal of the Sect to the wilderness, according
to the Manual of Discipline, was for the purpose of studying
the Law:

> And when these become a community in Israel, by these
> arrangements they shall be separated from the midst of the
> dwelling of the men of unrighteousness, to go to the wilder-
> ness to prepare there the way of Hu'ha',[4] as it is written, "In
> the wilderness prepare a way, . . . make straight in the desert
> a highway for our God." This is the study of the Law [which]
> He commanded by Moses, to do according to all that was
> revealed from time to time, and according to that which the
> prophets revealed by His Holy Spirit. (1QS 8:13-16)

Similarly, in the Damascus Document, the Law is associated
with the very origin of the Sect (cf. CD 6:4, p. 46 above).
The Books of the Law and the Searcher of the Law are found
figuratively in a prophecy from Amos and applied to the Sect
(CD 7:15-18). Stress upon the Law, the obligation to walk
according to the Law and not to deviate to the right or to
the left, and similar ideas are found throughout the Qumran
Literature.

The "Man of Understanding" (1QS 9:12-26) may be one
particular person in the Community charged with keeping the
knowledge of the truth and the judgment of righteousness
(perhaps the "Examiner"?), or this may be a description of
the ideal Qumranian.

---

[4] This cryptic word is obviously a surrogate for the divine Name which
was unutterable. Possibly it is an abbreviation of the words _hû' hā'ĕlōhîm_,
"He is God."

What is meant by "the Law" (or Torah) in the Qumran writings? The term may include ethical behavior, ritual acts and ceremonies, and other concepts.

*Good Conduct.* The positive virtues of the Mosaic Law are stressed in the Qumran writings: truth, righteousness, kindness or covenant love (*hésed*), justice, chasity, honesty, humility, and the like. These virtues and the opposite vices are mentioned repeatedly throughout the literature, but perhaps in the most concentrated expression in a passage where the "two spirits" are described (1QS 3:13 – 4:26). We shall return to this when we are considering the theological concepts of Qumran (see pp. 79f. below).

The spiritual concept of the Law was certainly present in Judaism; had it not been, Paul could never have argued successfully against rigid legalism. Something of the conflict between the more spiritual and the more legalistic views can also be seen reflected in the teachings of Hillel and Shammai. It is now clear that the Qumran sect also recognized the more positive application of the Law. Perhaps something of this is reflected in the expressions "well" and "wall": the first members of the covenant (those before the time of Qumran) "dug a well" (CD 3:16) — "the well is the Law" (CD 6:4). They also built a wall (CD 4:12), and "in His hating the builders of the wall, God's wrath was kindled" (CD 8:18). The aptness of this figure is obvious. The well was supposed to be a source of life, but access to it had been barred by those who erected all sorts of restrictions.

We should not hastily conclude, however, that the Qumranians had moved beyond all legalism.

*Legalism.* Some of the proscriptive attitude toward the Law is spelled out in the Damascus Document.

> (Woe to them) if they do not take care to do according to the interpretation of the Law for the evil end-time; and to separate themselves from the sons of the pit; and to abstain from the unclean wealth of wickedness (which has been acquired) by vow and by devoting and by the wealth of the Temple, and by (*sic*) robbing the poor of His people, to make widows their spoil and orphans they murder; and to separate between the unclean and the clean; and to make known (the difference) between the holy and the profane; and to keep the Sabbath day according to its interpretation and the appointed seasons and the day of fasting according

to the commandment of those entering into the New Covenant in the land of Damascus. (CD 6:14-19)

Columns 9-16 of the Damascus Document set forth the specific interpretations of the Sect on the following general subjects: vengeance (CD 9:2-8); the oath concerning lost property (9:9-15); offenses against the Law and witnesses thereto (9:16—10:3); judges (10:4-10); water purification (10:10-13); the Sabbath (10:14—11:18); defiling the Holy Place (11:18—12:2); exceptions in the case of persons possessed by demons or acting inadvertently (12:2-6); relationship with Gentiles (12:6-11); unclean food and objects (12:11-22); organization of the camps (12:22—13:7); duties of the Examiner (13:7-16); [broken section]; the order of rank (14:3-12); the common fund (14:12 [broken]); the oath of the covenant (15:1—16:2 [? broken toward the end]); the calendar (16:2-6); oaths and vows (16:6-[end broken away]).

It is obvious that there is no careful organization of the material. Dupont-Sommer observes, "This Code is essentially composite: it is a compilation, a digest, a collection of decisions which may date from different epochs."[5]

## The Sabbath

The study of the Qumran application of the Sabbath laws will be of particular interest, and will provide an important basis for comparison with the teachings of Jesus on the same subject.

Concerning the Sa[bba]th, to keep it according to its right:
Let no man do on the sixth day any work from the time when the orb of the sun is distant from the gate its fullness (i.e., one diameter above the horizon), for He is the One who said, "Keep the Sabbath day to sanctify it."
And on the Sabbath day let no man speak a bad or empty word.
Let him not exact any payment whatever from his fellow. Let him not judge concerning wealth or profit. Let him not speak with words of the occupation or the labor to be done in the morning.
Let no man walk about in the field to do the work of the desires of the Sabbath. Let a man walk outside his city no further than a thousand cubits.

5 Dupont-Sommer, *The Essene Writings from Qumran*, p. 142.

Let a man eat on the Sabbath day nothing except that which was prepared (previously); and what is perishing in the field he shall not eat. And let him not drink except (what) was in the camp; on the road, if he has gone down to wash, he may drink where he stands. And let him not draw with any vessel whatever.

Let him not send the son of a stranger to do his desire on the Sabbath day.

Let a man not take on him soiled clothing or (what was) brought on the back, except it be washed in water or rubbed with frankincense.

Let no man mingle any of his good will (with strangers) on the Sabbath day.

Let no man go after cattle to pasture it outside his city, except two thousand cubits. Let him not raise his hand to strike it with the fist. If it is rebellious, let him not take it out of his house.

Let no man take (anything) from his house outside, or bring (anything) outside into it. Let him not [o]pen a plastered vessel on the Sabbath. Let no man carry on him spices (or perfumes) to go out or to come in on the Sabbath. Let him not pick up a rock or dust in the house where he lives. Let no one tending an infant carry him to go out or to come in on the Sabbath. Let no man make his manservant or maidservant or hireling refuse (to do anything) on the Sabbath.

Let no man cause (assist) his cattle to bear on the Sabbath; and if it shall fall into a cistern or into a pit, let him not raise it on the Sabbath.

Let no man keep Sabbath in a place near gentiles on the Sabbath.

Let no man profane the Sabbath for the sake of wealth and profit on the Sabbath.

And every human being that shall fall into a source of water or into a reservoir, let no man go up with a ladder or a rope or a tool.

Let no man offer up a burnt offering on the altar on the Sabbath, except the Sabbath burnt offering, for thus it is written, "Besides the Sabbath [ . . . ]." (CD 10:14 — 11:18)

Again it is clear that there is no careful organization of material. Rather, it seems that the Sabbath code grew as the occasion presented new problems.

## Sacrifices

Did the Qumranians repudiate the sacrificial system when

they migrated from Jerusalem?[6] Or did they maintain some kind of sacrifice in the wilderness location? The discussion of this problem is not new, for it was thoroughly debated when the Damascus Document was first published (then known as the Zadokite fragments). With the discovery of the Qumran manuscripts, the discussion has been renewed.

A number of scholars, using questionable methodology, incline to the view that the Qumranians offered sacrifices. Josephus, in a statement that is admittedly obscure, is adduced to show "explicitly that the Essenes practiced separate sacrifice away from the Jerusalem Temple, in other words, at another geographic centre. . . ."[7] Feldman's handling of Josephus in this same passage is influenced by the interpretation of Qumran materials, "since . . . the Qumrân texts and archaeological evidence suggest that the sacrifice was practised. . . ."[8] Our study must be based on the texts, exactly as they stand, without emendation to fit *a priori* convictions. We shall discuss the Josephus passage later, but here we turn to the Qumran materials. The archeological evidence must be interpreted by the textual evidence, if possible, and not the reverse.

The Qumran Sect did not object to the sacrificial system as such. The War Scroll, indeed, pictures the resumption of the Temple worship including sacrifices at the end of time. The regular service of the priests is described as follows:

> And the heads of the priests shall take their place in order after the chief priest and his alternate, twelve heads to be ministering perpetually before God, and twenty-six heads of the courses shall serve in their courses. . . . These shall station themselves over the burnt offerings and over the sacrifices, to arrange a censer of sweet odor for the pleasure of God, to make atonement on behalf of all His Congregation, and to grow fat before Him perpetually at the table of glory. (1QM 2:1-6)

[6] One novel theory suggests that the Qumran sect originated in Egypt and migrated from there to the "city of the Sanctuary" which is identified by the protagonist as Qumran. Cf. S. H. Steckoll, "Qumran and the Temple of Leontopolis," *Revue de Qumrân* 6,21 (Feb. 1967), p. 68. The theory is ingenious if not fantastic.

[7] S. H. Steckoll, *art. cit.*, p. 65, referring to Josephus *Antiquities* 18.1.5 §19.

[8] Josephus, *Jewish Antiquities, Books XVIII-XX*, translated by L. H. Feldman (*Loeb Classical Library;* 1965), pp. 16-17, note a.

The "ram of the sin-offering" (cf. Num. 5:8) is mentioned in the Damascus Document as an offering to atone for any object obtained unlawfully (CD 9:14). Two columns later we read:

> Let no man offer up a burnt offering on the altar on the Sabbath, except the Sabbath burnt offering. . . .
> Let no man send to the altar a burnt offering or a cereal offering or frankincense or wood by a man defiled by one of the defilements to let him defile the altar. (CD 11:17-20)
> Let no man sell clean cattle or fowl to gentiles in order that they may not sacrifice them. (CD 12:8-9)

The meaning of this last provision is not clear; perhaps it was enacted because of attempts to avoid sacrificing. A few columns later we read another provision concerning sacrifices:

> Let no man vow to the altar anything taken by force. (CD 16:13)

According to the first archeological reports, no altar had been found at Qumran. A quantity of burnt or partially burnt animal bones which had been buried in earthenware jars was announced,[9] and upon examination proved to be the fore-quarters of sheep, lambs, goats, calves, and a few cows — mostly sheep and goats.[10] According to Steckoll, these are precisely the animals sacrificed at the "extremely rare ceremony of the consecration of a Temple."[11] Steckoll, however, takes no note of de Vaux' evidence that the bones were from different periods — which would certainly be fatal to any theory of the consecration of a Temple![12] It is generally agreed that the bones were from some sacred meals. We shall discuss the sacred meal (1QSa 2:17-22; 1QS 6:3-5) in connection with the messianic beliefs of the Community (pp. 100f. below).

The Manual of Discipline makes no mention of sacrifices. Some scholars are therefore inclined to date the Manual of Discipline later, and to date the Damascus Document prior to

---

[9] R. de Vaux, "Fouilles de Khirbet Qumrân," *Revue Biblique* 60 (1956), pp. 549f.

[10] F. E. Zeuner, "Notes on Qumrân," *Palestine Exploration Quarterly* (1960), pp. 27-36.

[11] Steckoll, *art. cit.*, p. 56.

[12] R. de Vaux, *L'Archéologie et les manuscrits de la Mer Morte* (1961), pp. 10f.

the migration of the Sect from Jerusalem. Such a theory needs confirmatory evidence.

The discovery of an altar at Qumran has been announced by Steckoll.[13] De Vaux promptly denied that this was a new discovery, stated that it was found by him in 1955, and added "this stone is surely not an altar."[14] We must again insist that the interpretation of an archeological discovery is properly made by the texts when texts are present.

## Spiritual Sacrifices

It seems clear from the Manual of Discipline that a spiritual view of sacrifices was also found, and perhaps was prevailing, at Qumran. The following passage is significant.

> When these things happen in Israel according to all these regulations, to found a spirit of holiness according to eternal truth, to make atonement for the guilt of rebellion and the infidelity of sin, and to (establish) good will on earth apart from the flesh of burnt offerings and apart from the fat of sacrifice, and the offering of the lips for judgment as a sweet savor of righteousness, and perfection of way as the voluntary gift of a cereal offering of good will. (1QS 9:3-5)

The passage is not without its difficulties. The word translated "apart from" (*min*) can also be translated "some" or "part of." Accordingly the sentence could be translated, "to (establish) good will on earth (by means of) some flesh of burnt offerings and some fat of sacrifice." The context, however, seems to indicate a contrast, and the "offering of the lips" and the "perfection of way" are intended to take the place of animal and cereal sacrifices.

This would be entirely in keeping with the teaching of the Old Testament.[15] With the Dispersion the Jews were able to accommodate their religion to the Synagogue and to learn

13 He refers to the announcement in *Mada'*, January 1956, pp. 246f., to which I have not had access. He describes the altar, gives an isometric sketch, and publishes a photograph of the altar in the article to which I have referred (n. 6 above).

14 R. de Vaux, "Post-Scriptum," *Revue Biblique* 75 (1968), pp. 204f. Steckoll's reply, rather contentious, is found in "Marginal Notes on the Qumran Excavations," *Revue de Qumrân* 7,25 (Dec. 1969), pp. 36f.

15 Cf. Amos 5:21-22; Hosea 6:6; Micah 6:6-8; Isaiah 1:11-20; and Psalm 51:16-17. There is no need of a Zoroastrian or Pythagorean explanation; cf. Dupont-Sommer, *The Essene Writings from Qumran*, p. 93 n. 1.

to live without the perpetual sacrifice of the Temple. This process, sometimes regarded as part of the "Hellenization" of the Jews, helped to prepare the Jewish people for the time when the Temple would no longer be standing and sacrifices would no longer be possible. At the same time it prepared the way for the more spiritual attitude of the "Hellenists" in the early Christian Church and ultimately for the attitude of Paul and of the author of the Epistle to the Hebrews.

Not only in the Dispersion, but even in the shadow of the Temple in Jerusalem, the Jews lived without sacrifices (cf. Acts 6:9; 9:29). Moreover, it is almost impossible to understand the development of rabbinical Judaism, unless we recognize the presence of a spiritualizing tendency in Pharisaic Judaism. Qumran helps us understand this development.

## Ritual Washing or Baptism

The discovery of Khirbet Qumrân with its complex system of aqueducts and water reservoirs serves to focus attention on the question, Were the Qumranians a baptist sect? Unfortunately, the literature from Qumran provides little help in answering the question, and most of that has to be gotten from negative statements.

> Let him (i.e. the perverse man who has not entered into the covenant) not enter into the water to touch the Purity of the men of holiness, for they shall not be pure except they have repented of their wickedness, for uncleanness (is) in all who transgress His word. (1QS 5:13-14)

The man who despises to enter the Community,

> shall not be reckoned with the upright, and his knowledge and his strength and his wealth shall not come into the Congregation of the Community. . . . He shall not be declared innocent by atonement, and he shall not be cleansed by waters of impurity, and he shall not be sanctified by seas and rivers, and he shall not be cleansed by all the waters of washing. Unclean, unclean he shall be all the days of his despising the judgments of God in order not to be disciplined in the Community of His Counsel. (1QS 3:1-6)

However the waters of cleansing, or ritual bathing, were not in themselves able to cleanse man from sin; the rite was not sacramental in the sense that it worked apart from the conscious will of the man.

> For in the spirit of the Counsel of the Truth of God the
> ways of man shall receive atonement for all his iniquities to
> look on the Light of life, and with a holy spirit to be united
> in His truth he shall be cleansed from all his iniquities, and
> with a spirit of uprightness and humility his sin shall be
> atoned, and in the humility of his soul toward all the stat-
> utes of God his flesh shall be cleansed, to be sprinkled with
> waters of impurity and to be cleansed with waters of pound-
> ing (— washing?). (1QS 3:6-9)

A passage in the Damascus Document may shed additional
light on ritual bathing.

> Concerning purification in water:
> Let no man wash in filthy water or in too little to cover a
> man. Let him not cleanse a vessel in it. And any pool in a rock
> in which there is not enough to cover (a man) and which an
> unclean person has touched, it is unclean: its waters are like
> the waters of a vessel. (CD 10:10-13)

On the basis of this passage, Allegro thinks it "more likely
that the sectarians would have preferred the running water of
the Jordan . . . or even of 'Ain Feshkha to the south, to the
static tanks in the Settlement."[16]

## The Purity

The passage concerning admission to the Community contains references to "the Purity of the Many" and "the Drink
of the Many."[17] The precise identification of these items or
qualities is not yet possible. The word *ṭohŏrā* in rabbinical
usage refers to ritually clean articles such as vessels, utensils,
garments, and particularly food. It seems reasonable to suggest that the Purity and the Drink were parts of a sacred meal,
sacred food and sacred drink, from which novices and members under discipline for serious violations were barred.

## Holy Days of the Calendar

Both in the Old Testament and in the Qumran writings
the observance of holy days is part of the religious life. Sab-
baths, new moons, holy days, years, and exact epochs are men-

16 J. M. Allegro, *The Dead Sea Scrolls* (Baltimore: Penguin Books,
1956), p. 90.
17 1QS 6:16-17, 20-21, p. 53 above. Other references are found in 1QS
7:3, 10-20; 8:17-18, 24-25; and CD 9:21-23. For a more detailed study see
my *Amazing Dead Sea Scrolls*, pp. 86-90.

tioned in the Dead Sea Scrolls. The Day of Atonement was important in the history of the Sect (cf. 1QpHab 11:7). Other holy days of the Jewish year were observed, as is now clear from the *Mishmaroth* texts.

One of the vows of admission was "not to advance the times and not to retard (them) from any of their appointed seasons" (1QS 1:14-15). In the Habukkuk Commentary there is a reference to the Wicked Priest who persecuted the Teacher of Righteousness, and then

> at the end of the appointed time of the resting on the Day of Atonement he appeared unto them to swallow them up and to cause them to stumble on the day of the fast, the Sabbath of their rest. (1QpHab 11:4-7)

This statement makes sense only if the Day of Atonement was observed by the Qumranians at a different time than it was by official Judaism.

The most extensive studies have been published by Mlle A. Jaubert.[18] For our purposes we need only point out that the Qumranians apparently used a lunar calendar (354 days in the year, with intercalary months as needed to keep the year in phase with the sun) and a solar calendar (364 days, with an intercalary day).[18a] The lunar calendar was the calendar of normative Judaism; the solar calendar was preserved in the Book of Jubilees. The *Mishmaroth* texts from Cave Four contain a synchronization of the two calendars and the twenty-six priestly courses (cf. 1QM 2:2) through a complete six-year cycle. The same texts mention the annual feasts: Passover, Feast of Wave Offering, Feast of Weeks, Day of Remembrance (and not New Year's Day), Day of Expiations, and Feast of Tabernacles.[19]

## The Ceremony of Passing Over into the Covenant

The opening columns of the Manual of Discipline describe

[18] A. Jaubert, *La date de la Cène* (Paris: Lecoffre, 1957; 159 pp.). Eugen Ruckstuhl, *Chronology of the Last Days of Jesus* (New York: Desclée, 1965), has built on this work in a study that deserves careful reading, especially pp. 72-140. For other titles on the subject, see my *Bibliography of the Dead Sea Scrolls 1948-1957*, §§3356-3367.

[18a] There is no indication of any attempt to harmonize this solar calendar with the actual solar year.

[19] Cf. J. T. Milik, *Ten Years of Discovery in the Wilderness of Judaea* (Studies in Biblical Theology, No. 26; London: SCM, 1959), pp. 107-113.

a ceremony that could be called, using Qumranian terminology, "entering" or "passing over into the Covenant" (1QS
1:16, 18, 23; 2:10, 12, 18). The ceremony was an annual
occasion, if we have interpreted it correctly: "Thus they shall
do year by year all the days of the dominion of Belial" (1QS
2:19).

There was also an annual examination (1QS 5:24, p. 51
above) with promotion or demotion. The postulant, likewise,
was examined for a year, and the novice for a second year
(1QS 6:13-23, p. 53 above). It is possible that these examinations were held, together with the ceremony of passing over
into the Covenant, at the same time. One scholar has suggested that it was in connection with the Feast of Weeks — a
suggestion that commends itself the more since Pentecost (or
Weeks) is the festival commemorating the giving of the Law
at Sinai. The Day of Atonement might equally well be considered, for in Jewish thought this is the day when the heavenly
books of good and evil deeds are balanced, and man receives
God's gracious atonement for another year.

## Punishment and Excommunication

A detailed list of punishments and fines for offenses against
the Community is given in the Manual of Discipline (1QS
6:24—7:25). It covers such matters as: lying concerning property, answering disrespectfully, using the divine name, inter-
rupting a fellow, sleeping during sessions of the Many or
leaving without permission, going naked, spitting in the session of the Many, laughing stupidly and loudly, etc. Fines are
expressed in terms of days or months; the exact meaning is
not clear, but it may refer to exclusion from the sessions or
from the sacred meals.

For more serious offenses there was banishment from the
Community. Murmuring against a brother or slandering him
brought temporary exclusion, but the same offense against the
Many or the Community was punished by permanent exclusion: "they shall send him away and he shall not return again"
(1QS 7:17). A member who betrayed the truth and walked
in stubbornness of heart was sent away for two years, and the
process of his readmission sounds similar to the admission of
a new member:

If he returns (or repents), he shall be punished two years; in the first he shall not touch the Purity of the Many, and in the second he shall not touch the Drink of the Many, and after all the men of the Community he shall sit. And when two years of days are fulfilled, the Many shall ask concerning his affairs, and if they shall cause him to approach, then he shall be written in his position, and afterwards he may ask concerning his judgment. (1QS 7:19-21)

However, if the man had been a member of the Council of the Community for more than ten years and had become guilty of the same crime, he was banished permanently, and

any man from the men of the Co[mmunity who shall min]gle with him in his purity or in his wealth, wh[ich is not by authority of] the Many, his judgment (or case) shall be like him, to [be sent away . . . ]. (1QS 7:24-25)

## Summary

The Qumranians were men who voluntarily separated themselves from the world. They turned their property over to the Community and had all things, including their mind and strength, in common. It is perhaps not accurate to call them a monastic order, since there were no vows of poverty or celibacy. In fact, provision is made in the literature for the presence of women and children in the camp and for the instruction of youths from early childhood.

They were devoted to the study of the Law of Moses. For them the Law meant a way of life, including the positive virtues as well as the negative prohibitions. Their literature contains many legalistic details, particularly with reference to the Sabbath, and in some points their Sabbatarian laws are more rigid than any known from any other Jewish source.

They did not stress the sacrifices of the altar, although provision is made in the literature for limited participation. The development of spiritual sacrifices is noteworthy. Ritual washing may have partly taken the place of the sacrificial system, and it is possible that a sacred meal also was a substitute for animal sacrifices.

They observed the calendar of the Book of Jubilees, synchronizing it with the official calendar to keep their priestly courses functioning properly.

Annual examinations, punishments, and even exclusion from the Sect, underscore the serious application of their discipline to their life in the Community.

## CHAPTER FIVE

# THE QUMRAN DOCTRINE OF GOD— "THE GOD OF KNOWLEDGE"

Beliefs develop slowly. Even those of us who speak of "revealed religion" do not think that it was delivered all at one time in nicely bound volumes arranged according to theological subjects. Man learns slowly, and as he learns he is able to progress to the next stage. When we say that God revealed truth to man, we recognize that God was fitting His revelations to this learning process. Theology develops as man seeks to arrange the scattered details in some orderly manner.

To speak of the "theology of Qumran" is therefore idealistic. We have found no systematic theologies, and the texts we have found suggest that the Qumranians had not yet developed any systematic theologians. Therefore when we attempt to arrange their beliefs in some semblance of system, we are imposing to a certain extent our own thought categories.

The customary divisions of theology are: the doctrine of God (Theology proper), the nature of man (Anthropology), and the relationship between God and man, or salvation (Soteriology). We shall follow in general this outline.

## The Qumran Doctrine of God

The Qumran Covenanters were Jews; therefore they believed in the God of the Old Testament, the God who had revealed Himself and His will through the prophets to Israel. On this is based the Qumran "argument from history" found in the Damascus Document (cf. CD 2:14—3:12). The Qumranians were moreover a sect that had separated from Jerusalem, gone into the desert (or to Damascus), and "entered the New Covenant"; therefore we should find points at which the Qumranians deviate from the beliefs of normative Judaism. This is "sectarian Judaism."

The following extended passage from the War Scroll gives us a fairly comprehensive idea of the Qumran doctrine of God. He is the God of Israel:

> Who is there like Thee, O God of Israel, in H[eave]n and on earth, who shall do according to Thy great deeds and Thy mighty heroism? And who is there like Thy people Israel whom Thou hast chosen for Thyself from all the peoples of the lands: a people of holy ones of the Covenant and instructed in the Statute, of enlightened ones of un[derstanding and knowledge] who both hear an honored voice and see angels of holiness, whose ear has been opened and who hear deep things? (1QM 10:8-11)

He is the Lord of creation:

> [For Thou hast spread] the sail of the clouds, the host of luminaries, and the burden of the winds (or spirits) and the dominion of the holy ones, storehouses of [Thy] gl[ory]. [Thou art the One forming] forests, and creating earth and the statutes of its divisions into wilderness and the land of the Arabah and all its produce with [its] fr[uit and] its [ . . . ], the circle of seas and the reservoirs of the rivers and the valley of the deeps, the deeds of beasts and winged ones, the model of man and [his] his[tory and] his [see]d, the mixture of language and the scattering of peoples, the dwelling place of families and the inheritance of lands [ . . . ], the appointed times of holiness and the seasons of the years and the end-times of eternity. [*About 3 lines too fragmentary for translation.*] (1QM 10:11-15)

He is the God of history:

> But to Thee is the war, and in the strength of Thy hand have their corpses been eviscerated so there is no burying (them). And Goliath the Gittite, a mighty hero, Thou didst deliver into the hand of David Thy Servant; for he trusted in Thy great name and not in sword and spear.
>
> For to Thee is the war, and the Philistines he su[bdued] many times in Thy holy name. And also by the hand of our kings Thou didst save us many times for Thy mercy's sake, and not according to our deeds which we made evil, nor (according to) our rebellious actions. (1QM 11:1-4)

He is the God of the Qumran covenanters:

> To Thee is the war and from [Thee] the power, and not
> ours; and not our strength and the might of our hands have
> done valor, but in Thy strength and in the might of Thy
> great valor.
>
> A[s] Thou didst declare to us formerly, saying, "A star shall
> proceed from Jacob, a sceptre shall rise from Israel, and he
> shall crush the temples (of the foreheads) of Moab and he shall
> destroy all the sons of Seth; and he shall go down from Jacob
> and cause the survivor [from the] city to perish, and the enemy
> shall be a possession, and Israel shall do valiantly." And by
> the hands of Thine anointed ones who see Thy testimonies
> Thou hast declared to us the [en]d of the wars of Thy hands,
> to be glorified by our enemies, to cause the troops of Belial to
> fall, seven nations of vanity, by the hand of Thy redeemed
> poor, in [ . . . ] and in peace by marvellous might. (1QM 11:4-9)

> And the melted heart (has become) a doorway of hope. And
> Thou wilt do to them as Pharaoh and as the officers of his char-
> iots in the [R]ed Sea. And the smitten in spirit Thou wilt
> cause to pass by like a torch of fire in the sheaves consuming
> (the) wicked, and not turning back until finishing (the) guilty.
>
> And formerly [Thou didst] cause to he[ar the appointed
> seas]on of the strength of Thy hand on the Kittim, saying,
> "Asshur shall fall by the sword that is not of man, and a sword
> that is not human shall devour him." For by the hand of the
> poor Thou wilt deliver up the [enem]ies of all the lands and
> by the hand of those who are bowed in dust, to bring low the
> mighty ones of the peoples, and to bring back the recompense
> of the wicked on [ . . . ], to justify the judgment of Thy truth
> on all the sons of men, and to make for Thyself an eternal
> name on the people of [ . . . ] the wars, and to be exalted and
> sanctified in the eyes of the rest of the nations, to know [*about
> 4 lines too broken for translation*]. (1QM 11:9-15)

A passage with numerous similarities will be found in the
Thanksgiving Hymns (1QH 1:6-20). Material for reconstruct-
ing the Qumran doctrine of God will be found throughout the
literature.

## Qumran Dualism

The term "Dualism" is used in many ways: in philosophy,
it is used of the matter-spirit dualism of the universe; in religion, of the ethical good-evil dualism, and also of the cosmo-

logical dualism of a supreme Good Being versus an equal Evil Being. Ethical dualism is found in the Bible: the two ways set before man (Prov. 2:13-15), the conflict between light and darkness (John 1:5), etc. Cosmological dualism is found in its classical form in Zoroastrianism, a religion that originated in Persia: Angra Mainyu (later Ahriman), the creator of evil, is opposed by Ahura Mazda (Ormuzd), the creator of good. But Zoroastrianism is not a perfect dualism, for whereas the two Spirits are coeval — that is, they have both existed from the beginning — they are not both eternal, for Ormuzd shall in the end triumph over Ahriman.

Elements of cosmological dualism, at least in modified form, are found in the Biblical doctrine of Satan, who is struggling against God much as Ahriman opposes Ormuzd. There is an important difference, however, for whereas Ormuzd is coeval with Ahriman, Satan is a creature of God.

Frequently a part of dualism, but not necessarily so, is the concept of lesser beings — spirits, angels, demons — who serve the supreme Being. Spirits and angels are mentioned in the Old Testament; angels, demons, and other spiritual beings are mentioned in the New Testament.

The struggle between these two hosts of beings can take place in the heavens; or it can take place on earth, with the subjugation or deliverance of man as its object; or man can be portrayed as entering into the conflict, to aid the forces of good or the forces of evil as he wills.

Against this brief background, the following passage from the Manual of Discipline is illuminating. First there is a statement of purpose:

> For the enlightened man, to understand and to teach all the sons of light in the generations of all the sons of man as to all kinds of their spirits in their signs, as to their deeds in their generations, and as to the visitation of their afflictions with the end-times of their reward. (1QS 3:13-15)

God is supreme over all:

> From the God of knowledge (comes) all that is and that is to be; and before their being He established all their purpose, and when they came into being for their testimony as the purpose of His glory, they fulfill their work and there is no changing. In His hand are the judgments of all, and it is He who shall provide for them in all their desires. (1QS 3:15-17)

God created two spirits:

> And it is He who created man to have dominion over the planet, and He appointed to him two spirits to walk in them until the appointed time of His visitation: they are the spirits of truth and unrighteousness (or error).
>
> In the abode of light are the generations of truth, and from the wellspring of darkness are the generations of unrighteousness. And in the hand of the Prince of Lights is the dominion of all the sons of unrighteousness, and in the ways of darkness they shall walk. (1QS 3:17-21)

The Angel of Darkness opposes God and is opposed by Him:

> And by the Angel of Darkness is the misleading (or straying) of all the sons of righteousness, and all their sins and their iniquities and their guilt and their rebellious deeds are in his dominion, according to the mysteries of God, until His end-time. And all their afflictions and the appointed times of their anguish are in the dominion of His adversary (or Mastema); and all the spirits of his lot (exist) to cause the sons of light to stumble, but the God of Israel and the angel of His truth (are) a help to all the sons of light.
>
> And it is He who created the spirits of light and darkness, and upon them He founded all His deeds, [and on] their [ways] every work [and on their ways every visitat]ion.
>
> One (spirit) God has loved for all the ages of eternity, and in all its actions He will be pleased for ever. One (spirit), He has loathed its secret council, and all its ways He hates in perpetuity. (1QS 3:21—4:1)

The way of the spirit of truth is described:

> And these are their ways in the world: to give light in the heart of man, and to make straight before him all the ways of true righteousness; and to put his heart in fear of the judgments; and a spirit of humility, and slowness to anger, and breadth of mercy, and eternal goodness, and enlightenment and understanding and mighty wisdom trusting in all the works of God and leaning on the multitude of His mercy, and a spirit of knowledge in all the purpose of doing, and zeal of the judgments of righteousness, and the purpose of holiness with firm purpose, and greatness of mercy unto all the sons of truth, and glorious purity loathing all the idols of impurity, and modesty to walk in all prudence; and to hide for truth the mysteries of knowledge. (1QS 4:2-6)
>
> These are the secret councils of the spirit for the sons of truth in the world. And the visitation of all who walk in it

> for healing, and abundance of peace in length of days, to yield
> seed with all the blessing of eternity, and eternal rejoicing in
> perpetual life, and perfection of glory with a garment of
> splendor in eternal light. (1QS 4:6-8)

The way of the spirit of unrighteousness is also described:

> And to the spirit of unrighteousness, greediness and negli-
> gence in the work of righteousness, wickedness and falsehood,
> pride and haughty heart, lying and deceit, cruelty and much
> hypocrisy, quickness of anger and much stupidity and pre-
> sumptuous zeal, loathesome works in the spirit of fornication
> and ways of impurity in deeds of uncleanness, and a tongue
> of insults, blindness of eyes and heaviness of ear, stiffness of
> neck and hardness of heart, to walk in all the ways of darkness
> and the cunningness of wickedness. (1QS 4:9-11)

The two spirits influence all of this life:

> In these (two spirits) are the generations of all the sons of
> men, and in their divisions are all the hosts (of men) for their
> generations. And in their ways they shall walk, and every effect
> of their deeds (shall be) in their (i.e. the spirits') divisions
> according to the inheritance of a man, between much and little,
> for all the times of eternity. For God appointed them (i.e. the
> spirits) in equal parts until the final end, and He set eternal
> enmity between their divisions. Loathing of truth are the
> actions of unrighteousness, and loathing of unrighteousness are
> all the ways of truth: and a contending zeal is upon all their
> judgments, for they do not walk in unity.
>
> But God in the mysteries of His enlightenment and in the
> wisdom of His glory has appointed an end to the existence of
> unrighteousness, and in the time of visitation He will destroy
> it forever. (1QS 4:15-19)
>
> To this moment the spirits of truth and unrighteousness con-
> tend in the heart of man: they walk in wisdom and folly. And
> according to the inheritance of a man in truth and righteous-
> ness, so he hates unrighteousness; and according to his posses-
> sion in the lot of unrighteousness, he does wickedness in it and
> so he loathes truth. (1QS 4:23-25)

But God has decreed their times and their works:

> For in equal measure God appointed them (the spirits) until
> the end He has decreed, and to make new. It is He who knew
> the effect of their deeds for all the times of [their appointment]
> and He shall cause them to inherit the sons of man, to know
> good [and evil. And it is He who c]ast the lots for every

living thing, according to his spirit in [the day of] visitation.
(1QS 4:25-26)

There are a number of important observations to make on this passage.

First and foremost is the rigid monism that pervades the entire section. God is supreme. There is never any question but that God has created all things and God will finish all things according to His own plan. Several scholars have suggested that there is marked Zoroastrian influence on Qumran theology, particularly in the dualism of the two spirits. But this is not Zoroastrian dualism. If there is in the Scrolls other evidence of Zoroastrian influence — in my opinion quite indirect and removed — it has certainly been refined by the monism of the Old Testament. If the Qumranians received certain peculiar doctrines from Zoroastrian sources, then this passage seems to be a polemic against Zoroastrian dualism.

Second, both spirits are created beings, created by God. The two Spirits of Zoroastrianism are uncreated. "Light" and "darkness" are, to be sure, found in Zoroastrianism, and Ahura Mazda is associated with light (has he not given us the word for the mazda lamp?) — but it takes more than this to prove derivation or even relationship. The contrast between light and darkness is so obvious to anyone who can see, that many have drawn upon these terms to express their ideas.

The resulting works of these two spirits upon men can be compared to the "deeds of the flesh" and the "fruits of the Spirit" in Paul's writings; we shall return to this when we consider the relationship between Paul and Qumran. Likewise the idea of light and darkness will be considered when we discuss the relationship between the Johannine writings and Qumran.

The doctrine of man in this passage is very important; we shall return to it when we turn to the Qumran concept of man.

## Satan, Belial, Mastema, and the Angels

In the Old Testament, the passages referring to Satan and angels are usually dated to the period after the Exile, and the doctrines are traced to Zoroastrian influence. In the intertestamental period there was an elaboration of the doctrines. We therefore are prepared to find an elaborate doctrine of these spiritual beings in Qumran writings.

The word "Satan" is found only in a fragment of a hymn, where it seems to be a common noun: "you shall rebuke every destroying adversary (Satan)."[1]

A more common name for the adversary of God is "Belial," which occurs nearly forty times, mostly in the War Scroll (16x) and the Thanksgiving Hymns (13x). In the Damascus Document, Belial is opposed to "the Prince of Lights":

> For formerly Moses and Aaron stood by the hand of the Prince of Lights, and Belial raised Jannes and his brother by his craftiness. (CD 5:17-19)[2]

In the passage quoted above (1QS 3:20-21, p. 79) the Prince of Lights is opposed by the Angel of Darkness; it therefore seems reasonable to identify the Angel of Darkness with Belial.

God's adversary is also called "Mastema," a word which, like "Satan," can be used either as a common noun or a proper noun:

> And all their afflictions and the appointed times of their anguish are in the dominion of His adversary (or Mastema). (1QS 3:23)

> And on the day when man sets it on his soul to return to the Law of Moses the angel of the adversary (the Mastema) will turn away from him, if he establishes his words. (CD 16:5)[3]

"Mastema" and "Belial" seem to used in a parallelism in the War Scroll, in a passage which presents a problem of translation:

> And Thou hast made Belial for destruction (or, to destroy?) the angel Mastema WBḤR [    ]. (1QM 13:10-11)

Unfortunately, the break in the following word makes translation uncertain. In my opinion the sentence ends after the word Mastema — which makes a parallelism impossible and favors the translation, "Thou hast made Belial to destroy the angel Mastema." I admit that this does not seem to be consistent with the usage of Mastema in other passages, especially 1QS 3:23 quoted above (cf. also p. 79).

[1] 1QH fragment 4:6 (Habermann, *megillôt midbar yehûdā,* p. 136); cf. Zech. 3:2.

[2] Cf. the reference to Jannes and Jambres in 2 Tim. 3:8.

[3] Cf. the expression "the angel Satan" in 2 Cor. 12:7. The word Mastema occurs also in 1QM 13:4, 11.

The following passages contain information concerning the doctrine of angels. They serve God in Heaven:

> For the multitude of [the]se holy ones in Heaven and the hosts of angels in Thy holy habitation of p[raise] Thy [name], and the elect of a holy people Thou hast appointed for Thyself in [ . . . and the numb]er of the names of all their hosts with Thee in Thy holy dwelling, and the a[ngels of heav]en in Thy holy habitation, and the favors of [Thy] ble[ssing] and the covenant of Thy peace, Thou hast engraved them with the stylus of life, to rule [over them] in all the appointed times of eternity, and to muster the h[osts of] Thine [ele]ct by thousands and tens of thousands, together with their holy ones and [the host] of Thine angels, and for a possession of (Thy?) hand in the war [ . . . ] those who rise from earth, the covenant of Thy judgment and with the elect of heaven [Thy] ble[ssings.] (1QM 12:1-5)

They also serve the Covenanters:

> And Thou, God, art e[stablished] in the glory of Thy Kingdom and the congregation of Thy holy ones is in our midst for an etern[al] help. [Before] us contempt for kings, derision and mockery for the mighty ones. The Holy One, the Lord and the King of glory is with us, the people of (or, together with) the holy ones. The mig[hty ones of] the host of angels are in our muster, and the hero of the wa[r] in our congregation, and the host of his spirits with our marching men, and [ou]r horses are [like] clouds and like the thickness of dew to cover the earth, and like a flood of showers to water (with) judgment all its produce. (1QM 12:6-9)

God is Ruler over all angels and spirits:

> Th[ou O God] hast [redeemed] us for Thyself, an eternal people, and in the lot of light Thou hast cast us for Thy truth. And the Prince of Light formerly Thou didst muster to help us, and [Thou hast] cho[sen the sons of righteousnes]s and all the spirits of truth in his dominion. And Thou hast made Belial for destruction, the angel Mastema. And [Thou hast] chosen [with] his [help] and with his counsel to make wickedness and to make guilt. And all the spirits of his lot, the angels of woe, in the statutes of darkness they shall walk, and unto him shall be their [desi]re together. And we in the lot of Thy truth shall be glad in Thy strength, and we shall rejoice in Thy salvation, and we shall exult in [Thy] he[lp and we shall —?— in] Thy [p]eace. (1QM 13:9-13)

The angels Michael the prince, Gabriel, Sariel, and Raphael are mentioned in the War Scroll (1QM 9:15-16). In the final battle, the outcome is secured by Michael:

> And He shall send an eternal help to the lot of His [redempt]ion in the strength of the mighty angel Michael in eternal light, to illumine with gladness the h[ouse of Is]rael, peace and blessing to the lot of God, to exalt among the gods ( = angels?) the ministry of Michael and the dominion of Israel over all flesh. (1QM 17:6-8)

## CHAPTER SIX

# THE QUMRAN DOCTRINE OF MAN—
# "A SLICE OF CLAY"

Man feels the need of "salvation." He may not use this word, but every effort he makes to improve his lot, whether it be education, science, or construction, is a way of saying, "Things are not yet perfect; they could be better."

There are three, and it would seem only three ways of salvation. Man can save himself: this is Humanism. He can work with God for his salvation: this is sometimes called synergism. Or he must depend entirely upon God to bring in the "golden age": this is salvation by grace. The Bible, Old and New Testaments, Jews and Christians, Protestants and Catholics, Eastern and Western Catholicism — *all* have always unanimously repudiated Humanism as a possible option. Events of recent decades tend to confirm the belief that man must have help from God if he is to achieve a perfect order. The choice between some form of synergism and pure grace has not been so clearly defined: both Judaism and Christianity have long debated it without a final answer.

If man must depend upon God, whether for part or all of his salvation, how can he know what God expects of him? This is the problem of the knowledge of God. Does God speak through dreams, or angels, or specially selected men? This is revelation in its broadest sense. Is the knowledge communicated to all men, or just to a chosen number? This introduces the matter of election. Is it secret, hidden from all except a select few? This is esoteric knowledge. So develops the complex problem of the knowledge of God.

And if man's salvation depends entirely upon God's grace, then all of these questions must be asked, and in addition still others. Is man a free agent, able to make his own decisions, or is he "elect" or "reprobate" solely by the will of God? The question of determinism enters, and with it the correlate of free will. Is the choice anterior to man's actions, or does it involve his moral behavior? Are good works the response to God's election or are they the work of God's redemption in him? Each question leads in turn to others.

The men of Qumran, like men of all places and ages, asked these questions. Their answers are not always unequivocal, and to us they may not always be satisfactory, but they are interesting and important.

## The Qumran Doctrine of Man

The most extensive passages are found in the devotional portions of the Qumran writings: the hymn at the end of the Manual of Discipline, and the scroll of Thanksgiving Hymns.

In the Manual of Discipline we find the following passage:

> As for me, to man is wickedness and to the secret council of flesh is unrighteousness; my iniquities, my rebellions, my sins, along with the perversions of my heart (belong) to the secret council of vermin and those who walk in darkness. For to man is his way, and the frail being cannot establish his steps; but to God is judgment, and from His hand is perfection of the way. And by His knowledge everything has come into existence, and everything exists by His purpose. He shall establish it, and without Him it shall not be done.
>
> As for me, if I stagger, the mercies of God are my salvation for ever. And if I stumble by the iniquity of flesh, my judgment is in the righteousness of God: it shall stand perpetually. And if He shall unloose my distress, then from destruction He will rescue my soul, and He will establish my steps on the way. By His tender mercies He has caused me to approach, and by His covenant love He will bring in my judgment. By His true righteousness [He] will judge me, and in the abundance of His goodness He will make atonement on behalf of all my iniquities, and by His righteousness He will cleanse me from the impurity of man and the sin of humankind. (1QS 11:9-15)

Similar to it is the following passage from the Thanksgiving Hymns:

> And what then is man — even earth is he, and from clay he
> has been sliced, and to dust is his return — that Thou shouldst
> enlighten him with wonders like these, and by the secret of
> G[od] Thou shouldst inform him?
>
> As for me, (I am) dust and ash; what shall I plan (?) if Thou
> hast not desired it, and what shall I consider if it is not Thy
> will? How shall I take strength if Thou hast not made me to
> stand? And how shall I have understanding if Thou hast not
> formed (it) for me? And how shall I speak if Thou hast not
> opened my mouth? And how shall I reply if Thou hast not
> enlightened me? . . . What therefore is he who returns to his
> dust that he should retain [strengt]h? Only for Thy glory hast
> Thou made all these. (1QH 10:3-8, 12)

Similar ideas are found in other hymns (cf. 1QH 4:29-37;
9:14-18; 13:13-21; 18:21-29).

This is devotional literature, and man always tends to be
more humble in the presence of Deity. If we had a scientific
or philosophical treatise on the human being from Qumran
we might find a different approach. But in the extant literature, man is the creature of God, with nothing in himself that
God has not graciously given him. Man is not the master of
his own way. In fact, something quite similar to "double pre-
destination" is found in one passage:

> Only Thou hast [created] the righteous, and from the womb
> Thou hast established him for the appointed time of (Thy)
> will, to be kept in Thy covenant and to walk in all (Thy way),
> [and to have p]ity upon him in the multitude of Thy tender
> mercies, and to unloose all the anguish of his soul, for age-
> long salvation and eternal peace, and without any lack. And
> Thou hast raised up from flesh his glory.
>
> And the wicked men Thou hast created for [the end-times
> of] Thine [ang]er, and from the womb Thou hast sanctified
> them for the day of slaughter. For they walk in the way of
> no good and they despise [Thy] c[ovenant. Thy word] their
> spirit loathes, and they have not delighted in anything Thou
> hast commanded, and they have chosen what Thou hast hated.
> (1QM 15:14-19)

We have already read the passage concerning the "two
spirits" in connection with the Qumran doctrine of God.[1] It
will repay reading again, this time noting the doctrine of man.
There is an "enlightened" man; all he has, he received from

---

[1] Cf. 1QS 3:13—4:26, pp. 78-80 above.

God; he is to have dominion over the earth. Man in general
is led by two spirits; the blessings and virtues are from the
spirit of light, the evils from the spirit of unrighteousness.
Finally, God purifies the enlightened man who has been led
by the spirit of truth.

The utter sinfulness of man is brought out in a passage
in the Manual of Discipline. He cannot be cleansed by any
means as long as he scorns the ordinances of God and refuses
to be taught by the Community. When he accepts the truth
from the Community, then he can be cleansed:

> And he shall establish his steps to walk perfectly in all the
> ways of God, as He commanded with reference to the ap-
> pointed times of His testimonies. And he shall not turn aside
> to the right or to the left, and he is not permitted to step one
> step from all His ways. Then he will be favored with atone-
> ments of sweet savor before God, and the covenant of an
> eternal Community shall be his (?). (1QS 3:9-12)[2]

## Salvation, Justification, and Good Works

Man's salvation depends upon God's willingness to forgive:
this was the lesson of history and the remnant of Israel (CD
1:4). It is also the lesson of human experience.

> As for me, I know that not to man is righteousness nor to the
> son of man is perfection of way. To God most high are all
> the works of righteousness, and the way of man is not estab-
> lished except by the spirit God fashioned for him, to perfect
> a way for the sons of men, that they may know all His works
> in the might of His power and in the multitude of His mercies
> unto all the sons of His pleasure. (1QH 4:30-33)

At the same time, human responsibility is not absent. There
is strong emphasis on good works and on repentance throughout the Qumran documents. The following passage from the
Manual of Discipline is representative:

> For they are not reckoned in His covenant, for they did not
> seek and they did not inquire after His statutes to know the
> hidden things in which they have strayed with resulting guilt,
> while the revealed things they have done high-handedly . . . .
> (1QS 5:11-12)

[2] For the preceding lines, see p. 71 above. The last clause here is difficult; the author seems to have changed his intended subject to an indirect
object.

Is there a doctrine of justification in Qumran theology like the Pauline doctrine? A number of scholars believe they have found it. One scholar does so by translating *mišpāṭ* "justification" in several passages; but the contexts do not require such translation, and the history of the word in Hebrew usage does not support it. Others point to the passage in the Habakkuk Commentary, where the same verse which Paul uses to support his doctrine is used by the Qumranians:

> Its interpretation: concerning all doers of the Law in the house of Judah whom God will deliver from the house of judgment for the sake of their toil and their faith in the teacher of righteousness. (1QpHab 8:1-3)

We shall discuss this at greater length when we study the relationship of Paul with Qumran writings. For the moment let us note that forgiveness in Qumran seems to be God's willingness to grant to man the spirit by which man is able to keep God's Law; it does not seem to be God's willingness to look upon man as "righteous" apart from good works. Even in the passage just quoted we note that it concerns "all doers of the Law."

The requirements of those who entered the New Covenant are set forth in several places in the Scrolls. We have already examined the complicated legal system, particularly the Sabbath laws. A summary of the essential obligations is quoted on pp. 64f. above (CD 6:14-19).

## Gnosis and Gnosticism

In a number of the passages cited there are repeated references to "knowledge," "mysteries," "truth," and similar terms. Several scholars refer to this as "Gnosticism," and some have traced it to Zoroastrianism. K. G. Kuhn says, "This Gnostic structure of the new text can scarcely have sprung up from Jewish tradition."[3] Dupont-Sommer remarks, "As a matter of fact, the idea of Knowledge, Gnosis, impregnates the whole of Qumran thought and mysticism . . . ."[4]

First, we need a clear idea of what Gnosticism is; then we can evaluate these statements.

[3] K. G. Kuhn, "Die in Palästina gefundenen hebräischen Texte und das Neue Testament," *Zeitschrift für Theologie und Kirche* 47 (1950), p. 211.

[4] Dupont-Sommer, *The Essene Writings from Qumran*, p. 332.

Gnosticism is in the first place a philosophical dualism (see pp. 77f.) with an added ethical concept. It starts with the idea that the universe is composed of matter and spirit, and usually adds the belief that matter is evil and only spirit is good. The supreme spiritual power or being of the Universe — let us call him or it "God" for convenience — is essentially good, and therefore could have had no part in the creation of matter which is evil. Creation therefore took place through a series of "emanations" and a Demiurge; thus "God" is removed from matter by these intermediaries.

Secondly, Gnosticism, as the name implies, claims a secret or esoteric knowledge by which man is able to achieve "salvation" from the material world of evil and enter the spiritual realm of good. This knowledge is not communicated to any except those who are duly initiated into the system.

Both elements are necessary if the system is properly to be labelled "Gnosticism." The secret or esoteric knowledge seems to be part of Qumran belief; but what of philosophical dualism?

God is called "the God of Knowledge" (1QS 3:15). There is a body of hidden knowledge that is revealed to those who enter into the covenant:

> When these are established in the foundation of the Community two years of days in perfection of way, they shall be separated (as) holiness in the midst of the Counsel of the men of the Community. And every matter (or word) which is hidden from Israel which has (!) been found by the man who is seeking, let him not hide it from these out of fear of a spirit of backsliding. (1QS 8:11-12)

This true knowledge is to be kept from the men of unrighteousness and revealed only to those chosen of the way (1QS 9:17-18). God has opened the ears of the Covenanters to wonderful mysteries (1QH 1:21).

If the Thanksgiving Hymns are the work of the Teacher of Righteousness, or even if they represent the convictions of some other individual, then someone was made an interpreter of knowledge concerning the wonderful mysteries (1QH 2:13), and it was through his mouth that God opened the fountain of knowledge to those who were enlightened (1QH 2:17-18; cf. 1QH 4:27-29). It is of course possible that this was the conviction of every member of the Community in ideal, and that the Hymns were the devotional expression of all members.

In the Book of Mysteries the nature of this mystery is spelled out a bit more clearly:

> And this is for you the sign that it shall be: when those born of unrighteousness are shut up, wickedness shall depart before righteousness as the dep[arting of darknes]s before light; and as smoke vanishes and i[s no] more, so shall wickedness vanish for ever and righteousness shall be revealed like the su[n], the fixed position of the world. And all those who hold the marvelous mysteries (without the right to do so) shall be no more. And knowledge shall fill the world, and folly is not there for e[ver]. (1QMyst [= 1Q27]:5-8)

## The Secret Knowledge of Qumran

It is not difficult to learn the secrets of the mysteries of God revealed to Qumran: they are written throughout the literature. For example, we read in the Habakkuk Commentary:

> And God told Habakkuk to write the things which are going to come on the last generation, but the conclusion of the end-time He did not make known to him. And where He said, "That the one who reads it shall run" — its interpretation (is) about the teacher of righteousness to whom God made known all the mysteries of the words of His servants the prophets. "For there is yet another vision pertaining to the appointed time; it shall speak of the end and it will not deceive" — its interpretation (is) that the final end-time will be lengthened and it will exceed everything that the prophets told, for the mysteries of God are marvelous. (1QpHab 7:1-8)

In the Manual of Discipline, the "mysteries of His (God's) enlightenment" and the "wisdom of His glory" are similarly defined:

> God . . . has appointed an end to the existence of unrighteousness, and in the time of visitation He will destroy it forever. And then shall go forth perpetually the truth of the world . . . . (1QS 4:18-19)

In the Thanksgiving Hymns, there is an extended passage, beginning with the words, "And what am I, that Thou [hast made known] to me the secret of Thy truth and hast enlightened me with Thy marvelous works?" (1QH 11:3-4). It continues to speak about "knowledge," the "secret of Thy truth," and "marvelous mysteries," and then immediately goes on to say,

> and because of Thy glory Thou hast cleansed man from rebellion to be sanctified for Thee from all unclean abominations and from the guilt of disloyalty, to be united [with] the sons of Thy truth and in the lot with Thy holy ones. (1QH 11:10-12)

Repeated reading of the Qumran texts will show, I am convinced, that the secret knowledge almost always has to do with the salvation of the Qumranians in the end-time. In some cases, however, it seems to pertain to the calendar of Qumran (cf. 1QS 10:1-8).

I can find nothing like philosophical (matter-spirit) dualism in the Dead Sea Scrolls, hence I believe it can only lead to confusion to use the term "Gnosticism."[5]

---

[5] I have previously expressed an objection to further watering-down of the term "Gnosticism," and suggested that we need new terminology. To call pre-Gnostic non-Hellenistic Gnosticism by the name "Gnosticism" simply confuses the matter. Cf. my *Amazing Dead Sea Scrolls,* pp. 139-150, for fuller discussion. For more recent literature cf. R. M. Grant, ed., *Gnosticism: An Anthology* (London: Collins, 1961; 254 pp.), and H. W. Huppenbauer, *Der Mensch zwischen zwei Welten. Der Dualismus der Texte von Qumran (Höhle I) und der Damaskusfragmente. Ein Beitrag zur Vorgeschichte der Evangelien* (Zürich: Zwingli, 1959; 132 pp.).

## CHAPTER SEVEN

# QUMRAN ESCHATOLOGY—
# "THE LAST GENERATION"

It is always of interest to know "how the story comes out" — and this is true also of religious systems. Is there a paradise of bright-eyed maidens? or a happy hunting ground? or a garden with vines and fig trees? or the exquisite delight of sheer nothingness? or the mystic bliss of oneness with God? Each religion has its particular doctrine of the end (or Eschatology). Sometimes they seem weird to us, and often we get the impression that man is building his own heaven out of the fondest of his unrealized hopes and dreams. But life is largely determined by dreams and ambitions, and once hope is taken from a man he quickly degenerates to the animal level.

## The End-Time Community

The Qumranians believed that they were the last generation, living on the very edge of the end of the world.[1] The Rule of the Congregation begins with the words,

[1] The expression, "the end of the world," is probably misleading. More accurate would be "the end of the age," which is based on the view that there is a succession of ages in the course of redemption-history. See the article by J. Carmignac, "La notion d'eschatologie dans la Bible et à Qumrân," *Revue de Qumrân* 7,25 (Dec. 1969), pp. 17-32. While Carmignac has given us a very helpful study of the Hebrew expressions *'aḥarón, 'aḥarît,* and *'aḥarît hayyāmîm,* and the Greek term *eschaton,* he has failed to take up the Greek term *aiōn,* "a segment of time, an age," which seems to be precisely the term for which he is groping.

> This is the order for all the Congregation of Israel in the last days when they are [gath]ered [into Community to wa]lk according to the judgment of the sons of Zadok and the men of their covenant. (1QSa 1:1-2)

At the beginning of the Damascus Document we find the words, "he will make known to the last generations what He has done in the last generation with the Congregation of traitors" (CD 1:10-13). Similar expressions will be found in other documents.

The most sustained and extensive picture, however, is given in the War Scroll,[2] which is essentially a description of the final war at the end of the age. The judgment can be summarized in a brief sentence: the final destruction of the gentile nations and the triumph of the people of the New Covenant (i.e. the Qumranians).

One of the features of the end-time Community, as we have already seen, was the knowledge which God had revealed to them through their teacher. In a later chapter we shall consider this figure, the Teacher of Righteousness.

## The Judgment

The Qumran writings speak of a "Day of Vengeance" (1QS 10:19), a "Day of Slaughter" (1QH 15:17), a "Day of Judgment" (1QpHab 13:2-3), and an hour of subjecting the enemy (1QM 17:5-6). The purpose is God's glory: "For the sake of Thy being glorified in the judgment of the wicked" (1QH 2:24). The wicked have been set apart from their mother's womb for the Day of Slaughter (1QH 15:17-21). This is the end of an "age," the age when the wicked tread upon God's people.

The time of judgment will be a time of distress for Israel, a time of war against all the nations (or Gentiles), and a time

[2] Until 11Q Temple is published, we cannot speculate on whether it will prove to be more significant than 1QM. According to Yadin, who is preparing the manuscript for publication, "The scroll's temple is not, strictly speaking, the eschatological, 'ready-made,' God-built temple which is the subject among other things of the Qumran *pesharim* ('that is the house which He will make thee in the end of the days'). At the same time, it can be assumed that the sect believed that the future God-built temple would take the same plan." Y. Yadin, "The Temple Scroll," in D. N. Freedman and J. C. Greenfield, eds., *New Directions in Biblical Archaeology*, p. 163.

of destruction for the wicked (1QM 15:1-2). The war is described in outline in a portion of the Hymns that is too broken to translate in full; it begins,

> And then the sword of God shall hasten in the end-time of judgment, and all the sons of His t[rut]h shall rise up to finish [the sons of] sin, and all the sons of guilt shall not be any more. And the Hero shall bend his bow, and He shall open (= raise) the siege . . . . (1QH 6:29-30)

After a description of the course of battle it concludes,

> They shall completely trample (them), and there is no rem[nant] . . . [ . . ] to all the mighty men of the wars there is no refuge; for to God Most High [ . . . ]. (1QH 6:31-33)

The curses of God are pronounced on the ungodly in vigorous terms:

> Cursed be thou in all thy guilty works of wickedness! May God appoint thee fright by the hand of all the avengers of vengeance! May He visit upon thee annihilation by the hand of all who pay recompense of rewards! Cursed be thou without mercies as the darkness of thy deeds, and damned be thou as the gloom of eternal fire! May God not be gracious to thee when thou callest, and may He not forgive, making atonement for thine iniquity! May He lift the face of His wrath for vengeance upon thee, and may there be for thee no peace on the mouth of all who hold to (the promise of) the Fathers! (1QS 2:5-9)

More of the same kind of language follows several lines later (1QS 2:14-17). The description in the passage concerning the two spirits summarizes the significant details of final judgment:

> And the visitation of all who walk in it (i.e. the spirit of unrighteousness) is for the multitude of afflictions by all the angels of woe, for eternal destruction by the anger of the fury of the God of vengeance, for perpetual fright and eternal shame with complete disgrace in the fire of dark regions, and all their times for all their generations in sorrowful mourning and bitter misfortune, existence in darkness until their annihilation, without remnant or escape to them. (1QS 4:11-14)

The most graphic description of the destruction by fire is given in the following passage from the Thanksgiving Hymns:

> And the rivers of Belial shall go over all (the) high banks, like fire eating in all their canals (?), to destroy every tree, green

or dry, from their channels; and it goes about with sparks of fire until all who drink them are nothing. In the pits of bitumen (?) it eats, and in the expanse of dry land; the foundations of the mountains (are given) to the conflagration and the roots of flint to rivers of pitch. And it consumes unto the great deep, and the rivers of Belial break through to Abaddon, and the dark places[3] of earth roars on account of the calamity which has happened to the planet, and all its beings cry out, and all who are on it riot, and they melt in g[re]at calamity. For God thunders with the tumult of His power, and His holy habitation resounds with His glorious truth, and the host of Heaven give their voice, [and] the eternal depths (?) melt and tremble. And the war of the mighty ones of Heaven goes about the world, and it does not return until the finish; and it is decreed for ever, and nothing (is) like it. (1QM 3:29-36)

The actual destruction of the wicked seems to be accomplished by the sons of light, or the Community, according to some passages (cf. 1QM 1:1-13; 11:9-11); in other passages it is attributed to Belial (cf. CD 8:2) or to the angels of destruction (CD 2:6).

The reason for the final judgment, mentioned in the War Scroll, is "to recompense for their evil all the nations of vanity" (1QM 6:6).

## The Rewards of the Righteous

For the people of God, the time of the end will be a time of salvation:

[Th]is shall be a time of salvation for the people of God, and the end-time of dominion for all the men of His lot and the ages of annihilation for all the lot of Belial. (1QM 1:5)

It will be a time of "peace and blessing to the lot of God" (1QM 17:7). The man of Qumran could sing,

Thou hast helped my spirit, Thou hast lifted up my horn on high, and I shall shine in seven-fold l[ight]. (1QH 7:23-24)[4]

---

[3] Emending MḤŠBY to read MḤŠKY. However, the same word occurs in the next line where the context requires some meaning such as "thinking beings." Millar Burrows translates "sentient beings" in both lines.

[4] Dupont-Sommer refers this passage to the Teacher of Righteousness, saying that he "announces his luminous transfiguration," and comparing it with the Transfiguration of Jesus. Cf. *The Essene Writings from Qumran*, p. 224 n. 5.

It will be a time of purification:

> And then shall go forth perpetually the truth of the world, for it has wallowed in the ways of wickedness in the dominion of unrighteousness until the time of the judgment decreed. But then God will purify with His truth all the deeds of man, and He will refine for Himself some of the sons of man to make perfect every spirit of unrighteousness from the depths of (?) his flesh, and to cleanse him with a spirit of holiness from all the actions of wickedness. And He will sprinkle upon him a spirit of truth as waters of impurity (to cleanse him) from all false loathing and wallowing in a spirit of impurity, to make the upright understand with the knowledge of the Most High and the wisdom of the sons of Heaven, to give enlightenment to those who are perfect in the way. For God has chosen them for an eternal covenant, and to them is all the glory of man, and there is no unrighteousness, and all the deeds of deceit have become shame. (1QS 4:19-23)

Man was made to rule over the earth (1QS 3:17-18), and this seems to be the ultimate hope of the Qumranian, according to a portion of the War Scroll:

> Arise, Mighty One; lead captive Thy captivity, Man of glory; take Thy plunder, Thou doer of valor! Put Thy hand on the neck of Thine enemies, and Thy foot on the mountains of (the) slain! Smite the gentiles Thine adversaries, and let Thy sword consume the flesh of the guilty.
>
> Fill Thy land with glory and Thine inheritance with blessing: a multitude of cattle in Thy fields, silver and gold and precious stones in Thy pala[c]es! O Zion, rejoice greatly! Make thine appearance with singing, O Jerusalem! Exult, all you cities of Judah! Open [Thy] gat[es] continually, to bring in the wealth of the gentiles unto Thee, and their kings shall serve Thee and all who oppress Thee shall bow down before Thee; and the dust [of Thy feet they shall lick. O Daughters] of My people, shout with the sound of singing, adorn yourselves with ornaments of glory, and rule over the [kin]g[dom until the King of I]srael [shall appear] to reign for ever. (1QM 12:9-15)[5]

Man will live a thousand generations (CD 7:6). The redeemed will be an eternal house:

---

[5] Some of the restoration is based on the parallel passage, 1QM 19:1-8; the balance follows Habermann, *megillôt midbar yehûdā*, p. 104. I have reservations about the restoration of the final line quoted.

This is the house which [the Lord will build in the la]tter days as it it written in the Book, "[In the temple, O Lord, which] Thy hands [have establi]shed, the Lord will reign for ever and ever." This is the house where no [ . . . ] shall enter, nor the Ammonite, nor the Moabite, nor the bastard, nor the son of a stranger, from that time and for ever; but the holy ones of the Name sh[all b]e [ . . . ] for ever,[6] continually He shall be seen above it. And strangers shall no more lay it waste, as in former times they laid waste the Tem[ple of Is]rael in their sin. And He said to build for Him a temple of man, to be burning incense in it to Him in the presence of those who do the Law.[7] (4QFlor 1:2-7)

## The Messiah

One of the most important and most frequently discussed subjects in Dead Sea Scroll eschatology is the messianic belief. Unfortunately, the term "messiah" has become quite indefinite, and we find included in the discussion messianic forerunners, eschatological personalities, and sometimes even a person who has none other than a priestly office.[8]

The development of the messianic idea has been traced by several writers, and their works should be studied by anyone who desires a better understanding of the origins and complexities of messianism.[9] The following terms may help in this respect:

[6] The passage is difficult. It would make better sense to restore YH[W]H rather than YH[Y]H, and read "the Lord will dwell there forever . . ."; but the sacred name seems never to be used in the Qumran texts outside of actual quotations from Scripture.

[7] It is necessary to read LW' = LW, and BW' = BW in order to get a meaningful translation. The meaning of "a temple of man" is debatable: does it mean man-made, or does it mean a temple consisting of men rather than one built of stones? The latter idea seems to me to be too advanced for Qumran theology. The former, however, is redundant.

[8] I have attempted a clarification of the problem in a study, "The Messianic Idea in Qumran," in *Studies and Essays in Honor of Abraham A. Neuman* (Leiden: Brill, 1962), pp. 343-364. A number of the following points have been drawn from that study, with the kind permission of the copyright owners.

[9] Cf. J. Klausner, *The Messianic Idea in Israel* (New York: Macmillan, 1955; 543 pp.); S. Mowinckel, *He That Cometh* (New York: Abingdon, 1954; 528 pp.); H. Ringgren, *The Messiah in the Old Testament* (London: SCM, 1956; 71 pp.); and E. O'Doherty, "The Organic Development of Messianic Revelation," *Catholic Biblical Quarterly* 19 (1957), pp. 16-25.

The *soteriological* hope: the constant hope of the Lord's redemptive activity in the various phases of history;

The *eschatological* hope: the hope of a final intervention by which the Kingdom of God is established;

The *messianic* hope: the expectation of a specific person, the "Anointed" (or "Messiah") of the Lord, who is to serve as the ideal King.[10]

It may be well to make a finer distinction in the category of the *eschatological* hope, by limiting the *messianic* hope to the ideal King who is to rise up within Israel, and by using the term *apocalyptic* to describe the irruption into history of a heavenly "Son of Man."[11]

Normative Judaism, it is generally admitted, developed from a general soteriological hope — found as early as there was an Israelite faith — to an eschatological hope. The eschatological hope is certainly found as early as the eighth-century prophets (cf. Isa. 11:1-10; 9:67, etc.). This developed into a messianic hope in the intertestamental period or perhaps somewhat earlier. The Son of Man or apocalyptic concept did not come into normative Judaism, but developed in sectarian Judaism.[12]

Where does Qumran eschatology fit into this complex development? The Community believed that it was living in the end of days, hence it certainly had developed an "eschatological" hope — but was it "messianic" or "apocalyptic" or both? And if it was messianic, what kind of Messiah did the Qumranians expect? For among sectarian Jews in the late intertestamental period the messianic idea had further devel-

10 From J. Coppens, in *L'Attente du Messie* (Paris: Desclée de Brouwer, 1954), pp. 35-38.

11 This distinction is blurred in Christianity, where Jesus is looked upon as both Lord and Christ — i.e., as the divine Redeemer sent from Heaven and as the Son of David who grew up in Israel. Sometimes an attempt is made to distinguish between these two figures by referring one to the first and the other to the second Advent of Christ. But this certainly will not hold, for (1) doctrinally the Christian Church has always maintained that both the divine and the human natures were found in Jesus from the time of the incarnation in Mary's womb, and (2) the "Son of David" aspect of Christ's messianic kingship will certainly not be realized until after His appearance as "Son of Man" on the clouds at the Second Advent.

12 This last point may be debated, depending on how much the development of the idea is found in Daniel. I think we have to admit that the foundations of the New Testament Son of Man concept, at least, can be traced to Daniel — but the New Testament represents sectarian Judaism!

oped to include a Messiah son of David, a Messiah son of
Joseph, and a Messiah from the tribe of Levi.

## The Messiah of Aaron

A number of scholars find two Messiahs in the Qumran
texts: the Messiah of Israel, or Davidic Messiah, which is the
familiar messianic figure, and a Messiah of Aaron, or priestly
Messiah, who seems to have the priority over the Davidic
Messiah.

The theory was advanced when the Zadokite Fragments —
now the Damascus Document — were first published, and with
the discovery of the Manual of Discipline among the Dead
Sea Scrolls, the theory was repeated with a new emphasis.
The basis in the Damascus Document had been the expression
"the Messiah of Aaron and Israel," which certain scholars
emended to read "the Messiahs of Aaron and Israel." When
the Manual of Discipline was published, the expression "the
Messiahs (sic) of Aaron and Israel" was found (1QS 9:11), confirming (so scholars concluded) the emendation that had long
ago been suggested for the Damascus Document. The "Messiah of Aaron," according to this view, was the priestly Messiah, and the "Messiah of Israel" was the lay (or Davidic)
Messiah.

The theory of a priestly Messiah does not rest merely on
the passage in the Manual of Discipline and the emended passages in the Damascus Document. The "Chief Priest and his
second" are mentioned in the War Scroll (1QM 2:1). However, a list of other "chiefs" is found in the following lines,
none of whom is an eschatological figure. Later in the same
scroll a war is described in which the anointed priests (in the
plural!) perform priestly functions, but nothing "messianic."
And still later, when the people are finally delivered from their
enemies, the priests are praying, but it is Michael who de-
livers the people (cf. 1QM 15:4-5; 17:6).

Much more important is a passage in the Order of the
Congregation, referring to what is sometimes called "the messianic banquet." Two principal persons are present at the
meal, one called the "Chief Priest," and the other the "Messiah of Israel." The Chief Priest seems to have the place of
priority. The text in full is as follows:

[This is the sessi]on of the men of the name, [the called ones of the] appointed time to the Counsel of the Community: If (or when) [God (?)] shall beget the Messiah with them, (then) shall enter [the] chief [priest], all of the Congregation of Israel, and all the fathers of the sons of Aaron the priests, [those called to] the appointed time of the men of the name, and they shall sit b[efore him, each] according to his glory (rank or importance).

And after (wards) shall [enter the Messi]ah of Israel, and there shall sit before him the head[s] of the t[housands of Israel, eac]h according to his glory according to [their] s[tanding] in their camps and in their journeyings, and all the chiefs of the f[athers of the Congregati]on with the wise men of [the Congregation of Holiness] shall sit before them, each according to his glory.

And if to the table of Community (or, to a common table) [they] shall be assembled [or to drink the new] wine, he (?) shall arrange the common table. [When they pour the] new wine to drink, [let no] one [stretch forth] his hand on the first (?) of the bread and [the new wine] before the priest, fo[r he shall] bless the first of the bread and the new win[e, and he shall stretch forth] his hand on the bread of the presence (?).

And after (wards) the Messiah of Israel shall stretch forth his hand on the bread, [and after] they [shall bles]s, all the Congregation of the Community, e[ach according to] his glory.

And according to this statute [they] shall do for every ar[rangement when] they [shall be assembl]ed up to ten me[n]. (1QSa 2:11-23)

It is obvious that there are many broken places in the text, some of them at crucial points. There are also several words of doubtful meaning or difficult to interpret, and at two or three places the syntax presents problems. This is not the place to go into the details.[13] Certain facts, however, can be pointed out: (1) the Priest plays a prominent part; (2) the "Messiah of Aaron" is not mentioned, at least not by this title, here or anywhere else in the Qumran texts; (3) the Messiah (or anointed) of Israel is present and seems to rank after the Priest; (4) bread and new (sweet) wine are mentioned specifically and solely; (5) the ritual applies to every occasion

13 I have discussed various problems in this connection in the following writings: *Amazing Dead Sea Scrolls*, pp. 157-162; " 'The Messiahs of Aaron and Israel,' " in *Vetus Testamentum* 6 (1956), pp. 425-429; and "The Messianic Idea in Qumran," in *Studies and Essays in Honor of Abraham A. Neuman*, pp. 354-356.

when ten men are assembled. One other fact can be added, not apparent in this passage: the entire fragment is "the Order for all the Congregation of Israel" — including women and children (1QSa 1:4) — for any meeting of significance, whether for judgment or advice or military mission (1QSa 1:25-26).

The marked similarity between the passage just quoted and a passage in the Manual of Discipline (1QS 6:2-8) should be pointed out. In each case the meeting is called a "session." In each case there is mention of "stretching forth of the hand" to bless, and also mention of the bread, the wine, the arranging of the table, the presence of a priest, and a quorum of ten. There seems to be no convincing reason to call it a "messianic banquet." Yet, as Burrows has pointed out, what is the Messiah of Israel doing there?

So we come back to the expression "the Messiahs of Aaron and Israel." The expression "the Messiah of Aaron" has not been found in the Qumran texts. The expression "the Messiahs of Aaron and Israel" has been found in only one place, 1QS 9:11. It can be found in the Damascus Document (three times) only by emending the text. These facts must now be placed beside additional facts.

A fragment of the Damascus Document from Cave Four (4QD$^b$ = CD 14:19) clearly reads in the singular, "the Messiah of Aaron and Israel," exactly as the Cairo exemplar. This explodes once and for all the theory of a medieval scribal emendation of the Damascus Document from a plural to a singular, and therefore destroys the basis for a modern emendation of the singular to a plural. In my opinion this holds not only for CD 14:19 but for the other passages as well — for if one reading had not been emended, then likewise the others had not been emended.

This leaves us with the passage in the Manual of Discipline (1QS 9:11), where we have the plural reading, "the Messiahs of Aaron and Israel." A fragment of this document also was found in Cave Four (4QS$^e$) — and this omits the passage entirely, going from the words in 1QS 8:16 immediately to the words in 1QS 9:12. This does not destroy the evidence from 1QS 9:11 — but by suggesting that there is a textual problem at this point it raises a question as to its value as evidence.

There is, in my opinion, no sufficient basis to find a "Messiah of Aaron," or priestly Messiah, in the Dead Sea Scrolls.

## The Messiah of Israel

The "Messiah of Israel" is mentioned in the Order of the Congregation (1QSa 2:14, 27, and "Messiah" in 2:12; see p. 101 above). If the suggested restoration in the same passage is valid, "If (or when) [God] begets the Messiah," we may consider it to be a reference to Psalm 2:6 (Masoretic Text 2:7), which was commonly applied to the Davidic Messiah.

In a fragment from Qumran known as the Patriarchal Blessings, which is a commentary on Genesis 49:10, we read,

> A ruler shall [not] depart from the tribe of Judah while Israel has dominion (?), [ . . . ] —?— not to David. For "the staff" is the covenant of kingship, [and the thousan]ds of Israel they are "the feet," until the coming of the Messiah of Righteousness, the sprout of David, for to him and to his seed has been given the covenant of kingship unto the generations of eternity. . . . (4QPatrBless 2-5)

In another fragment known as the Florilegium the Davidic descent is again indicated:

> This is the sprout of David, the one standing with the Seeker of the Law who [shall arise] in Zi[on in the la]tter days, as it is written, "And I will raise up the tabernacle of David which is falling"—that is the tabernacle of David which is fall[ing and whi]ch shall stand to save Israel. (4QFlor 1:11-13)

These and other brief references show that the Messiah of Israel was the Messiah of David, not different, so far as we can reconstruct the Qumran picture, from the Messiah of normative Judaism.

The War Scroll is generally interpreted as describing the eschatological war; it is therefore remarkable that there is in it no mention of a Messiah.

## The Son of Man

One very important fact to be noted is that there is no "Son of Man" concept in the Dead Sea Scrolls so far published. This is the more remarkable in view of two facts: the Son of Man concept belongs to the apocalyptic movement in Judaism, and Qumran is usually placed within this movement; again, the Son of Man, or Heavenly Redeemer, concept is usually traced to Zoroastrian sources, and Qumran likewise has been connected with Zoroastrianism. Yet Qumran does not refer to the

Son of Man. Eleven different manuscripts of the Book of Enoch are represented in the fragments from the Qumran caves. These fragments represent all parts of Enoch except Book II (the Similitudes) — and it is only in Book II that the Son of Man doctrine is set forth. It would appear then either that Book II was not yet part of the Book of Enoch or that the Qumran Community excised Book II from its documents.

From this it appears that Qumran eschatology was messianic but not apocalyptic — at least so far as the Son of Man concept is concerned. We have already seen that in the last great battle, Michael the archangel appears as the deliverer (1QM 17:6).

## Other Eschatological Persons

A prophet like Moses is mentioned in Deuteronomy 18:18, and according to Malachi 4:5 Elijah was to appear before the Day of the Lord. Around these two figures some literature and much tradition developed, some of which is reflected in the questions which were asked of John the Baptist (John 1:21). It is possible that these two eschatological figures are represented in the "two anointed ones" of Zechariah 4:12-14, and further possible that the two-Messiah theory developed from the passage in Zechariah.

Something of this complex development probably was found at Qumran, although it is difficult to work out the details from the extant literature. The "Teacher of Righteousness" is one of the eschatological figures, and to him we shall devote a separate chapter. Other names or terms that are found include: the "Seeker (or Interpreter) of the Law," the "Star," the "Scepter," the "Staff (or Commander or Lawgiver)," the "Prince of the Congregation," and others.

Scholars have attempted to identify these figures with the eschatological characters found in Judaism of the intertestamental period, but there is no general agreement. Dupont-Sommer seems to compress all the figures except the Messiah of Israel into the Teacher of Righteousness,[14] and by finding three "antichrists" in Qumran, he is even able to impose upon the Teacher of Righteousness the triple quality "of Prophet, lay Messiah and priestly Messiah."[15] The theory seems to destroy itself.

[14] Cf. Dupont-Sommer, *The Essene Writings from Qumran*, pp. 358-367.
[15] *Ibid.*, p. 318.

The eschatology of Qumran is complex and not well worked out. But then, what system of eschatology is? Certainly Christianity has its share of divergent interpretations, as does Judaism. We Christians do well to remind ourselves that those who had worked out elaborate messianic systems completely failed to recognize Jesus when He came — and yet some of us go on working out our own detailed eschatologies. So far as Qumran eschatology is concerned, I am willing to admit that I have not yet fit it into a neat system.

## Summary

Qumran theology is not well worked out but it is possible to make several observations. The Qumran doctrine of God is basically that of the Old Testament. There is a more developed concept of dualism, but this is basically consistent with the Old Testament and does not need to be explained by referring it to a non-Jewish source such as Zoroastrianism.

The doctrine of the Adversary (Belial or Mastema) and the doctrine of angels are more thoroughly developed than anything we find in the Old Testament. They are in keeping, however, with the development of the concepts in the intertestamental period.

The concept of man is basically that of the Old Testament. Salvation is centered in the covenant grace of God, and this is specifically referred to the Sect; this, however, is developed from the Old Testament concept of the "remnant." Knowledge of the mysteries as found in Qumran writings has to do almost exclusively with the mystery of the Community and the salvation which comes to those who belong to its fellowship. The fundamental elements of Gnosticism are not present, and only by stretching the definition can we call Qumran a Gnostic group.

The Community had a strong sense of living in the end-time. Its messianic concepts, however, were not well developed. The Messiah, to the extent that he is described in the texts, is the Davidic Messiah, developing out of the Old Testament prophecies. The presence of a Priestly Messiah (or Messiah of Aaron) in Qumran theology is all but impossible to demonstrate. The final punishment is to be by fire, and the final blessings of the righteous appear to be earthly and materialistic.

## CHAPTER EIGHT

# THE TEACHER OF RIGHTEOUSNESS IN THE QUMRAN TEXTS

Of the Teacher of Righteousness, Dupont-Sommer says: he is "without doubt the most astonishing of the revelations of the Dead Sea Scrolls"; "the interpreter *par excellence,* the supreme Hierophant of divine Gnosis"; "as it were a new Moses" who was not only "to restore the true covenant of Israel, but also to bring salvation to the nations; the "Saviour-Messiah . . . born in distress"; "the man of sorrows," who in these sorrows "should build his glorious Church," of which "he is the sap, the very life of the Church—his Church." "The place he occupies in the writings of Qumran is such that in almost every chapter I have had occasion to speak of him. . . ."[1]

In the face of such all-embracing claims, it is necessary for us to devote a full study to the Teacher of Righteousness in the Qumran Literature.

## The Teacher of Righteousness in the Habakkuk Commentary

Much of the material concerning the Teacher of Righteousness is derived from the Habakkuk Commentary. There the expression *môrè haṣṣédeq* ("the teacher of righteousness" or perhaps "the righteous teacher") occurs seven times. Because of the importance of these texts we shall give them in context.

[1] Dupont-Sommer, *The Essene Writings from Qumran,* pp. 262, 358-368, *passim.*

The Teacher was a priest who received from God understanding to interpret the words of the prophets:

> [ . . . ] the traitors with the Man of Falsehood, for [they have] not [believed the interpretation of] the Teacher of Righteousness from the mouth of God; . . . who will not believe when they hear all that is c[oming on] the last generation from the mouth of the priest to whom God gave in [his heart understandin]g to interpret all the words of His servants the prophets. (1QpHab 2:1-3, 6-9)

> Its interpretation, concerning the Teacher of Righteousness whom God caused to know all the mysteries of the words of His servants the prophets. (1QpHab 7:4-5)

Doers of the Law in the house of Judah, almost certainly meaning the members of the Community, will be delivered from judgment because of their work and their faith in the Teacher:

> Its interpretation, concerning all the doers of the Law in the house of Judah whom God will deliver from the house of judgment for the sake of their toil and their faith in the Teacher of Righteousness. (1QpHab 8:1-3)

The Teacher of Righteousness was opposed, persecuted, pursued, and probably "swallowed up" by the Wicked Priest:

> Its interpretation, concerning the Wicked Priest who pursued the Teacher of Righteousness to swallow him up in the anger of his wrath at the house of his exile, and in the end of the appointed time (= feast) of rest of the day of Atonement he appeared unto them to swallow them up and to cause them to stumble on the day of fasting, the Sabbath of their rest. (1QpHab 11:4-8)

> ["The wicked" is the Wicked Priest, and "the righteous"] is the Teacher of Righteousness [ . . . ]. (1QpHab 1:12)

The "house of Absalom" — the meaning is in question — did not help the Teacher:

> Its interpretation, concerning the house of Absalom and the men of their counsel who were silent at the rebuke of the Teacher of Righteousness, and who did not help him against the Man of Falsehood who despised the Law in the midst of all their c[ongregation]. (1QpHab 5:9-12)

God allowed the Wicked Priest to be punished:

> Its interpretation, concerning the [Wick]ed Priest whom, in

the iniquity of (= because of the iniquity done to) the Teacher of Righteousness and the men of his counsel, God gave unto the h[ands of] his [ene]mies to humble him . . . . (1QpHab 9:9-10)

## The Teacher of Righteousness in the Damascus Document

In the Damascus Document, there is no common form of the expression; rather we find the following expressions: *môrè ṣédeq* ("a teacher of righteousness"), *môrè hayyāḥîd* ("the unique teacher" or perhaps "the teacher of the Community"), *yôrè haṣṣédeq* ("the one teaching (?) righteousness"), *yôrè hayyāḥîd* ("the one teaching (?) the Community (?)" or "the unique teacher"), and *môrê* ("a teacher"). Again, we print the passages in context.

In former times men did not listen to their Teacher — but in the light of the context this surely means God Himself:

> And they did not listen to the voice of their Maker, the commandment of their Teacher. (CD 3:7-8)

Then God remembered His covenant and raised up a remnant of them, a sprout from Israel and from Aaron (cf. CD 1:3-7):

> Then they understood their iniquity, and they knew that they were guilty men. But they were like blind men, like men groping their way, for twenty years. And God considered their deeds — that they sought Him with a whole heart — and He raised up for them a teacher of righteousness to guide them in the way of His heart. (CD 1:8-11)

The men of the Community heeded the teachings of the Teacher:

> All who cling to these judgments to go out and come in according to the Law, and have listened to the voice of a teacher, and have confessed before God, "We have [sinned] . . . ." (CD 20:27-28 [Habermann 8:50-51])
>
> . . . and they have been chastened by the first judgments by which the men of the unique (one) (or, men of the Community?) were judged, and they gave ear to the voice of the teacher of righteousness and they did not leave the statutes of righteousness . . . . (CD 20:31-32 [Habermann 8:54-56])

The unique teacher, probably to be identified with the

Teacher of Righteousness, was "gathered in," probably meaning that he died:

> All the men who entered the New Covenant in the land of Damascus, then turned back and acted treacherously and turned away from the well of living water, they shall not be reckoned in the secret council of the people, and in its writing they shall not be written, from the day of the gathering of the unique teacher (or, teacher of the Community?) until the rising of a messiah from Aaron and Israel. (CD 19:33—20:1 [Habermann 8:21-24])

> And from the day of the gathering of the one teaching the Community (?) (or, the unique teacher?) until the completion of all the men of war who went with the Man of Falsehood, about forty years. (CD 20:13 15 [Habermann 8:36-38])

The rising of the Teacher of Righteousness was anticipated. It is not clear whether this means the resurrection of the one who died, or the rising up of another, particularly since the title in this case is not *môrè haṣṣédeq* but *yôrè haṣṣédeq* ("one teaching [?] righteousness"):

> . . . to walk in them in all the end-time of wickedness, and without them they will not attain to the rising of the Teacher of Righteousness in the last days. (CD 6:10-11)

## The Remaining Texts Containing the Expression

A fragment of a commentary on Psalm 37 indicates that the Teacher was a priest, confirming the interpretation of 1QpHab 2:1-3, 6-9 given above (p. 107), and also indicates that the Teacher was chosen by God to build the Community:

> Its interpretation, concerning the priest, the Teacher of [Righteousness whom] [ . . . ] He established him to build for Him the Congregation of His elect . . . . (4QpPs37 [on 37:23-24; Habermann 3:34-35; Dupont-Sommer 1:15-16])

The name is found in a fragment of a commentary on Micah, without context and therefore of no value:

> [ . . . concernin]g the Teacher of Righteousness, he is [ . . . ]. (1QpMic 16)

This represents the full body of material in the Scrolls on the Teacher of Righteousness. That some scholars have been able to find so exceedingly much more about the Teacher is due to two facts: (1) they identify the Teacher with one or more of the other figures, such as the "priest," the "seeker of the Law," the "star," and the "lawgiver"; (2) they accept many of the Thanksgiving Hymns as autobiographical compositions of the Teacher. Sound methodology requires that we work first from the clearly identifiable passages. Having set these down, we may now turn to other passages in which the Teacher may be intended.

## The Teacher of Righteousness in the War Scroll

The Teacher of Righteousness is not mentioned by name in the War Scroll. Dupont-Sommer finds a reference to him in the expression, "the venerated (Being)":

> And who is like Thy people Israel . . . who hear the voice of the venerated (Being) and see the angels of holiness; of those whose ear is opened and who hear profound things? (1QM 10:10, translation by Dupont-Sommer)

In a note he says, "Who is this 'venerated Being'? Obviously the expression is applicable to God; but in the sect it is also applicable to the Teacher of Righteousness." Then on the basis of passages in the Damascus Document which speak of heeding or hearing the voice of the Teacher (CD 20:28, 32), he continues, "The parallelism seems to me to suggest that in the present text the 'venerated Being' is the Teacher of Righteousness."[2]

The passage, however, says considerably less than the French savant finds in it. The Hebrew is simply *šōm'ē qôl nikbād,* "hearers of an honored voice"; there is no definite article and no reason to understand *nikbād* as a noun, much less a proper noun. The parallel stichos says *werō'ē mal'ăkè qōdeš,* "and seers of angels of holiness (= holy angels)" — and according to the rules of Hebrew parallelism we should interpret "honored voice" and "holy angels" in parallel categories. It is highly probable that "honored voice" refers to a heavenly voice. The passages in the Damascus Document (see p. 108 above) can hardly be used to control this passage since the contexts are entirely different. My own translation is given

2 Dupont-Sommer, *The Essene Writings from Qumran,* p. 184 n. 5.

above in its full context (p. 76) and can be studied at this point.

This is the only passage in the War Scroll that Dupont-Sommer interprets as applying to the Teacher of Righteousness, which is significant, for the War Scroll was written, according to Dupont-Sommer, after 63 B.C., or (by his own dating) after the death of the Teacher. The War Scroll, moreover, has to do with the great battle at the end of the age. Now if the Teacher had become such a venerated Being and if he was expected to return at the end of the age, we should have expected to find him in the War Scroll. It would be unthinkable, for example, not to find Jesus Christ in the Book of Revelation.

The "Star" and the "Sceptre" are mentioned in the War Scroll, and Dupont-Sommer notes that in the Damascus Document, where the same scriptural quotation is used, these figures are identified with the Seeker of the Law and the Prince of the Congregation, respectively. In the War Scroll, however, the parallelism of the passage is preserved, and a verbal form in the singular is used, indicating that the "Star" is also the "Sceptre":

> A star has marched forth from Jacob,
>     A sceptre has arisen from Israel;
> And he will shatter the temples of Moab,
>     And destroy all the Sons of Seth.
>                 (1QM 11:6; cf. Num. 24:17-19)

In the Damascus Document this citation is used as follows:

> And the star is the Seeker of the Law who is coming to Damascus; as it is written, "A star has marched forth from Jacob, and a sceptre has arisen from Israel." The sceptre is Prince of all the Congregation, and when he arises he will destroy all the sons of Seth. (CD 7:18-21)

To attempt any identification of this passage with the Teacher of Righteousness is precarious.

## The Teacher of Righteousness in the Thanksgiving Hymns

The Teacher is not mentioned by name in the Thanksgiving Hymns. Yet it is in these poems that Dupont-Sommer finds his greatest amount of material on this figure.[3] Calling this scroll "the jewel of all the mystical literature from Qumran," Dupont-Sommer asks:

> Who was this writer? To my mind, he unquestionably presents himself in several of the canticles as the leader of the sect of the Covenant: he is the Teacher who teaches, the Father who cares for his children and feeds them, the Source of living waters, the Builder of the Community of the Elect, the Gardener of the eternal Planting. How is it possible to avoid concluding that such a person must be the Teacher of Righteousness himself whom the *Damascus Document* and the biblical Commentaries from Qumran (notably the Commentary on Habakkuk) present as the founder and lawgiver of the sect, the Prophet *par excellence,* whose tragic destiny and exceptional prestige they describe.[4]

Many of Dupont-Sommer's ideas are found sprinkled through the footnotes to his translations of the Hymns in *The Essene Writings from Qumran*. The following is a representative, but not exhaustive, selection. The Teacher of Righteousness was "the bearer of divine revelation" (p. 205 n. 2), "the interpreter of Knowledge" (p. 206 n. 1), "God's messenger" (p. 252 n. 3) sent "to fulfill (?) the Law" (p. 218 n. 2). The birth of this "Saviour-Messiah" (p. 207, title of Hymn E) is intertwined with the "myth of the Mother of the Messiah" which is also found in Isaiah 7:14 and Revelation 12 (p. 208 nn. 1-4). He was the "first-born" of his church (p. 208 n. 4). He was a sign of contradiction, whose ministry brought sin to those who resisted, but healing and salvation to those who believed, hence he was, like Jesus, "set for the fall and rising of many in Israel" (p. 205 n. 2).

The church which he, the Teacher of Righteousness, founded was a "building" built on rock, an impregnable refuge (p. 220 nn. 1-2); it was his body (p. 222 n. 1). He was a father, even like a mother (p. 224 n. 2). He was the spring of living

---

[3] Other scholars also find much autobiographical material in the *Hôdāyôt*. For example, Gert Jeremias, *Der Lehrer der Gerechtigkeit* (Göttingen: Vandenhoeck & Ruprecht, 1963), pp. 94-104, ascribes the following portions to the Teacher of Righteousness: 1QH 2:1-19, 31-39; 4:5 — 7:25; 8:4-40. I shall return to this point below (pp. 115f.).

[4] Dupont-Sommer, *The Essene Writings from Qumran,* p. 200. We have already seen, pp. 106-109 above, that such extravagant claims for the Commentaries and the Damascus Document cannot be substantiated in fact.

water (pp. 225 n. 2, 227 n. 5, 228 n. 4), but was in himself deprived of this life-giving water (p. 229 n. 5).

He was despised (p. 226 n. 6), a dishonored and afflicted Just Man (p. 227 n. 1), like a root out of dry ground (p. 227 n. 3), mistreated at the hands of wicked persecutors (p. 227 n. 7). He was the Servant of the Lord (p. 252 n. 1), who came to preach repentance, teach divine laws, and announce the Gospel (p. 252 n. 6), in the manner of Isaiah 61:1-2 (p. 252 n. 7) "Not only was he to restore the true Covenant of Israel, but also to bring salvation to the nations" (p. 363).

He was the all-powerful gardener by whose hand God ensures the growth of the Church (p. 229 n. 1). He was the "Shoot" of Israel 11:1 (p. 219 n. 2), but this "Shoot" was also the Community, the spout from the eternal planting (pp. 222 n. 5, 226 n. 3), which was "the Church founded by the Teacher of Righteousness" and "which will become an immense tree spreading over the whole earth" (p. 226 n. 5).

He announced beforehand "his luminous transfiguration," to be compared with the transfiguration of Jesus (p. 224 n. 5). Most important, he announced that he will rule as conqueror and lord (p. 224 n. 4).

This is an imposing array of revelation concerning the Teacher of Righteousness, and to consider each point in the light of its context in the Thanksgiving Hymns — which is the only proper way to handle the material — would require a volume in itself. However, most of the material under consideration here had previously appeared in a work devoted entirely to the Thanksgiving Hymns, and replies to many of Dupont-Sommer's suggestions have been published by several scholars.[5]

We can avoid the necessity of getting bogged down in these problems if we bear in mind one important fact: *everything that Dupont-Sommer finds in these Hymns about the Teacher of Righteousness is based on the twofold assumption that the author was the Teacher of Righteousness or one of his disciples and that the references in the first person are all related to the Teacher.* If this hypothesis is false, the entire case col-

[5] A. Dupont-Sommer, *Le Livre des Hymnes découvert près de la mer Morte (1QH). Traduction intégrale avec introduction et notes* (Paris: Adrien-Maisonneuve, 1957; 120 pp.). For titles see my *Bibliography of the Dead Sea Scrolls 1948-1957,* §§2275ff., 3850ff.

lapses. This is indeed a tremendous weight to be supported by a slender thread![6]

Other scholars, with more caution, have been willing to grant that the Hymns contain autobiographical elements of the Teacher of Righteousness. We cannot therefore dismiss the whole problem as the invention of the French scholar, but we must examine it in more detail.

Some passages in the Hôdāyôt are clearly based on the canonical Scriptures of the Hebrew Bible. Expressions concerning persecution by enemies, deliverance by the Lord, and the like, can be found frequently in the Psalms. It is therefore not sound methodology to insist that similar statements in the Thanksgiving Hymns refer to the persecution and martyrdom of the Teacher of Righteousness. Confidence that the Lord reveals His secrets, makes known His way, or teaches His knowledge, is likewise expressed in the Psalms. Similar passages in the Thanksgiving Hymns should not be made the basis for theories of Gnostic or esoteric secrets. References to the "congregation," the "assembly," the "counsel," and the "council" are found often in the Psalms. To translate any of these terms "church" in the Thanksgiving Hymns is to read into the Qumran writings a specialized meaning that has come from the New Testament; after all, we do not know what Hebrew or Aramaic word lies behind the Greek word ekklēsia used in the New Testament.[6a] Even the striking figures of "building" and "planting" are found in the Old Testament, notably in Jeremiah.

When we have removed all passages that can be reasonably explained as reflections of the Biblical Psalms, we may have a residual body of autobiographical material that describes a deeply religious person who is conscious of the spiritual leadership conferred on him by God. It does not seem unreasonable to suppose that this is the Teacher of Righteousness.

[6]It would be comparatively easy to go through the Biblical Psalms and select from the passages in the first person a similar body of material, and then arrange this material into an "autobiographical" portrait of the author. To whom should we then attribute the Psalms? To Moses, the outstanding spiritual leader and founder of the Israelite religion? To David? To Isaiah? Shall we conclude, since his name is not used, that like the divine Name it was too sacred to be uttered? Would Dupont-Sommer himself, an excellent critical scholar, permit such methodology with the Biblical Psalms?

[6a] Cf. Kittel, Theological Dictionary of the New Testament, III, 524.

The most striking of these passages are now given in full or in extensive excerpts.

> And I was a snare for transgressors, but healing for all who repent of transgression; prudence for the simple, and firm inclination for all the hasty of heart. And Thou hast appointed me shame and mockery to the treacherous, a counsel of truth and understanding to those whose way is straight. And I was on account of the evil of the wicked ones slander on the lips of the violent ones; jesters gnashed their teeth. And I was a song to transgressors, and against me the congregation of the wicked became agitated and made noise like tempest of the seas when their waves roar: mud and mire they cast up. And Thou hast appointed me a banner for the righteous elect, and an interpreter of knowledge in wonderful mysteries to test the [seekers] of truth and to try those who love instruction. (1QH 2:8-14)

> And by me Thou hast illumined the face of many, and Thou hast strengthened (them) until (they were) numberless. For Thou hast caused me to know by Thy wondrous mysteries, and by Thy wonderful secret Thou hast made strong with me ('immādî), and Thou hast done wondrously in the presence of many, for the sake of Thy glory, and to make known to all the living Thy might. Who (that is) flesh is like this? And what creature of clay (is able) to magnify wonders? And he is in iniquity from the womb, and unto old age in the guilt of unfaithfulness. As for me, I know that not to man is righteousness, and not to a human being is perfection of way. To God most high are all the works of righteousness, and the way of man shall not stand except by the spirit God fashioned for him. (1QH 4:27-31)

> And Thou, my God, hast put in my mouth something like an autumn rain for all [the sons of men?], and a spring of living water which shall not disappoint. (1QH 8:16)

> Do not take away Thy hand [from Thy people that there may] be to them one who grows strong in Thy covenant and who stands before Thee. [ . . . spri]ng Thou hast opened in the mouth of Thy servant and by his tongue Thou hast prescribed (or, engraved) upon a line [ . . . to proc]laim to the creature apart from his understanding and to speak eloquently (or, to interpret) with these things to dust like me. And Thou hast opened a sp[ring] to admonish the creature of clay (concerning) his way and the guilt of one born of woman according to his works, and to open a s[pring . . . ] Thy truth to the creature whom Thou hast ordained by Thy power, to [ . . . ] according to Thy truth one proclaiming good tidings [ . . . ]

Thy goodness, to proclaim good tidings to the humble concerning the multitude of Thy mercies [*too fragmentary for
translation*]. (1QH 18:9-14)

Of course each interpreter must reach his own conclusions
on the basis of the text. In my opinion, these passages add but
little to what we have already learned about the Teacher of
Righteousness in the texts where his identity is not hypothetical. He was dedicated to the law of God: he was persecuted
by wicked men because of his convictions; he was the faithful
teacher of his followers. His "knowledge" of "mysteries"
seems to refer to his characteristic method of interpreting the
Scriptures. His proclamation of the "gospel" or good tidings
is probably drawn from Isaiah, which was one of the favorite
books of the Sect. Far from claiming to be of unusual origin
or to have received unusual powers, he seems to place himself
on a level with all sinful flesh, and ascribes to God whatever
spiritual illumination and power he might have.

The last of the passages just quoted (1QH 18:9-14) has
elicited from Dupont-Sommer the following note: "The psalmist lifts the veil completely on the identification of the 'servant';
it is indeed himself."[7] I fail to find, however, any specific use
of the term "servant" in this passage which would indicate
that the author considered himself to be the Servant of the
Lord depicted in Isaiah's prophecy.

## Summary

The material in the Scrolls concerning the Teacher of
Righteousness is extremely little. Passages in which he is
named beyond any question of interpretation give us very few
details concerning his life and ministry. Passages in which he
is probably indicated (such as, for example, those including
the words, "the teacher," or "the unique teacher," add very
little more. If we draw upon some of the Thanksgiving Hymns
for "autobiographical" material, we increase the quantity of
data but at the same time we open the door to the admission
of subjective interpretation without providing objective controls. In the next chapter we shall try to analyze the complex
picture of the Teacher as it has been drawn by several scholars,
and attempt to separate the subjective material so far as
possible.

[7] Dupont-Sommer, *The Essene Writings from Qumran*, p. 252 n. 5.

## CHAPTER NINE

# THE TEACHER OF RIGHTEOUSNESS IN COMPOSITE PORTRAIT

When Michel published his large volume on the Teacher of Righteousness in 1954, he was able to establish only the following facts from the texts:[1]

> The Teacher of Righteousness was probably a priest (1QpHab 2:8), although nothing in the Damascus Document leads to this conclusion;

> The Teacher was a prophet and knew the secrets of the prophets (1QpHab 7·1-8), and he had the special gift of interpreting the prophets (1QpHab 2:5-10), but he is nowhere called a "prophet";

> He was possibly considered as a judge (1QpHab 13:2-3); however, the *crux interpretum* in the passage can be read either as "elect one" or "elect ones," altering the meaning basically; he is never called a "judge";

> He may have been called the "elect"; if not, at least the Community members were called the "elect ones" and he by virtue of membership in the Community would therefore be "elect";

> He died (CD 19:35; 20:14), but the manner of death is not indicated, and the death is not directly mentioned;

> Persecution of the Sect by the Wicked Priest, resulting in extermination of the members (1QpHab 11:5; 12:6), suggests that the Teacher died a violent death.

Fourteen years later, Walter Grundmann could publish the following statement:

[1] A. Michel, *Le Maître de Justice* (Avignon: Aubanel, 1954), pp. 267-271.

The name of this Teacher of Righteousness and the period of Jewish history in which he lived remain, now as before, open questions; but his personality is coming more sharply into focus. We see a man who is hemmed about with conflict and persecuted for the sake of his doctrine and the attitude this compels him to adopt towards contemporary issues; who founded an order of brethren and gave it a rule, a doctrine and a way of life; who may well be the architect of the much discussed buildings of the monastic settlement at Qumran; who knows that all mankind is fallen and guilty, and who is made herald and minstrel of the mercy and grace of a saving God on which his life is based.[2]

If we examine Michel's statements carefully, we note that he has cautiously qualified each point with "probably" or "possibly" or otherwise indicated that it is not firmly established. Grundmann's summary, on the other hand, contains many items that are stated as facts without qualification. Previously, Grundmann had characterized the Teacher of Righteousness as "the last of the prophets" and "the touchstone of salvation or damnation."[3]

Scholars have put together an elaborate picture of the Teacher of Righteousness including many hypotheses which range from highly probable suggestions to preposterous fabrications without basis in fact or reasonability. In this chapter we want to take apart the composite picture and analyze the details, in order that we may be able to conserve what commends itself and reject the rest.

## Was the Teacher of Righteousness the Founder of the Sect?

That the Teacher of Righteousness founded the Qumran Sect is nowhere stated in the texts from Qumran. Bruce makes a cautious statement: "If he was not actually the founder of the community, it was certainly he who impressed upon it those features which distinguished it from other pious groups" of the same period.[4] It is possible, however, to be more defi-

[2] W. Grundmann, "The Teacher of Righteousness of Qumran and the Question of Justification by Faith in the Theology of the Apostle Paul," in *Paul and Qumran*, ed. Jerome Murphy-O'Connor (Chicago: Priory, 1968), pp. 95f.

[3] *Ibid.*, p. 95.

[4] F. F. Bruce, *The Teacher of Righteousness in the Qumran Texts* (London: Tyndale, 1957), p. 7.

nite than this in the light of a passage in the Damascus Document (CD 1:5-11, see p. 45 above), and state that the Teacher of Righteousness did not found the Sect. We could, of course, assume that the Damascus Document refers to a time prior to the founding of the Sect — perhaps a reform movement or a schism was already developing — and then assume further that the actual Qumran Community was founded by the Teacher. In any event it would have to be admitted that the movement was under way about twenty years before the Teacher of Righteousness came into the picture (CD 1:10).

To compare the Teacher of Righteousness with Jesus in this respect is to disregard all textual evidence concerning either figure, for only by complete disregard of the text could it be said that Christianity started as a reform movement years before Jesus began to shape its thought.

## Was the Teacher of Righteousness a Prophet?

The Teacher of Righteousness was the principal spokesman of the Qumran Community, but whether he should be called "prophet" is a matter of interpretation. The term is never used of him in the texts. There is no passage describing any revelation that God gave to him. He is best described as an interpreter of the prophets.

Bruce makes an important observation in this connection. In the Book of Daniel, God communicates the "mystery" (rāz) to one person and the "interpretation" (pēšer) to another. Only when the mystery and the interpretation are brought together can the revelation of God be understood. This same principle, says Bruce, underlies Qumran exegesis (interpretation of Scripture). The mystery was communicated to the prophets, and the interpretation to the Teacher of Righteousness.[5] However, it is also possible to say that the mystery was communicated to the interpreter, since he completed the interpretation of the mystery, and in this sense we must understand certain statements in the Scrolls:[6]

> For Thou hast uncovered my ear to wonderful mysteries. (1QH 1:22)

[5] F. F. Bruce, *Biblical Exegesis in the Qumran Texts* (Grand Rapids: Eerdmans, 1959), pp. 8f.
[6] *Ibid.*, p. 18; cf. 1QpHab 7:4-5 and Dan. 2:28.

And Thou hast appointed me an ensign to the chosen ones
of righteousness and an interpreter of knowledge in the wonderful mysteries. (1QH 2:13)

For Thou hast caused me to know Thy marvelous mysteries.
(1QH 4:27-28)

The Teacher of Righteousness never placed his words
alongside those of the prophets, or suggested that he spoke
with equal authority. He nowhere claimed to "fulfill" the Law
and the prophets.

## Was the Teacher of Righteousness a Priest?

Frank Cross points out that: "The Essenes of Qumran
were a priestly party. Their leader was a priest."[7]   When
Michel made his statement, he said, "The Teacher of Righteousness was probably a priest."[8]  We must remember that
Michel's statement was made before material from Cave Four
was available. In the Commentary on Psalm 37, we read the
following interpretation on Ps. 37:23-24:

Its interpretation: Concerning the priest, the teacher of [Right-
eousness . . . ] YHWH [ . . . ] he established him to build
for him (?) the congregation of his choosing [ . . . ]. (4QpPs37
2:15-16, Habermann 3:34-35, Dupont-Sommer 1:15-16)

The passage is broken, but the restoration is not unreasonable. Two points should be noted. The word "teacher" is
clearly read, but "righteousness" is restored in the broken
manuscript. This priest was established (H-stem of KWN), as
Carmignac points out, "to build" (libnôt) the congregation,
and not "to found" it.[9]

## Was the Teacher of Righteousness a Lawgiver?

We have come across references to the "Seeker of the Law"
(dôrēš hattôrā). In the Damascus Document he is identified
with "the Staff" (CD 6:7-9) and with "the Star" (CD 7:18-20).
More important is the question of his identification with the
Teacher of Righteousness.

[7] F. M. Cross, "Early History of the Qumran Community," in *New Hori-
zons in Biblical Archaeology*, p. 77.

[8] See n. 1, p. 117 above.

[9] Cf. *Les Textes de Qumrân*, II, ed. J. Carmignac, É. Cothenet, and H.
Lignée (Paris: Letouzey et Ané, 1963), p. 125 n. 27.

Dupont-Sommer first suggests that the term "may refer to the Teacher of Righteousness, the Seeker of the Law and Prophet *par excellence.*"[10] Then he makes a positive identification: "The 'Seeker of the Law' is the Teacher of Righteousness."[11] From there he goes on to refer to him as "the Lawgiver, the new Moses, who 'could have said, like Jesus the Nazarene: "Think not that I am come to abolish the Law and the prophets; I am not come to abolish but to fulfill. . . ," ' "[12]

However, it is not clearly established that the Seeker of the Law was the Teacher of Righteousness. Moreover, the Teacher never sets his own statements authoritatively over against accepted interpretations as Jesus did. And it is not clear that he was looked upon as the Lawgiver, a new Moses. As for the statement that "he could have said, like Jesus . . .," what historian can seriously consider such hypothecations?

To support his suggestion that the Teacher of Righteousness was the new Moses, Dupont-Sommer presents a quotation from Josephus:

> The name of the Lawgiver is, after God, a great object of veneration among them, and if any man blasphemes against the Lawgiver he is punished with death. (*Jewish War* 2.8.9 §145)

In a footnote, Dupont-Sommer says: "It is generally explained that this Lawgiver is Moses. But I myself think rather that it refers to the Lawgiver of the sect, i.e. its Founder."[13] Again, the French savant moves from a cautious footnote to a bold assertion in the body of the text: "His [i.e. the Teacher of Righteousness'] name is unknown. As a mark of respect, his adherents refrained from uttering or writing it, just as the Jews then did with regard to the name of Yahweh. It is no doubt to this that Josephus alludes in his accounts of the Essenes (*Jewish War,* II, 8, 9, §145). . . ."[14]

10 Dupont-Sommer, *The Essene Writings from Qumran,* p. 91 n. 6.
11 *Ibid.,* p. 131 n. 3.
12 *Ibid.,* pp. 147f. This technique is used by Dupont-Sommer several times on different subjects. He makes a cautious suggestion in a footnote, repeats it more positively two or three times in subsequent footnotes, and finally moves it into the text as a settled conclusion. I suggest that this be called the "subliminal" approach to scholarship!
13 *Ibid.,* p. 31 n. 3.
14 *Ibid.,* p. 358. Dupont-Sommer made the same suggestion in his footnotes on pp. 87 and 88.

The conclusion rests upon the following hypotheses: (1) that the Essenes described by Josephus are identical with the Qumran Community; (2) that the "Lawgiver" in Josephus is the Teacher of Righteousness rather than Moses; (3) that the Teacher of Righteousness is the Seeker of the Law; and (4) that the Seeker of the Law is actually a new Lawgiver, a second Moses. We need to remind ourselves that it is contrary to the principles of sound scholarship to build a hypothesis on a hypothesis.

There is no indication in the Qumran texts that the Teacher of Righteousness, or anyone else, was looked upon as a new Lawgiver, a second Moses. An "Interpreter" or "Seeker" of the Law is not a lawgiver; in fact, the very name of the office suggests that the Law itself is the final authority. It is highly probable that if anyone in the Qumran Community had presumed to speak as a new Lawgiver he would have been charged with speaking against the Law, in the same way that Stephen was (Acts 6:11, 13).

## Was the Teacher of Righteousness Crucified?

Dupont-Sommer has consistently held that the Teacher of Righteousness was put to death.[15] John M. Allegro has suggested that this death was by crucifixion.[16] These statements need careful study.

The "Man of Scoffing (or Mockery)" (CD 1:14) persecuted the Qumranians with the sword. According to Dupont-Sommer (*The Essene Writings from Qumran*), this person is the "Man of Lies," the "Prophet of Lies," and the "Wicked Priest," historically to be identified with Hyrcanus II, High Priest in Jerusalem (p. 122 n. 4). Since this was "by the sword," it was a bloody persecution, and "doubtless led to martyrdom and, in particular, to the death of the Teacher of Righteousness himself" (p. 123 n. 1).

The trial was probably before the Sanhedrin (based on a doubtful identification of "the House of Absalom" in 1QpHab 5:11-12 with the Sanhedrin), and was conducted without any intervention by the Teacher on his own behalf. The nature

---

[15] Dupont-Sommer, "Le Maître de justice fut-il mis à mort?" *Vetus Testamentum* 1 (1951), p. 215, and elsewhere in his writings.

[16] Allegro, *The Dead Sea Scrolls*, pp. 99f.

of the punishment, to judge from the expression "swallows up," was probably the death penalty (p. 261 n. 4).

Restoring a broken text in the Habakkuk Commentary, Dupont-Sommer reads "[persecuted the Teacher of Righteousness]" (1QpHab 8:17), and takes the passage that follows to refer to him: "[and they s]et upon him to smite him in virtue of the wicked judgments, and evil profaners committed horrors upon him and vengeance upon his body of flesh" (1QpHab 9:1-2). The scholar admits that others take the passage to refer to the Wicked Priest, mentioned in the preceding line (p. 264 n. 2). A few lines later, he takes the statement, "because he had done wickedly to His elect" (1QpHab 9:11-12), to refer to the Teacher of Righteousness, and notes, "this suggests that it was a bloody persecution" (p. 265 n. 1). Then in a note to 1QpHab 11:4, he says,

> This phrase informs us quite distinctly that the persecution of the Teacher of Righteousness was violent and "furious"; in the words of the text, the Wicked Priest gave free vent to "the anger of his fury," even going so far as to "swallow up" his enemy, i.e. — if we give this metaphor its usual meaning in Hebrew — to do away with him, to kill him. (p. 266 n. 3)

All of these footnotes finally lead to the conclusion embodied in the text: "In fact, the Qumran documents frequently mention a bloody persecution which raged against the sect, a persecution 'by the sword,' in the course of which the Teacher of Righteousness was finally arrested, judged, maltreated and very probably put to death" (p. 360).

Dupont-Sommer further notes that "the idea of the martyrdom of the Teacher of Righteousness gains more and more adherents," and points out that all who have identified the Teacher with Onias III, Jose ben Joezer, or Menahem, not to mention Onias the Just, cannot object to the theory, since all of these historical figures were martyred (p. 360 n. 1). It could be pointed out that the Teacher of Righteousness might have been none of these figures. Many a leader of a small schismatic group has appeared larger in the eyes of his followers than his place in history would justify. And if it be objected that the Qumran movement was not a small schismatic group but rather the large Essene movement, then it could equally well be stated that even Jesus Christ does not loom large in the pages of contemporary history. If we did not know the name of Jesus from Christian scriptures, with which of the historical figures of His period would we attempt to identify Him? Such methodology is patently unsound.

Allegro constructs his argument for the crucifixion as follows. He calls the Teacher "the true High Priest of Israel," arguing that "this was certainly to be his title when he arose to be the priestly Messiah of Israel," and goes on to say that "if he took it at this time, it could only have been interpreted as a deliberate attempt to overthrow the authority of Jannaeus."[17]

Jannaeus, continues Allegro, could not have tolerated such insurrection, and would therefore have to punish it by "a particularly dreadful punishment which he had learnt from his Gentile mercenaries. This was execution by crucifixion, or the hanging of a man alive from a stake until he died of starvation and exposure." Jannaeus actually allowed this atrocity in Jerusalem, according to Josephus (*Antiquities* 13.14.2 §380), but was later opposed by Demetrius III. The Nahum Commentary from Qumran, Allegro reminds us, mentions a Demetrius (4QpNah 1:2) and also a "Lion of Wrath" (4Qp-Nah 1:6-8) who crucified political enemies. Allegro adds, "One might surmise that the Sectarians had particular cause to recall this activity of Jannaeus, since their Master had suffered the same cruel death, the recognized punishment of a rebel."[18]

Other scholars have identified the Demetrius of the Nahum Commentary with Demetrius I; therefore since the identification with Demetrius III is not yet definitely established, Allegro cannot use Josephus to support his theory. But even if this identification were established, the theory is an elaborate structure of hypotheses which can be broken down into the component parts: (1) that the Teacher was martyred; (2) that this was because his claims were of the nature of an insurrection; (3) that the one who punished him was Alexander Jannaeus; (4) that the Demetrius mentioned in the Nahum Com-

[17] Allegro, *The Dead Sea Scrolls*, pp. 98f. He is referring to Alexander Jannaeus, 104-78 B.C.

[18] *Ibid.*, pp. 99f. Allegro had previously broadcast a somewhat different form of this statement over the BBC (see *Time*, Feb. 6, 1956, p. 37), claiming that a Qumran text supported his position that the Teacher of Righteousness had been crucified. The remaining members of the international team of Qumran experts, of which Allegro was a member, immediately published a disavowal of his claim. Cf. "Certain Broadcast Statements of Mr. J. Allegro," *The Times* (London), Mar. 16, 1956, p. 11. See p. 20 above.

mentary (actually a restoration based on the last four letters of the name) was Demetrius III, a contemporary of Alexander Jannaeus; (5) that the punishment meted out in this case was the same as that mentioned by Josephus in other cases, namely crucifixion. In order for the theory to stand, all of these hypotheses must be established, and at present not a single one has been!

Discussing Allegro's claim, Professor Rowley says, "Of this crucifixion there is not the slightest mention in any of the texts, and we are nowhere told how the Teacher of Righteousness died."[19]

## The Resurrection of the Teacher of Righteousness

Dupont-Sommer bases his theory of a resurrection-appearance of the Teacher of Righteousness on the following text:

> The explanation of this concerns the Wicked Priest who persecuted the Teacher of Righteousness, swallowing him up in the anger of his fury in his place of exile. But at the time of the feast of rest of the Day of Atonement he appeared before them to swallow them up and to cause them to stumble on the Day of Fasting, their Sabbath of rest. (1QpHab 11:4-8, translation by Dupont-Sommer)

The subject of the verb "appeared," notes Dupont-Sommer, "can only be the Teacher of Righteousness, and not the Wicked Priest as some writers maintain. The victims of this 'apparition' (or 'revelation') were, in fact, the unfaithful Jews, and not the sectaries."[20] He supports this line of reasoning by pointing out that in a passage from the Thanksgiving Hymns (1QH 4:11-12) the same quotation from Habakkuk is applied to these misguided Jews. In the light of Qumran exegetical methodology, this argument is not particularly convincing. Far more important, however, is the construction of the passage in the Habakkuk Commentary. I translate it as follows:

> Its interpretation concerns the Wicked Priest who pursued (or persecuted) the Teacher of Righteousness to swallow him up in the anger of his wrath unto the place of his exile, and at the end of the appointed time of the rest of the day of

[19] H. H. Rowley, *The Dead Sea Scrolls and the New Testament* (London: S.P.C.K., 1957), p. 6. See also Burrows, *More Light on the Dead Sea Scrolls*, p. 217.

[20] Dupont-Sommer, *The Essene Writings from Qumran*, p. 266 n. 4.

Atonement he appeared unto them to swallow them up and to cause them to stumble on a day of fasting, the sabbath of their rest. (1QpHab 11:4-8)

There is no strong disjunctive word, such as would require the translation "but" after the words "the place of his exile," and such as would be required if a change of subject were intended. Moreover, the repetition of the word translated "to swallow up" suggests a continuity of the same subject. Perhaps more significant, if the subject of the second part is "the Teacher of Righteousness" there is then no logical antecedent for "them." If, on the other hand, the subject is "the Wicked Priest" expressed by the pronoun "he," then the word "them" would logically pertain to the men in the place of exile probably intending Qumran. Dupont-Sommer advanced his theory over twenty years ago, and it has gained no appreciable support from other scholars working in the field.[21]

Some scholars, while denying that there is any specific reference to the 'resurrection of the Teacher in past time, are willing to admit that his (future) resurrection would be included in the Sect's general belief in a final resurrection. This is of course reasonable, if the Sect had such a belief. We have already considered the theological ideas of the Qumranians, however, and we have found no explicit or implicit statement on this matter. Vermès discusses the matter and concludes that the Qumran texts contain no such statement because the members of the Sect expected to pass from this life into the resurrection life without passing through death, since they were the last generation. He supports this with a reference to Paul (1 Cor. 15:51).[22] But while it is stated in Paul, it is not stated in Qumran. We must therefore maintain an agnostic position on this point in Qumran theology, and so we cannot reason from general belief to specific faith concerning the resurrection of the Teacher.

[21] Dupont-Sommer, *The Dead Sea Scrolls*, pp. 27f. The French scholar has softened his presentation to some extent. In this earlier publication he allowed himself to say, "The very word used here, *hôphi'*, describes the appearance of Yahweh himself. Furthermore the biblical text here commented on contains the words: so that God may see their feasts; and this text is applied by the commentator to the Master: what an extraordinary apotheosis!" (*ibid.*, p. 44). Actually the word "God" is not in the text, as Dupont-Sommer's later publication clearly shows.

[22] Géza Vermès, *Discovery in the Judean Desert* (New York: Desclée, 1956), p. 119.

## The Return of the Teacher of Righteousness

The return of the Teacher of Righteousness, according to Dupont-Sommer, is set forth in the Damascus Document:

> . . . until the coming of the Teacher of Righteousness at the end of days. (CD 6:10-11)

In a footnote, Dupont-Sommer adds: "The Teacher of Righteousness is dead but will appear 'at the end of days,' i.e. at the end of the world, when 'all the time of wickedness' will have ended. This expectation of the Teacher's return, formulated so clearly here, was one of the fundamental articles of belief in the credo of the New Covenant" (*Essene Writings*, p. 131 n. 6).

This doctrine is found again in Manuscript B of the Damascus Document:

> "from the day when the Unique Teacher was taken, till the coming of the Anointed sprung from Aaron and Israel." (CD 19:1 = B 2:1)

Here the Messiah is identified with the Teacher to come; but Dupont-Sommer sidesteps the problem in a note, "there is nothing to contradict the identification of this Messiah with the Teacher of Righteousness himself, appearing at the end of time" (p. 139 n. 3). A few pages later, Dupont-Sommer moves his theory into the body of his book with the casual sentence: "While waiting for his glorious return, they must unceasingly listen to his voice and walk in his commandments" (p. 147).

It should be observed that no "credo" of the Qumran Sect has yet been published and no information of any such discovery has been announced. It should also be pointed out that the expectation of the Teacher's "return" does not seem to be formulated "so clearly" in this passage. The passage does not contain the usual words *môrè hassédeq,* "the teacher of righteousness," but *yôrè hassédeq,* which might be translated "the one teaching righteousness." This point should not be pressed, and I would be willing to accept the terms as synonymous; the fact remains, however, that some scholars feel there is an indicated difference in the two terms.

A far more important fact must be observed, namely that the "Teacher of Righteousness" may be an official title rather than the name of an individual. Several scholars feel that there are at least two "Teachers of Righteousness" indicated in the Scrolls: one early in the history of the Sect, and one to come at the end. At least one scholar seems to accept the title as one of "a stock set of masks" that were fit upon "a stock set of characters,"[23] in other words, the title of an office and not the title of a single person.[24]

In 1956 I wrote the following tentative conclusion:

> There is little doubt, as I understand the texts, that some out-standing figure of the recent past had so impressed the Com-munity that he became known as the Teacher of Righteousness. That he was expected to return is, to me, less clear. But that he represented an ideal so basically right that it had to be part of the messianic age seems to be a minimum interpreta-tion. Beyond this, I would prefer not to go at the present time.[25]

I have not yet found reason to go beyond that statement.

## The Teacher of Righteousness and the Mother of the Messiah

In the Thanksgiving Hymns there is a particularly difficult portion which has led to considerable speculation and few ex-treme statements. Dupont-Sommer calls it "one of the most important and most difficult to interpret of the whole collec-tion" (*Essene Writings*, p. 207 n. 1). In the notes to his transla-tion, the French scholar seems to limit his interpretation to the Community: "The Mother of the Messiah, i.e. the Com-munity . . ." (p. 208 n. 4). In his summary chapter on the Teacher of Righteousness, however, he applies this as a prophecy to the Teacher: "Before this supreme exaltation, the earthly destiny of the Teacher was horribly dramatic: the Savior-Messiah was to be born in distress, in 'the waves of death.' Such is the theme developed in one of the *Hymns*

[23] Theodor H. Gaster, *The Dead Sea Scriptures* (Garden City, N.Y.: Doubleday, 1956), pp. 27f.

[24] G. W. Buchanan, in a study of "The Priestly Teacher of Righteous-ness," says, "The most significant conclusion of this study is that the rab-binic reference to the priestly teacher of righteousness as a position rather than the description of a specific individual makes good sense when applied to the passages that mention the teacher of righteousness in the Dead Sea Scrolls" — *Revue de Qumrân* 6,24 (March 1969), p. 558.

[25] LaSor, *Amazing Dead Sea Scrolls*, p. 171.

(III, 7-18) revealing the highest summits of messianic speculation attained by the Essene sect" (p. 365).

The passage is full of graphic language, figures of speech,
and perhaps several plays on words. I offer this translation
with hesitancy and with no motive other than to provide a
basis for further discussion.

> I shall be in travail like a woman in labor bearing her first-
> born. For her pangs are overturned and travail is vehement
> upon her birth-stool to await the first-born of the pregnant
> one. For sons have come unto the birth-stools of death, and
> the one pregnant with a male child has become constricted in
> her travail. For on birth-stools of death she will give birth to
> a male, and with the pangs of Sheol he will burst forth from
> the womb of the pregnant one, a wonderful counselor with
> his might, and a male child shall be saved from (the) birth-
> stools. In his pregnancy (= when he was yet in the womb)
> all the birth-stools hastened and the travail of violence on
> those bearing them and shuddering to those pregnant with
> them, and when he was born all birth pangs were overturned
> in the womb (or, on the first-born?) of the pregnant one, and
> the one pregnant with a viper for travail of violence and birth-
> stools of the pit (or, destruction) for all the deeds of shud-
> dering.
>
> And the foundations (or, depths?) of (the) wall shout (?) like
> a ship on the face of the water, and the clouds roar with the
> voice of a multitude, and those that sit in dust like those who
> go down to the seas are terrified by the tumult of water. And
> their wise men are all of them like sailors in the depths of the
> sea, for all their wisdom is swallowed up in the tumult of the
> water, in the boiling of the deeps upon the confusion of the
> water [they are expelle]d by the height of the waves, and the
> breakers of the water with the tumult of their voice, and when
> they are expelled (the) h[eavens will be opened to let fly al]l
> (the) arrows of destruction. With their march to the deep they
> cause their voice to be heard, and the gates of [heaven?] shall
> be opened [on behalf of] the deeds of the viper, and the doors
> of the pit shall be closed on behalf of the one pregnant with
> unrighteousness, and the elect ones of eternity on behalf of
> all the spirits of the viper. (1QH 3:7-18)

To comment on this passage would require pages. The
word translated "birth-stool," for example, also means "break-
ers," and is so used in line 16. The word translated "firstborn"
($b^e k\hat{u}r$) can mean "in the crucible (or, womb)," which would
be supported by the form $mikk\hat{u}r$ ("from the womb") in line

10. Syntax is equally problematic. The figures of speech are almost kaleidoscopic, and the effect is confusing, to say the least. The only "messianic" hint in the passage, in my opinion, is the expression "wonderful counselor," from Isaiah 9:5-6. The contrast between the woman pregnant with a male child and the woman pregnant with a viper (line 12), also expressed as the woman pregnant with unrighteousness (line 18), may refer to the conflict between truth and unrighteousness. But to find a deeper reference to the Community or to the Messiah is eisegesis (reading into the text) and not exegesis (reading out of the text).

No commentator speaks with finality on this passage — all admit its great difficulty. It therefore is not correct to say that this is *not* a messianic passage; the only statement that can be made with certainty is to the effect that no doctrine should be based upon this passage unless it is clearly taught in other documents from Qumran.

## Summary

The material on the Teacher of Righteousness in the Dead Sea Scrolls is quite limited, and seems to provide little textual basis for the elaborate theories built around this figure. He was not the founder of the Sect, in its formative stage at least. He was not its Messiah. Rather, he was its teacher, its interpreter of the mysteries which had been committed to the prophets.

If we accept some of the Thanksgiving Hymns as containing biographical elements, we may conclude that the Teacher of Righteousness was a strongly motivated, deeply religious person, with a sense of human frailty and personal sin. He had insights into the purpose of God as revealed by the prophets, particularly Isaiah, which no other known religious leader of the intertestamental period had expressed.

But to speak of him as a divine Master, the Builder of a Church, the Mediator of a New Covenant, the Man of Sorrows, the Savior-Messiah, and similar extravagant terms, borders on the realm of sheer fancy. This can only be done by reading back into his life episodes which are clearly recorded about Jesus, but which are not recorded at all of the Teacher, and then to project this mythical creature to a proportion that neither history nor the texts of Qumran will support.

## CHAPTER TEN

# POSSIBLE NON-QUMRAN SOURCES CONCERNING QUMRAN

Our methodology has been clearly stated and carefully followed: we are seeking to describe the Qumran Community and its beliefs from the Qumran documents; then, when we have the picture as complete as we can make it, we shall compare it with Christianity.

The charge may be made, however, that in following this methodology we have overlooked an important body of source-materials, namely that which is written about the Essenes. I have maintained, and still maintain vigorously, that until there is positive identification of the Essenes and the Qumranians, nothing but confusion can result from mixing the Qumran and non-Qumran materials. However, I am equally anxious that no possible evidence should be overlooked, and it *is* a possibility — and must remain a possibility until the question is settled finally — that the materials concerning the Essenes refer to the Qumranians, if not specifically, then by inclusion of the Qumranians in a larger group. It is therefore in order to set down the facts about the Essenes that are known from non-Qumran sources. No attempt will be made to reconcile differences between the sources, and contradictory or conflicting statements will be presented in both or all forms when necessary.

## The Sources

The sources of information concerning the Essenes are:

Philo of Alexandria, *Let Every Good Man be Free,* and *Apology for the Jews (Hypothetica).* Philo lived in Egypt from c. 30 B.C. to some time after A.D. 40. He was therefore contemporary with the Qumranians, although geographically removed from them. His *Apology* is not extant, but parts of it are quoted by Eusebius. We shall refer to the works by brief titles: *Every Good Man,* and *Apology.*

Flavius Josephus (or Joseph ben Matthias), *War of the Jews,* and *Jewish Antiquities.* Josephus was born in A.D. 37, lived in Palestine the first half of his life, and records that he was determined to know the three Jewish sects (Pharisees, Sadducees, and Essenes) at first hand. He joined the Essenes when he was sixteen, but since he was already a confirmed Pharisee at nineteen, it is doubtful that he completed the necessary period of testing to become an Essene — for by his own description that took three years. He provides our most extensive source concerning the Essenes. We shall refer to his works by the brief titles: *War,* and *Antiquities.*

Pliny the Elder, *Natural History.* Pliny was a Roman who died in A.D. 79. He may have been in Palestine with Titus during the Jewish war against Rome.

A fourth author, Hippolytus of Rome, is sometimes quoted. His work, *A Refutation of All Heresies,* was written about A.D. 230, and the material on the Essenes seems to be based on Josephus.

## *The Essenes: General Description*

The Essenes (or Essaeans) were one of three "sects" of the Jews.[1] They left the cities of Palestine and lived in towns and villages.[2] A specific location is mentioned, namely west of the Dead Sea; "below" them was En Gedi,[3] and they were not far from Sodom.[4] They numbered about 4,000 members.[5]

They were without goods and property,[6] and without

[1] Josephus *War* 2.8.2 §119.
[2] Philo *Apology* 11.1; *Every Good Man* §76; Josephus *War* 2.8.4 §124.
[3] Pliny *Natural History* 5.15.73.
[4] Quoted in Synesius *Dio.* Cf. *Dio Chrysostom,* vol. 5, p. 379, in Loeb Classical Library.
[5] Philo *Every Good Man* §75; Josephus *Antiquities* 18.1.5 §20.
[6] Philo *Every Good Man* §77

house.[7] They lived frugally,[8] having only what was necessary for life.[9] They did not hoard silver and gold, and did not have vast domains.[10] They despised riches.[11] They had no slaves.[12] They worked in fields or at crafts which contributed to peace,[13] and would make no instrument of war.[14] They did not engage in commerce of any kind.[15]

## Communal Life

The Essenes lived a communal life,[16] dwelling in brotherhoods.[17] They ate together,[18] held property in common,[19] and had a common purse.[20] Wages were turned over to one person,[21] the administrator of the common fund.[22] They had a common store of clothing,[23] and always wore white clothing.[24]

## Marriage and Children

They banned marriage: "no Essene takes a woman."[25] Or they disdained marriage, but did not abolish it.[26] They were without women and without love,[27] and continence is listed as one of their virtues.[28] There were some Essenes, however, who evidently differed from the others in that they did marry.[29]

[7] Philo *Every Good Man* §85; *Apology* 11 4.
[8] Philo *Apology* 11.11.
[9] Philo *Every Good Man* §76.
[10] Philo *Every Good Man* §76.
[11] Josephus *War* 2.8.3 §122.
[12] Philo *Every Good Man* §76; Josephus *Antiquities* 18.1.5 §21.
[13] Philo *Every Good Man* §76; *Apology* 11.8-9.
[14] Philo *Every Good Man* §78.
[15] *Ibid.*
[16] Philo *Every Good Man* §85; Josephus *War* 2.8.3 §122.
[17] Philo *Apology* 11.5.
[18] Philo *Every Good Man* §86; *Apology* 11.5, 11.
[19] Josephus *Antiquities* 18.1.5 §20.
[20] Philo *Every Good Man* §86.
[21] Philo *Apology* 11.10.
[22] Josephus *War* 2.8.3 §123. Possibly this refers to the community, not to the fund.
[23] Philo *Every Good Man* §86; *Apology* 11.12.
[24] Josephus *War* 2.8.3 §123.
[25] Philo *Apology* 11.14; Josephus *Antiquities* 18.1.5 §21.
[26] Josephus *War* 2.8.2 §§120-121
[27] Pliny *Natural History* 5.15.73.
[28] Philo *Every God Man* §84.
[29] Josephus *War* 2.8.13 §160.

They had no children, no adolescents, not even young men.[30] They adopted children.[31] They renounced pleasure and resisted passions.[32] They treated the sick and the aged with special care.[33]

## Admission to the Essene Sect

Admission to the sect was a long process, consisting of one year as a postulant and an additional two years of limited participation in the community.[34] Then the novice took solemn oaths before he could touch the common food.[35] The oaths included his relationship to God and to fellow members, to hate the wicked and to love truth, to conceal nothing from the members and to reveal nothing to outsiders, to transmit the doctrines exactly as he received them.[36] When he entered, he surrendered his property to the sect.[37]

## A Typical Day in Essene Life

Josephus gives us a picture of a typical day in the life of the Essenes. They rose before dawn and recited prayers to the rising sun. Then each man attended to his craft until the fifth hour (11 a.m.). At that time the community assembled, put on linen loin-cloths, bathed in cold water, and then went to the special building restricted to members, and to a dining-hall that was further restricted to those who were pure. Bread and one bowlful of food were served. The priest said a prayer before anyone was permitted to touch the food, and another prayer after the meal. Then they laid aside the sacred garments and returned to work until evening. Dinner in the evening was in the same manner as the noon meal. They ate quietly, and they spoke only in turn. They ate and drank only what they needed to satisfy them.[38]

[30] Philo *Apology* 11.3.
[31] Josephus *War* 2.8.2 §120.
[32] *Ibid.*
[33] Philo *Every Good Man* §87; *Apology* 11.13.
[34] Josephus *War* 2.8.7 §§137-138.
[35] *Ibid.*, §139.
[36] *Ibid.*, §§139-142.
[37] *Ibid.*, 2.8.3 §122.
[38] *Ibid.*, 2.8.5 §§128-133.

## Religious Beliefs and Practice

The Essenes were not concerned with logic or natural philosophy, but they devoted themselves to ethics.[39] They concerned themselves with purity[40] and with holy minds.[41] They rejected oaths, and considered their word sufficient.[42] They did not offer sacrifices[43]— or else they did not send sacrifices to the Temple, but sacrificed among themselves.[44] They sent offerings to the Temple.[45] They considered oil a defilement.[46] They believed that their souls were immortal.[47]

They devoted themselves to the law of ethics, especially on the seventh day,[48] when they went to synagogues and sat according to age.[49] One would read and another explain, making use of symbols and the triple use of definitions.[50] On the Sabbath they would do no work.[51] They studied the works of the ancients, particularly becoming proficient in the knowledge of healing, of roots, and of stones.[52] They studied the holy books, and were skilled at predicting the future.[53] The name of the lawgiver was an object of great veneration.[54]

## Ranks, Precedence, and Discipline

The Essenes were divided into four lots or ranks,[55] and would do nothing unless ordered by superiors, with the exception of works of mercy.[56] They obeyed their elders.[57] When ten sat, one would not speak if the nine were opposed.[58] They

39 Philo *Every Good Man* §80.
40 *Ibid.*, §84.
41 *Ibid.*, §75.
42 *Ibid.*, §84; Josephus *War* 2.8.6 §135.
43 Philo *Every Good Man* §75.
44 Josephus *Antiquities* 18.1.5 §19.
45 *Ibid.*
46 Josephus *War* 2.8.3 §123.
47 Josephus *Antiquities* 18.1.5. §18; *War* 2.8.11 §154.
48 Philo *Every Good Man* §§80-81.
49 *Ibid.*, §81.
50 *Ibid.*, §§82-83.
51 Josephus *War* 2.8.9 §147.
52 *Ibid.*, 2.8.6 §136.
53 *Ibid.*, 2.8.12 §159.
54 *Ibid.*, 2.8.9 §145.
55 *Ibid.*, 2.8.10 §150.
56 *Ibid.*, 2.8.6 §134.
57 *Ibid.*, 2.8.9 §146.
58 *Ibid.*, §146.

refrained from spitting in assembly, or to the right.[59] Justice was dispensed at an assembly of one hundred members or more.[60] Expulsion from the group resulted from serious offenses, and the person expelled, because of his vows, usually starved.[61]

## Similarities between the Qumranians and the Essenes

Similarities between the Essenes as described in these sources and the Qumranians as described in Qumran sources are obvious at many points.

Both were, of course, Jewish sects. According to Josephus, there were three Jewish sects — Pharisees, Sadducees, and Essenes — and a number of writers have pointed out that the Qumranians were not Pharisees and were not Sadducees; therefore they must be Essenes. The flaw in this logic should be obvious; we know that there were more than these three sects.

The geographical location seems to be the same, and as several scholars have pointed out, the region is not suited to accommodate many such communities. However, J. P. Audet has made a detailed study of Pliny's use of the expression *infra hos*, and shows rather convincingly that it never means "south" or "downstream," but only "below." Audet therefore concludes that Pliny intended to locate the Essenes above En Gedi, that is, in the region above the cliffs west of En Gedi; Audet suggests that the location may have been at Hasason-Tamar.[62] This also fits the description given by Dio Chrysostom, "but not far from Sodom" — provided Sodom is to be located at the southern end of the Dead Sea, and not, as some believe, at the northern end.

Both groups renounced private property and lived an austere life. Both lived in communal settlements, eating together, having a common purse. Both had a supervisor of the common wealth.

In both cases admission was a process of trial and examination. Both had an oath of admission. Both hated the wicked

59 *Ibid.*, §147.
60 *Ibid.*, §145.
61 *Ibid.*, 2.8.8 §143.
62 Cf. J.-P. Audet, "Qumrân et la notice de Pline sur les Esséniens," *Revue Biblique* 68 (1961), pp. 346-387. But see the replies by E. M. Laperrousaz (*Revue Biblique* 69 [1962], pp. 369-380) and C. Burchard (*ibid.*, pp. 533-569).

and loved the members of the fellowship. Both kept the esoteric knowledge of their group from outsiders. In both groups
the new member surrendered his property to the sect.

Prayers, ritual bathing, common meals, study and interpretation of the Bible, and concern with purity marked the
daily life in each case. Both were careful to keep the Sabbath.
Both groups were divided into lots or ranks — although the
parallel is not quite as neat as we might wish. Both observed
the authority of elders and superiors. Both had injunctions
against spitting in assembly. Both had a minimum group of
ten. Both had laws of expulsion for serious offenses.

## The Differences between the Essenes and the Qumranians

The differences between the two groups — or perhaps we
should say, between the two sets of descriptions — are also noteworthy; these are not pointed out as often or as carefully as
the similarities have been. In fact, one sometimes gets the
impression that certain scholars are trying too hard to prove
their identity. Dupont-Sommer thinks he has found "a sort
of 'Essenophobia' with which most historians of Judaism and
primitive Christianity were for a long time afflicted."[63]   I
must confess that I have never felt any such "phobia," nor
was I aware of it when studying about the Essenes either before or after the Dead Sea Scrolls were discovered. I simply
felt that honest scholars were grappling with a problem and
were not convinced that the Essenes provided all the answers.
If suddenly the Dead Sea Scrolls furnished the necessary solutions, who would not rejoice that another problem was solved?
A few of us, however, feel that there are still some difficulties
that need to be ironed out.

Obviously the Qumranians could not be all of the Essenes,
but only a very small fraction of the "4,000 men" at most, and
only one of the numerous "towns and villages" mentioned in
the sources. The Damascus Document, of course, may provide the solution in its reference to camps (CD 7:6).

If the Qumranians worked at crafts, we know nothing
about it. Nor do we know their attitude toward war and im-
plements of war. We do know that they drew up a fully de-

---

[63] Dupont-Sommer, *The Essene Writings from Qumran*, p. 145.

tailed account of an army, weapons, maneuvers, and the like, for the War Scroll; and they do not sound much like pacifists— but that could be poetic license (cf. 1QS 9:16; 22-23; 10:18; 1QSa 1:19-21). There are indications that the Qumranians did engage in commerce (cf. CD 13:14-15).

We know nothing of a common store of clothing at Qumran. We know of no regulation concerning white clothing or of other personal items such as those mentioned in the Essene sources.

The Qumran Sect was not situated for married life, yet we know from its literature that provision was made for wives and children. There were young children; there were adolescents; there were young men. It is of course possible that these were the "marrying Essenes" to which Josephus refers.

Admission to the Essenes was a three-year process; to Qumran it took two years.

We know nothing of Qumranian prayers to the sun or of anything that Josephus might have misconstrued as such. We know nothing of daily bathing, but it would have been quite possible with the facilities for water storage at Qumran.

Philo's efforts to describe the philosophical interests of the Essenes may have been written out of a background that does not quite convey to us his meaning, but we must still record the fact that the Qumran writings do indeed contain something like a natural theology. Unlike the Essenes, the Qumranians did use oaths, and there are sections on oaths in their literature (CD 9:8-12; 15:1-10; 16:6-18). The Qumran attitude toward sacrifices is not entirely clear, but there is provision for sending sacrifices to the Temple; the Essene attitude toward sacrifices is also confused in the Essene sources. We know of no Qumran aversion to oil; in fact, oil of anointing is mentioned in the War Scroll (1QM 9:8).

The seating arrangement at Qumran was by rank and not, as in the Essene sources, by age; rank was, moreover, altered by annual examination.

We have no evidence that the Qumranians used a system of triple definitions in Biblical interpretation. There is a minimum amount of the use of symbols in Qumran writing. The Dead Sea Scrolls do not indicate that the Qumranians studied the knowledge of healing, roots, or stones. If they were expert at predicting future events, we have no record of it beyond the vague generalities found in some texts. In fact, modern historians are unable to get a consistent historical picture out of the Qumran texts.

The name of the Lawgiver may have been an object of great veneration at Qumran, but there is no direct statement to the effect. We must reject Dupont-Sommer's conclusion that Josephus was referring to the Teacher of Righteousness in his statement concerning the Lawgiver.

The division into four lots or ranks mentioned by Josephus is not clear: at Qumran it could be the priests, Levites, lay members, and proselytes. However, this does not seem to be Josephus' meaning; rather, he seems to refer to some kind of classification or rank (*moiras* in Greek means something like the Hebrew *góral*, "lot") assigned to the member who had just concluded his entrance examination.

There is no indication in Qumran literature that a member would do nothing unless ordered by a superior; there was, of course, a strong sense of rank and authority.

There is no indication that justice at Qumran was administered by a session of a hundred men; rather, it seems to have been administered by a council of fifteen (1QS 8:1) or ten (CD 9:4-5).

## Summary

How can we account for the differences, as well as the similarities, between the two sets of records?

We can assume that Philo, Josephus, and Pliny the Elder were wrong on the details where the two bodies of material differ. The Qumran records, we might maintain, are, after all, the primary sources. They were produced by the Qumranians, and the Qumranians would know better than outsiders the details of their organization. But this contains a hidden *a priori,* assuming what remains to be proven, i.e. that the Qumranians were Essenes. We can set aside the Essene sources only when we have a third body of material to control our assumptions.

Or we can assume that there were temporal developments that would explain the differences between Qumran and the Essenes. The non-Qumran sources are all later than the probable date of the Qumran sources, and this would allow time for differences to develop. Again, we need an independent control.

Or we can assume that there were geographical differences, and that the non-Qumran sources are describing Essenes located in some other community. This, however, overlooks two facts. First, the geographical location of Qumran and the geographical location described by Pliny have together been taken as one of the most convincing arguments for the identity of Qumran with the Essenes.[64] If we remove the geographical location of the Essenes from Qumran, we remove at the same time the support that Pliny is supposed to have given to the argument for identity. Second, the Qumran materials have been accepted, by many of the scholars who favor an Essene identification, as the source material for Essenism. Here at Qumran, we are told, were produced the sectarian writings of the Essenes. To Qumran, it has been suggested, Essenes came for an annual reunion. Yet some of the distinctive character-istics of the Essenes are not found at Qumran: the attitude toward oaths, the attitude toward sacrifices, and above all the attitude toward marriage. Obviously these things cannot all be true at the same time.

Or again we can assume that the literature at Qumran is not homogeneous, but that it represents different sub-groups of Essenism. But when we have reached this point we are in effect saying that in Qumran and in the non-Qumranian Es-sene sources we have nonhomogeneous portraits of a stream of Judaism that diverged from the main stream: part of it went to Qumran, part perhaps went to Damascus, part possibly to Hasason-Tamar above En Gedi, part to some village or town where Josephus met it, and so on. *But why label this "Essene"?* "Essene" is what Philo, Josephus, and Pliny have described for us — and what they have described is not exactly what we find at Qumran.

That both groups, the Essenes and the Qumranians, can be traced to the same origin is a truism: they were Jewish sects.

[64] Cross takes the geographical location as "virtually decisive" in the identification of the two groups; cf. "Early History of Qumran Com-munity" in *New Directions in Biblical Archaeology*, pp. 76f. I find his "reckless" (p. 77) willingness to "assume the identification and draw freely upon both classical and Qumran texts" in his discussion of Qumran strangely different from his careful critical methodology in Old Testament studies.

Our interest now, as historians, is to try to understand when and why they separated from the main stream of Judaism; then we want to know something of their subsequent development, including further divisions within the sectarian movement. We are not interested in psychoanalysis for Essenophobia, nor in subjective reconstructions of a Super-Essenism. We simply want to get as much of the record as straight as we possibly can from the objective materials available to us.

We shall therefore continue to treat Qumran as Qumran and the Essenes as Essenes. And since comparisons between Essenism and Christianity were wrung dry nearly a century ago, we shall limit our study to comparisons between the New Testament and the Dead Sea Scrolls.

## CHAPTER ELEVEN

# JOHN THE BAPTIST
# AND QUMRAN

One scholar of unquestioned fidelity to the Christian faith has written, "The discovery of the manuscripts has in an undeniable way confirmed the Baptist's contacts with the monks of Qumran, whom we know to be identical with the Essenes."[1] With only slightly less certainty, an archeologist of eminence stated, referring to the ruins at Qumran, "John the Baptist was almost certainly an Essene and must have studied and worked in this building."[2]

Now, as Millar Burrows has well expressed it, "There is no reason why one should be so reluctant to believe that John was or had been a member of their community. The only question is whether there is good reason to suppose that he was, or that he had anything to do with the sect."[3] We must not let our emotions control our logical processes. There must be one and only one objective: to solve the problem on the basis of the records. Does the available evidence prove that John was a member of Qumran or not? Or, if there is no clear answer to this question, does the evidence indicate that such a relationship was probable or improbable?

[1] Jean Daniélou, *The Dead Sea Scrolls and Primitive Christianity* (Baltimore: Helicon, 1958), p. 15.

[2] G. Lankester Harding, "Where Christ Himself May Have Studied: An Essene Monastery at Khirbet Qumran," *Illustrated London News* 227 (Sept. 3, 1955), pp. 370-381.

[3] Burrows, *More Light on the Dead Sea Scrolls*, pp. 56f.

We can dispose of the first question peremptorily. John the Baptist is not mentioned in the Qumran texts and Qumran is not mentioned in the New Testament or in Josephus, which are the only sources concerning John the Baptist. There is nothing in the Qumran texts or in any other known source that will in any way lead to a clear-cut decision either that John was or that he was not a member of the Qumran Sect. It therefore seems that Daniélou has overstated the case.

We are left, then, with the more general problem: Does the available evidence suggest that John was probably a member of Qumran, or does it suggest that he was not, or is it completely neutral?

## John the Baptist in the Sources

The only extant sources of material concerning John the Baptist are the New Testament and Josephus. In the New Testament, the fullest notices are found in Matthew and Luke. Josephus gives but one statement which concerns the imprisonment of John (*Antiquities* 18.5.2 §119). The material is not extensive, but we are able to form a sketch of the life and ministry of John from it.

John was born of a priestly family (Luke 1:5) about six months before Jesus was born (cf. 1:36). John's parents were well along in years (1:7), and there was an aura of the miraculous in the birth of the child. The father Zechariah was convinced that he had seen visions of an angel who told him that the child was to be dedicated as a Nazirite (1:15), that he would be similar to Elijah in his ministry, and that he was to prepare the people for the Lord (1:17, 68-79).

The child John was "in the desert" until he began his public ministry about the age of thirty (Luke 1:80; 3:23) — which was about A.D. 27 or 28 (cf. 3:1).

John's ministry did not last long — perhaps as little as six months — but it created a sensation among the Jewish people. According to Josephus, Herod feared that John's great influence over the people might lead him to raise a rebellion, and therefore Herod put him in the dungeon at Machaerus. The New Testament contains glowing statements about John from the lips of Jesus (cf. Luke 7:28). History places its stamp on the importance of John, for John-the-Baptist sects were scattered over the Near East, and followers of John can be found to the present time.[4]

The ministry of John the Baptist was striking. He was garbed in coarse clothing, and his diet was locusts — almost certainly the insect and not the fruit of the locust tree — and wild honey (Mark 1:6). He conducted his ministry at or near the Jordan river at a location or locations that cannot be positively identified. One place was "Bethany beyond the Jordan" (John 1:28) — but the name Bethany is noncommittal, for there were numerous places by that name, and there is a textual witness (of weak value, it is true) for the name Bethabara instead of Bethany. Bethabara, we might add, simply means "the place of the crossing," and could indicate any of several fords. John also baptized at "Aenon near Salim" (John 3:23), which is located, according to some scholars, near the headwaters of Wadi Far'ah, not far from the modern city of Nablus.

He taught his disciples to pray (cf. Luke 11:1), and disciplined them to fast (cf. Matt. 9:14). Particularly, he stressed the nearness of the Kingdom of God, and subordinated his own ministry to that of the One (certainly the Messiah) who was to come (Mark 1:7; cf. John 3:30). When Jesus came to be baptized, John hesitated to baptize Him, and later pointed Him out as the One for whom John was to prepare the way (Matt. 3:14; John 1:30).

The nature of his ministry attracted crowds (Matt. 3:5; cf. 11:7-10), and this led to an official investigation (cf. John 1: 19-23). He preached a stern message of repentance, saying, "The Kingdom of Heaven is at hand" (Matt. 3:2), and he baptized those who repented (3:6). He looked upon himself not as the Messiah, nor indeed as any of the other figures associated with the messianic concept (cf. John 1:19-23), but simply as the voice crying in the wilderness, in fulfillment of the words of Isaiah (cf. Matt. 3:3; Isa. 40:3). He dealt with specific problems and gave stern and rebuking answers (see Luke 3:12-14 and Matt. 14:1-2). Because of the forthright character of his preaching he incurred the enmity of the Herodian family, was put in prison, and then was executed (cf. Luke 3:19-20; Matt. 14:3-4; Mark 6:17-18).

---

[4] Cf. LaSor, *Amazing Dead Sea Scrolls*, pp. 203-206; *Great Personalities of the New Testament*, pp. 23-31.

Critical scholars reject some of these items, but there seems to be no strongly compelling reason to do so. The picture of John in the four Gospels is consistent and there is no contradictory material in any other sources. Brownlee, after restudying the New Testament portrait of John the Baptist in the light of the Qumran materials, concludes that "the most astonishing result of all is the validation of the Fourth Gospel as an authentic source concerning the Baptist."[5]

## Possible Contacts with Qumran: the Desert Tradition

From this body of material certain points have suggested a possible connection between John and Qumran.

First of all, there is the tradition that John grew up in the desert or wilderness (Luke 1:80; 3:2). The term "wilderness" is used to describe the arid region between the Jerusalem-Hebron road and the Dead Sea. There are few places in this wilderness that will support life; Qumran is one such place, hence it is reasonable to suppose that John grew up at Qumran.

Daniélou believes that the location is actually more definite than I have stated it here. The word "desert," he points out, "designates a specific place, for this is the very word used by the hermits of Qumran to designate the region where they dwelt."[6] How Daniélou can be so sure that the Greek word used by Luke is "the very word" as the Hebrew word used in the Dead Sea Scrolls he does not tell us. Further, Daniélou says that this desert is "a precise location which, as Pliny the Elder has noted . . . , was planted with palm trees and watered by springs."[7] However, it is not certain that Pliny was referring to Qumran. Audet has argued in favor of a location near En Gedi, and from personal observation I would say that the flora and the spring at En Gedi compare much more favorably with Pliny's description than does the present Qumran. What it was like in the days of the Qumran Sect, of course, we do not know.

[5] W. H. Brownlee, "John the Baptist in the New Light of Ancient Scrolls," in K. Stendahl, ed., *The Scrolls and the New Testament*, p. 52.
[6] Daniélou, *The Dead Sea Scrolls and Primitive Christianity*, p. 16.
[7] *Ibid.*, p. 16.

If John went to the wilderness when yet a very young boy, it is obvious that he had to be in someone's care. Scholars have suggested that his parents placed him in the custody of the Qumran "Essenes," reminding us of Josephus' statement: "Marriage they disdain, but they adopt other men's children, while yet pliable and docile, and regard them as their kin and mould them in accordance with their own principles."[8]

There are, however, some details that do not fit this theory. John's clothing was not the white linen of the Essenes, and his diet was not the diet of the Essenes. Moreover, it is difficult to understand how Zechariah and Elizabeth, who were of the priestly line — particularly Zechariah, who was an active member of the Jerusalem priesthood — would have committed the son for whom they had prayed and waited so long into the custody of a group so stately hostile to the Jerusalem priesthood.

Schubert has raised another embarrassing question for this theory. "If John spent his youth among the Essenes," he points out, "it is surprising, to say the least, that Josephus should leave this fact wholly unmentioned in his detailed account of John the Baptist in Ant. 18, 5, 2."[9] He goes on to suggest that there were others who lived in the desert, and reminds us of a man named Bannus, described by Josephus as one "who lived in the desert, wore clothing made of tree bark, ate wild herbs, and washed himself with cold water frequently during the day as well as at night for purification."[10] Josephus clearly distinguished this Bannus from the Essenes. Schubert points out that John's clothing was more like that of Bannus than that of the Essenes; on the other hand, the washings of Bannus were more like those of Qumran than the baptism of John.

## The Use of Scripture

Both in the Qumran texts and in the accounts of John the Baptist, Isaiah 40:3 is quoted: "In the wilderness prepare the way of the Lord: make ready in the desert a highway for

[8] Josephus *War* 2.8.2 §120.
[9] K. Schubert, *The Dead Sea Community* (London: Black, 1959), p. 128. I cannot agree that Josephus has given us a "detailed account of John the Baptist," but Schubert's point deserves consideration.
[10] Josephus *Life* 2 §11.

our God" (1QS 8:12-14; Matt. 3:3; John 1:23). Daniélou ventures the opinion that the similarity of content and expression "cannot be fortuitous."[11] It could be pointed out that when the same Scripture is quoted the content and expression will always be the same — it is the context, the use that is made of the Scripture, that is definitive. How was this passage used at Qumran? How did John use it?

To "prepare the way" to the Qumranian meant "to go into the desert," where they might receive instruction in the mysteries, and where they would be separated from the men who had not departed from unrighteousness (1QS 9:19-21). The "way" that they were to prepare in the desert was "the searching of the Law [which] (God) commanded by Moses" (1QS 8:12-16). No Qumranian on record said, "I am the voice of one crying . . . " — in fact, this part of the quotation from Isaiah does not appear in the Qumran texts.

To John, "to prepare the way" meant to leave the seclusion of the wilderness and to preach the gospel to men who needed to repent. "The way" for John was not the mere searching of the Law, but the preparation of the people for the Messiah by calling them to a realization of the significance of the Law in all areas of life. For this task, John was the "voice" crying in the wilderness (cf. Luke 3:3-17; John 1:19-27).

It is granted that the Hebrew in Isaiah is not phrased in the way just indicated. Both the poetic structure and the Masoretic accents indicate the following phrasing:

> A voice crying aloud,
>> In the wilderness prepare the way of the Lord,
>> Make straight in the desert a highway for our God.

But a study of the Gospels, particularly Mark 1:3-4, indicates that the verse was used in a slightly different way. John was the "voice crying in the wilderness," and Mark adds, "John the baptizer appeared in the wilderness." This slight divergence from the Hebrew in itself underscores the difference between John's use and the Qumranian use of this verse.

If John received the inspiration for his ministry from this verse of Scripture while a member of the Qumran Community — a possibility which is not ruled out by the foregoing dis-

[11] Daniélou, *The Dead Sea Scrolls and Primitive Christianity*, p. 17. Burrows remarks, "Surely this is pushing the argument too far" (*More Light on the Dead Sea Scrolls*, p. 57).

cussion — the fact remains that he used the verse with an entirely original application in his own ministry. It cannot be used, then, as basis for argument that John was brought up at Qumran.

## Ascetic Life

John's ascetic way of life has been compared with the asceticism of Qumran. He wore coarse clothing and ate locusts and wild honey. He "came neither eating nor drinking" (Matt. 11:18), and was probably under the Nazirite vow not to touch wine or strong drink (Luke 1:5). It is reasonable to infer that he was not married. The Qumran brotherhood has been described as a monastic or quasi-monastic sect,[12] living a rigorous life of self-discipline — although we need to remind ourselves again that many of the details have been read in from the Essene sources.

According to the Qumran texts, there was enforced community of goods, which might be described as "poverty." There were common meals, but nothing to indicate that they were austere — this idea comes from the Essene sources. There was strict discipline of life with much reading of the Torah. It cannot be maintained from the Qumran sources that there was enforced celibacy. Neither can it be maintained from the Qumran sources that other elements of the Nazirite vow — no use of the razor and no drinking of wine or strong drink — were imposed on the Qumranians.

On the other hand, there is no necessity to suppose that John got his ascetic ideas from Qumran. Nazirite vows are known in the Old Testament. Whether we accept the Lucan account of the angelic annunciation to Zechariah or not is beside the point: there is no reason to hold that John's parents could not have dedicated him, even as Hannah dedicated Samuel generations earlier, to the Nazirite vow (cf. 1 Sam. 1:11, 28). In fact, the language of the Hannah-Samuel story seems to be echoed at several points in the first chapter of Luke — which in itself may suggest that the dedication of John was in some way inspired by the Biblical narrative.

[12] The monasticism of the group has been based on 1QS 6:13-22; cf. *Discoveries in the Judean Desert,* vol. 1, p. 108. I find nothing in the passage to support the theory. The text is printed in full, pp. 52f. above, and may be examined in this connection.

## Baptism with Water

The baptism of John and the baptistic practices of the Qumran Community have been viewed as an indication of interrelationship. The whole matter of baptism in general, and the origin and nature of John's baptism in particular, are very complex, and we cannot enter into these subjects in any detail in this work.

The origin of John's baptism could in theory be traced to one of three and only three possible sources: (1) John got the idea from the Jews; or (2) he got it from some pagan source, directly or indirectly; or (3) he originated the idea. Now if John had either invented the idea, or gotten it from a non-Jewish source, the very novelty would have been offensive to the nation he was trying to reach. It is of the essence of Judaism that there be a line of "tradition" — in other words, that whatever is new can be shown to have its origin in what has already been received. There can be no discontinuity. This fact lies behind the preaching of John and it also lies behind the preaching of Jesus. The early Christian Church likewise insisted on demonstrating its organic relationship to the Old Testament. It is almost certain, then, that John received his idea of baptism from the Jews.

The most likely source was "proselyte baptism," which seems to have developed in the Jewish synagogues of the Diaspora, and which was designed to wash away the defilement of the Gentile who sought to become a Jewish convert. If this be so, John's insistence that all must be baptized who sought to enter the Kingdom of God would be striking, for in effect he would be saying that not only Gentiles but even Jews need to be converted to enter the Kingdom. This would certainly cut right across the popular view that said, "We are Abraham's children."[13]

Brownlee thinks that this "severe indictment of Jewish society as utterly corrupt and as outside the pale of God's people is precisely characteristic of the Essenes." Expanding this idea, discussing the ashes of the heifer, the "water for impurity," and the cisterns at Qumran, Brownlee concludes that "one's full admission into the community was probably marked by a bath which marked him off henceforth as be-

---

13 John 8:33, 39; cf. W. F. Flemington, *The New Testament Doctrine of Baptism* (London: S.P.C.K., 1953), p. 16.

longing to the 'holy men.' . . . This would be an exact parallel to John's extreme demand that everyone, not simply proselytes from the Gentile world, receive baptism."[14]

But it must be pointed out that there is nothing in any existing text, either from Qumran or from the Essene sources, to indicate that there was an initiatory bath. Hence, it is questionable whether the term "baptism" should be used for the ritual of water-purification either at Qumran or among the Essenes.[15]

Perhaps it will clarify the matter to point out that there are three characteristic types of ritual bathing or "baptism." (1) One is initiatory, that is, a symbolic rite required of anyone who wishes to enter the group. It does not have to be repeated. (2) Then there is a purificatory washing, symbolic of cleansing from impurity, physical or spiritual or both. This is sometimes administered by another person, but is usually self-administered. It is repeated as needed, in some cases daily (cf. the "hemerobaptists"). (3) Perhaps a modification of the second is therapeutic bathing, designed as a cure for diseases. This is performed and repeated only as needed.

In a sense John's baptism was initiatory, the symbol of repentance for those who wanted to enter the Kingdom of God. The ablutions at Qumran were purificatory rather than initiatory; the Essene baths were likewise purificatory and administered daily. There is no indication that in either group the first ritual washing was looked upon as initiatory. The Qumran texts, as a matter of fact, make it clear that the waters of purification were restricted to members in good standing, and were denied to those seeking admission to the Sect (1QS 5:13).

Professor Rowley correctly summarizes the differences between John's baptism and the washings of the Qumranians under three points: (1) John's baptism was initiatory; Qumran washing was not initiatory baptism. (2) John's baptism was

[14] W. H. Brownlee, art. cit., The Scrolls and the New Testament, pp. 37, 39.

[15] H. H. Rowley indeed says, "By baptism we mean a water rite of initiation, and only a rite of initiation" — "The Qumran Sect and Christian Origins," Bulletin of the John Rylands Library 44 (1961-1962), p. 141. For a full discussion of the various kinds of baptism (using the term broadly), cf. Josèph Thomas, Le mouvement baptiste en Palestine et Syrie (150 av. J.-C.—300 ap. J.-C.) (Gembloux, Belgium: Duculot, 1935; 455 pp.).

administered immediately upon repentance and profession of
faith; Qumran washing was denied until the end of the second
probationary period had been attained, i.e. after two years.
(3) The baptism of John was related to the coming of the
Messiah; there is no reference in any text from Qumran that
relates the purificatory washing of the Messiah, with the Teacher of Righteousness, or with any other figure, eschatological
or otherwise.[16]

## Baptism with the Spirit and with Fire

The New Testament records a saying by John to the effect
that the coming Messiah would baptize "with the Holy Spirit
and with fire" (cf. Matt. 3:11-12). The two parts of this expression have been studied as a basis for possible connection
between John and the Qumran Sect.

There is much stress on the "spirit" in the Qumran writings,
but whether it is to be understood as a divine Spirit, or even
more as a divine Person (as in the New Testament beyond any
question), is not always clear.

In the Manual of Discipline we find the statement, "And
he will sprinkle upon him a spirit of truth, like water for impurity" (1QS 4:21). Some scholars see a reference here to the
prophet-messiah, others to the Teacher of Righteousness; in
context it seems to me to refer to man as a member of the redeemed society, i.e. Qumran. (For context, see p. 97.) But in
any event, there is no need to look upon this passage as the
source of John's statement about baptizing with the Holy
Spirit, for in Ezekiel there is a passage containing all the details necessary to account both for John's words and for the
quotation in Qumran: sprinkling, cleansing, and the spirit
(cf. Ezek. 36:25-27).

Baptism with fire, particularly in the context of judgment
by fire (Matt. 3:12), has been taken by some scholars as an
idea of Zoroastrian origin.[17] The possible contacts between
Zoroastrianism and Qumran have been mentioned in passing

[16] Rowley, art. cit., pp. 140-143. For a fuller study, see Rowley's article,
"The Baptism of John and the Qumran Sect," in New Testament Essays:
Studies in Memory of T. W. Manson (Manchester: Manchester University
Press, 1959), pp. 218-229.

[17] Thus, e.g., Carl Kraeling, John the Baptist (New York: Scribner,
1951), p. 117; and building on his suggestion, W. H. Brownlee, art. cit.
(note 5 above), p. 42.

(pp. 78, 81), and I have indicated that I do not see evidence of direct Zoroastrian influence on Qumran theology. The picture of judgment by fire is found in the Thanksgiving Hymns (1QH 3:29-36, pp. 95f.). Brownlee says that it seems "Quite reasonable to suppose that the baptism of fire of which John spoke may have been in the torments of hell so vividly described here."[18]

This is curious logic! There is absolutely none of the imagery of either Qumran or Zoroastrianism in the New Testament passage. The word "fire" occurs in a quotation reported to be by John the Baptist, and into it are read the Zoroastrian river of molten metal and the Qumran rivers of Belial.

Once again it is possible to find in the Old Testament a sufficient possible source for John's words (as well as for the Qumran portrayal, to a limited extent). A "river of fire" is found in Daniel (7:10), and fire as a symbol of divine judgment is mentioned often in the Old Testament (Num. 11:1; 1 Kings 18:38; often in the Psalms). But the significant characteristic in John's figure has been overlooked: he was talking about the fire that consumes the chaff after the grain has been winnowed (Matt. 3:12). This figure seems to be taken completely from Isaiah 5:24. But where is it in Qumran or Zoroastrianism?

## Summary

John could have been a member of the Qumran Community. There is nothing to deny this possibility. But his attitude toward sinners seems to indicate either that he was not a Qumranian or that he had broken completely with the Qumranian viewpoint. Or John might have known of the Sect and picked up some ideas and expressions from their terminology. In either case, this would be an attractive explanation for the alleged similarities between Qumran and the Johannine writings — for these would in that case contain reflections of the Baptist through some of his disciples who subsequently became disciples of Jesus. This, however, is still in the realm of wishful thinking and is not objective scholarship.

On the other hand, the prophetic spirit of John the Baptist — which was recognized by his contemporaries, including

18 Brownlee, art. cit., p. 42.

Herod, the Pharisees, and the people, if we can put any confidence at all in the only extant records we have about John — would be sufficient to account for him and for all that he did.[19]

How the Spirit works we do not know. We have enough records of men who claimed that they were, or were believed by others to have been, filled with the Spirit, that we can make a few observations. The Spirit uses holy men; the Spirit makes use of contemporary situations; the Spirit particularly works through the Scriptures. We find in John something of each of these elements.

---

[19] See Mark 6:20; Matt. 14:5; 21:26. Josephus' very brief statement confirms this popular feeling, *Antiquities* 18.5.2 §117.

## CHAPTER TWELVE

# THE EARLY CHURCH AND QUMRAN

Soon after the publication of the Manual of Discipline scholars began to point out comparisons between the Qumran Community and the early Christian Church. Some of these works tended to prove a dependence upon Qumran on the part of the early Church; some were obviously trying to disprove any such dependence; but most of them were simply trying to explore areas in which problems have long existed or fill in details in the historical framework in which both Qumran and the Church developed.

This material has grown to a vast quantity. We can only consider part of it, and I shall attempt to select that which is most significant.

## The "Church Idea"

Millar Burrows has pointed out that "the church idea, the concept of a spiritual group, the true people of God, distinct from the Jewish nation as such," is more important, when we compare the two movements, than mere details of organization and ritual. Krister Stendahl, using different terms, emphasizes the same fact: whereas the Pharisees and Sadducees were "parties" within Judaism, the Essenes and Christianity must be distinguished as "sects."[1]

[1] Burrows, *The Dead Sea Scrolls* (New York: Viking, 1955), p. 332; K. Stendahl, ed., *The Scrolls and the New Testament*, pp. 7-10. Josephus, we might add, uses the term *hairesis*, "sect," to describe the Pharisees and the Sadducees (*Antiquities* 13.5.9 §171). The term is used of Christianity (Acts 24:5; 28:22). Because "sect" often suggests "heresy" it has fallen into disuse in the sense in which it is used by Josephus and the New Testament.

In the Qumran viewpoint as well as in early Christian thought, official or normative Judaism had failed and stood under the judgment of God. The new sect, in each case, consisted of the "elect," or those who were seeking to fulfill the obligations of true religion. Both sects were end-time or eschatological movements, convinced that the judgment of God was about to be visited upon His people. Both groups, in other words, could be looked upon, from within their own individual frame of reference, as the Kingdom of God.[2]

In the case of Christianity, these points are clearly stated. John the Baptist sounded the keynote: "Repent, for the kingdom of heaven is at hand" (Matt. 3:2). Jesus took up the same theme when He began to preach (Matt. 4:17). And although Peter does not use the expression, "The Kingdom of God" in his Pentecostal sermon, there can be little doubt that it was in his mind, for after drawing on the promises of the messianic age, he declared, "Repent, and be baptized every one of you . . ." (Acts 2:38). The sectarian character of the Church is stated by Peter before the Sanhedrin: "And there is salvation in no one else, for there is no other name under heaven given among men by which we must be saved" (Acts 4:12, referring to Jesus; cf. 4:10). The eschatological character of the Christian fellowship is indicated in Peter's statement of the promise in Deuteronomy 18:15-16 and the claim that "the prophets proclaimed these days."

There is no explicit statement that the first Christians looked upon themselves as the community of the New Covenant, but by the time of the writing of Second Corinthians, Paul could speak of Christians as "ministers of a new covenant" (2 Cor. 3:6) and one or two decades later the author of the Epistle to the Hebrews was referring to Jesus as "the surety of a better covenant" (Heb. 7:22) and "the mediator of a new covenant" (Heb. 12:24), supporting the concept with a long quotation from Jeremiah (Heb. 8:8-12; 10:16-17; cf. Jer. 31: 31-34). That this concept was found in the early Church is strongly suggested by the words of the institution of the Lord's Supper quoted in the Synoptics and in First Corinthians, "This is my blood of the covenant" or "This cup is the new covenant

[2] Obviously I am attempting to avoid personal Christian convictions; rather I am seeking to get inside the movements. For a careful study see Lucetta Mowry, *The Dead Sea Scrolls and the Early Church* (Chicago: University of Chicago Press, 1962), ch. 2.

in my blood" (Matt. 26:28; Mark 14:24; Luke 22:20; I Cor.
11:25). The statement appears to have gained a liturgical
usage prior to the sources of these writings, in other words,
within the first two decades of the Church's existence.

I have found no reference to "the Kingdom of God" in the
Qumran texts. However, a hymn recorded twice in the War
Scroll deals with the Kingdom: God is referred to as "a God
standing erect in Thy kingly glory" (1QM 12:6); the splendors
of the age are described, and the daughters of the people are
called upon to "shout with the sound of exultation, adorn
yourselves with ornaments of glory, and rule over the kingdom" (1QM 12:14; 19:8). Both portions are considerably
broken away, but the restorations can be made on the basis of
the close verbal agreement of the two passages. However, the
hymn deals with the kingdom to be established after the eschatological war described in the scroll, and does not refer to
the Qumran Community prior to that time.

Neither have I found any direct call to repentance in the
Scrolls, although the use of the expression, "the penitents of
the desert" (4QpPs37 2:1 [Habermann, fragment 3:19], suggests that repentance was requirement for admission to the
Sect. The frequent use of the verb šûb, "turn, repent," supports this suggestion.

But if the exact terms are not used, there can be no doubt
that the basic idea of the Community was eschatological and
exclusivistic. The origin of the Sect is traced to the "remnant"
which God had left (CD 1:4-7). God's willingness to forgive
is directed to "those who repent of transgression" (CD 2:5).
Likewise, the ritual of initiation includes an act of repentance
(1QS 1:24-25). The expression "covenant" or "new covenant"
is used to describe the Sect. Its members are "the men who
have entered into the new covenant in the Land of Damascus"
(CD 8:21), or simply "those who enter the covenant" (CD
9:2-3). The covenant is called "the covenant of repentance"
(CD 19:16), and "the covenant and contract which they had
ratified in the land of Damascus, namely (the) new covenant"
(CD 20:12). It was not only a new covenant; it was a permanent one: "to lay a foundation of truth for Israel for a community of an eternal covenant" (1QS 5:6). The prominence

of this term is seen in that the word *b<sup>e</sup>rît*, "covenant," occurs about 110 times in the Qumran writings.[2a]

These similarities between Qumran and the early Church do not necessarily imply any connection between the two, for the concepts are found in the Old Testament. The concept of the "remnant" was clearly set forth by Isaiah, and the concept of the "new covenant" by Jeremiah. Any group seeking to justify its existence and its claim to be the "true Israel" would certainly make use of these and similar passages.

## Membership in the Fellowship

In details of membership there are more points of contrast than points of comparison between the two sects.

*Admission.* Anyone desiring to enter the Qumran Community was obligated to pass through an increasingly difficult period of probation, lasting two years, with examinations at least at beginning, middle, and end.

Admission to the Christian fellowship was immediate. There was no novitiate, no trial period. This is clearly manifest at many points and without any exception. On the day of Pentecost, three thousand were admitted upon profession of faith and baptism (Acts 2:37-41). The Ethiopian (Acts 8: 34-38), Cornelius (Acts 10:44-48), and the Philippian jailor (Acts 16:30-33) were similarly admitted. Even more significant is the decision of the Jerusalem Conference, which after a serious debate of the requirements of membership excluded any trial membership or process of testing (Acts 15:23-29).

*Community of Property.* Assigning personal property or wealth to the Community was obligatory for anyone wishing to enter the Qumran fellowship. The property was conveyed tentatively during the novitiate and permanently at the time of entering the Community.

Community of property was not obligatory in the Christian fellowship. A number of scholars have singled out the examples of the Jerusalem fellowship, Barnabas, and, by way of contrast, Ananias and Sapphira, and have suggested that the early Church required of its members something similar to the Qumran obligation. But a study of the New Testament texts will not support this position. In the description of the

[2a] This figure is taken from Habermann's concordance. The figure will doubtless be larger when a complete count is available.

Jerusalem fellowship, there is no indication that the community of goods was obligatory: "And all who believed were together and had all things in common; and they sold their possessions and goods and distributed them to all, as any had need" (Acts 2:44-45). Likewise, the contribution of Barnabas is described as an act of generosity:

> Far as many as were possessors of land or houses sold them, and brought the proceeds of what was sold and laid it at the apostles' feet; and distribution was made to each as any had need. Thus Joseph who was surnamed by the apostles Barnabas . . . sold a field which belonged to him, and brought the money and laid it at the apostles' feet. (Acts 4:34-37)

In the case of Ananias and Sapphira, the text clearly states that there was no obligation either before or after selling the property to turn its value over to the apostles: "While it remained unsold, did it not remain your own? And after it was sold, was it not at your disposal?" (Acts 5:4).

The most significant point, however, seems to have been overlooked. Membership in Qumran required signing over the property before admission was possible; in the case of the early Church, there is nothing of the sort — the instances cited, even if it could be demonstrated that the community of goods was obligatory, all involved those who were already members of the Community.

If more proof is required, the decision of the Jerusalem Conference can again be cited: the Church refused to impose any obligation beyond those specified — and community of property was not specified (cf. Acts 15:28-29).

*Poverty.* Closely related to the point just discussed is the question of the attitude toward poverty in the two communities. A number of scholars have emphasized the place of poverty in the Qumran Community, in my opinion beyond what the texts will support. It is readily admitted that both Qumran and the early Church were opposed to greed and were aware of the dangers of riches. But to say that either group regarded poverty as charismatic is certainly stretching the textual evidence.

*Testing, Rank, and Promotion.* The Qumran Community was structured according to "lot" or "glory," each person having his allotted place or rank. The rank was assigned when he was admitted to membership, and was advanced or retarded according to his achievement as determined by annual test.

Nothing even remotely resembling this is found in the early Church. Rather, the idea of rank or precedence is contrary to the principles taught by Jesus:

> You know that the rulers of the Gentiles lord it over them, and their great men exercise authority over them. It shall not be so among you; but whoever would be great among you must be your servant, and whoever would be first among you must be your slave . . . . (Matt. 20:25 27)

In the early Church all seem to have been admitted equally, and there is no record of tests or examinations. The entire structure of legalism by which promotion or demotion was determined in Qumran, is denied consistently and repeatedly by Christ and the Apostles.

*Excommunication.* For offenses against the brotherhood, Qumranians were fined or punished, and for grave offenses they were temporarily or permanently banished from the community.

Discipline is found in the early Church, but there is no record of fines or excommunication. The First Epistle of Paul to the Corinthians deals at length with problems of disciplinary nature in the church at Corinth. In one case Paul counsels, "to deliver this man to Satan for the destruction of the flesh, that his spirit may be saved in the day of the Lord Jesus" (1 Cor. 5:5). The meaning of this has puzzled scholars; the spirit of it, however, is redemptive and not exclusivistic, for the goal was the salvation of the soul of the offender. The same spirit pervades the epistle, and reaches its climax in chapter 12 with the figure of the Church as a body, each part of which needs the other (1 Cor. 12:14-27), and in chapter 13, the exquisite description of Christian love.

## Organization

Details of organization in the Qumran Community are found in the texts, but we have been unable to piece them together into an integrated table of organization. We have considered material on the Twelve and the Three, the Examiner, and other officials (cf. pp. 54-57 above).

In the early Church the picture is likewise not clear, which can quickly be demonstrated by the fact that various types of

ecclesiastical systems in the modern Church all find justification for their structures in the New Testament. Obviously we
cannot solve the problem here, and anything that I may say
about the organization of the early Church can be challenged
by others who understand the New Testament in a different
way.[3] We must be content, therefore, to compare some of the
details.

*The Twelve and the Three.* A number of scholars have
pointed out the similarity between the council of twelve men
in Qumran and the twelve apostles in the early Church. Some,
it seems, have tried various ways to force the two bodies into
close agreement, such as comparing the three priests of the
Qumran body with the three "pillars" of the early Church,
etc. Such methodology is always questionable.

The Qumran body under consideration was composed of
"twelve men and three priests" (1QS 8:1). Its purpose was to
practice truth, righteousness, etc., to guard faith, and to make
satisfaction for iniquity. No distinctive name is used of this
body: it is either called "the Counsel of the Community" —
a name which seems to be used of the entire Community in
other passages — or it is an unnamed body in the Counsel of
the Community. The wording suggests a total of fifteen persons rather than twelve.

In the early Church there was a distinctive body with a distinctive name: the Twelve, or the Twelve Apostles. The purpose of these men was to witness to the world concerning what
they had seen and heard during the days of Jesus' ministry
including His death and resurrection (Acts 1:8, 21-22). They
refused to be sidetracked by administrative details (Acts 6:2-4).
There is no record that they met as a council; the only council
meeting recorded in the New Testament is in Acts 15, and
this was presided over by James who was not one of the Twelve.

During the days of Jesus' ministry there was a group of
three — the "inner circle" so called — who were present on certain particular occasions and thereby received special training: Peter, James (not the James of Acts 15, for this one had
already been killed in Acts 12:2), and John. There is no place
of prominence given to these three as a group in the records

[3] For a helpful study, see Bo Reicke, "The Constitution of the Primitive Church in the Light of Jewish Document," in *The Scrolls and the
New Testament*, pp. 143-156.

of the early Church. In Galatians Paul mentions three persons in the Jerusalem Church "who were reputed to be pillars" (Gal. 2:9): James, Cephas (Peter), and John. There can be little doubt that this James is the James of Acts 15, known as "the brother of the Lord," and not "the brother of John" (Gal. 1:19; cf. Acts 12:2). These three were not priests, hence cannot be compared to the three priests of Qumran. There is no record that they ever acted as a body. They were simply prominent "pillars" in the Jerusalem Church. On occasion Jesus rebuked each of the "inner circle" for their presumption (Mark 10:35-45; Matt. 16:23). Paul found it necessary to rebuke Peter, and by implication also James (Gal. 2:11-14). John does not figure in the Jerusalem Conference (Acts 15).

The number twelve in itself is not sufficiently distinctive to prove any interdependence, for the concept of the twelve tribes of Israel obviously lay behind the figure in each case. In Qumran the chiefs of the tribes are expressly mentioned in connection with the convocation of the Assembly (1QSa 1:28-29). Twelve chiefs of the Levites are mentioned, "one per tribe" (1QM 2:2-3). Likewise, Jesus definitely associated the twelve apostolic offices with the twelve tribes (Matt. 19:28; cf. Luke 22:30, clearly an independent tradition). In the Book of Revelation, the Twelve Tribes and the Twelve Apostles are joined in the imagery of the Holy City (Rev. 21:12-14).

*The Bishop.* In Qumran there was a figure known as the $m^e baqq\bar{e}r$, translated sometimes "Superintendent" or "Supervisor"; I have translated it "Examiner." His position is described rather fully in the texts (pp. 55f. above). He has sometimes been compared with the bishop in the early Church.

The office of bishop in the early Church is the center of much controversy in ecclesiological discussion. Some Christians hold that the "bishop" is the same as the "elder" or "presbyter." They point out that Paul mentions only two offices in his letter to Timothy, namely bishops and deacons (1 Tim. 3:2, 8). Others hold that the bishop is an administrative or supervisory official over the presbyters or priests. Regardless of the origin or development of the office, it will be granted, I think, that the New Testament does not list duties of the bishop comparable to those of the Qumran $m^e baqq\bar{e}r$. Whether there was any influence of Qumranian ideas or experience in the early Church is a matter of speculation and not of record;

it is not improbable, nor is there any reason why a Christian should find such a thought objectionable.

## Worship and Ritual

Both in the Dead Sea Scrolls and in the New Testament there is a minimum of detailed description of worship.[4] At Qumran there was much devotion to reading the Law. Prayers and singing are not described. There is a passing reference to the sending of sacrifices or gifts to the Temple. Baptism or ritual washing was not administered upon admission but was probably self-administered as the need for cleansing was felt. Some cultic meal with the outline of the ritual including the blessing of the bread and the new wine is described.

In the early Church the reading of the Scriptures certainly had a prominent place, for we find constant reference to Old Testament figures and quotations. There is, however, no indication of continuous or extended reading of the Scriptures in the early Church.

The early Church devoted itself much to prayer: there is frequent reference to the fact, and a number of prayers are recorded in the New Testament. In several instances the prayers were reported to be instrumental in miraculous healing, deliverance, or other miraculous deeds. Likewise the singing of psalms and hymns is mentioned in connection with the early Church. There is, however, no body of literature in the early Church comparable to the Thanksgiving Hymns from Qumran.

The preaching of the gospel — which included the redemptive activity of God in history, its culmination in the death and resurrection of Jesus of Nazareth, and an appeal for men to repent and believe in Jesus for the forgiveness of sins — was one of the central activities of the early Church: probably we should say it was the center as well as the circumference of the Church's work. A number of sermons or outlines of sermons are included in Acts. There is nothing comparable in the Qumran record.

In the early Church two streams were found: those who maintained their worship at the Temple, and those who wor-

---

[4] Mowry, however, is able to devote an entire chapter to the subject: (*The Dead Sea Scrolls and the Early Church,* ch. 9) as does H. Ringgren (*The Faith of Qumran* [Philadelphia: Fortress, 1963], ch. 7).

shipped in the synagogues. Because of interpenetration of Jews and Gentiles in the synagogues and in the gentile areas, Gentiles came into the Christian Church and gradually became the majority element. The Jerusalem Conference in Acts 15 centered about the problem of what to do with gentile converts: to compel them to become Jews ("to be circumcised") or not. The early Church decided not to compel Gentiles to become Jews in order to become Christians.[5] At the same time, as long as the Temple was standing, Christian Jews maintained faithful attendance at its services; even Paul, who is sometimes accused of turning Christianity into a gentile religion, was careful to go to the Temple to worship when he returned to Jerusalem, and indeed planned his journeys so as to be in Jerusalem for the feast of Pentecost (Acts 20:16). Because James the brother of the Lord was so careful to keep the Law, some ventured the opinion that Jerusalem was destroyed as punishment for its murder of James.[6] In Qumran any fellowship with Gentiles would have been unthinkable — as indeed it was in segments of the early Church.

We have already discussed baptism in connection with John the Baptist (pp. 149-151 above). The early Church administered baptism to all converts upon profession of faith and repentance of sin. The act was not considered as purificatory and was not repeated. In the case of the disciples of John the Baptist at Ephesus, who had only been baptized in the baptism of John, the New Testament records that they were baptized in the name of Jesus when they received the gospel of Jesus (Acts 19:5). The reason for a second baptism in this case is clearly stated.

In the early Church the Eucharist or Lord's Supper was perhaps a daily service (if "the breaking of bread" refers to the Lord's Supper, Acts 2:42, 46). Later it was held on the first day of the week (Acts 20:7). There are indications that a common meal or "love feast" (agápē) was held prior to the actual communion service (1 Cor. 11:21; Jude 12). The institution of the Supper is recorded in First Corinthians (11:23-26), and the sources of the accounts in the Gospels would certainly

[5] See ch. 21 of my *Church Alive* (Glendale: Regal Books, 1972) for the development of this problem.

[6] Origen (*Against Celsus* 1.47) and Eusebius (*Ecclesiastical History* 2.23) attributed this to Josephus. However, no such statement is extant in Josephus.

seem to be as early (cf. Mark 14:22-25; Matt. 26:26-29).[7] The elements of the Supper were bread and wine, as in the Qumran meal, and several scholars have suggested a connection.

However, it should be noted that the elements in the Christian Lord's Supper are related by a very early tradition to the body and blood of Jesus, or to His redeeming sacrifice. In my opinion it is impossible to remove this interpretive significance, hence it must be traced back to Jesus Himself. No such theological significance is given to the Qumran meal.

It is not difficult to find the origin of the elements of the two meals. Bread and wine are elements of the Jewish Passover, and the Passover can certainly be the ritual that suggested both the Qumran and the Christian rites, whether we look upon the Last Supper as a Passover or not.[8] The very symbolism of the closing part of the Haggadah quite naturally leads to an eschatological attitude, and this in turn could provide the reason for adapting this part of the service as Jesus did.

The closing portion of the Seder centers about the uneaten matzah (or unleavened bread) and the cup that has been reserved for Elijah the forerunner of the Messiah. The closing words are, "Next year in Jerusalem." I find the suggestion attractive that Jesus took the cup "after supper," i.e. Elijah's cup, and the bread that had been kept to the end, and with these instituted the Supper. The words "Next year in Jerusalem," belonging to the Dispersion, quite naturally gave way to "Until the Kingdom of God shall come," or perhaps "Until I

[7] Luke's account (Luke 22:14-20) obviously does not come from Mark. It also seems to be independent of Paul. In other words there are, in my opinion, three traditions of the institution of the Lord's Supper in the New Testament, already divergent within twenty-five years of the actual event. We are forced to conclude that the actual form of the institution was still earlier than these traditions, hence not a creation of the Church of a later generation. For a thought-provoking discussion, see K. G. Kuhn, "The Lord's Supper and the Communal Meal at Qumran," in *The Scrolls and the New Testament,* pp. 65-93.

[8] A number of scholars have pointed out that the Passover is basically a family feast, designed to be held in the home and to instruct the children in the elementary facts of the Lord's redemptive activity in Israel. The Last Supper violated this family character by taking the Twelve away from their families. I am inclined to believe that this in itself was part of Jesus' purpose in keeping "this feast" with His disciples. He was, in effect, establishing a new family. He had previously indicated that earthly ties were considered inferior to those of the Kingdom (cf. Mark 3:33-35; Luke 11:27-28).

come in My Kingdom." This is speculation, but it is intended
to show that the Passover was sufficient to account for the
Lord's Supper. In a similar manner it could account for the
Qumran meal, without the elements of sacrifice and second
coming, for it would still have its eschatological character.

## The Holy Spirit

The Qumran texts refer frequently to the "spirit." The
word *rûaḥ*, "spirit," occurs well over a hundred times, not always, of course, referring to the spirit of God, and sometimes
meaning simply "wind." We have considered the Qumran doctrine of the two spirits (pp. 78-81 above). In the early Church
likewise there is strong emphasis upon the Spirit or Holy Spirit.

According to the early chapters of the Book of Acts, the
Apostles were instructed by Jesus to refrain from their apostolic witness until they had received the promised Spirit (Acts
1:4-5). Several days after the Ascension, on the Day of Pentecost, the promise was received. The account is given in considerable detail (Acts 2:1-12): there was a sound of wind filling
the house; something like tongues of fire appeared on each one
present; and they began to speak with other tongues, so that
pilgrims in the city, who were attracted by the disturbance,
heard the message each in his own language. This is called
the Pentecostal miracle of glossolalia, or speaking with tongues.
Peter explained the event as the fulfillment of the prophecy
of Joel (Acts 2:16-21; Joel 2:28-32). From that moment the
Church was conscious of the presence of the Spirit in all its
actions and deliberations. There is nothing in the Qumran
documents that in the slightest way resembles Pentecost in
the early Church. There is no record of the coming of the
Spirit, no claim of speaking with tongues, and no claim of the
fulfillment of Joel's prophecy. This last is perhaps of significance in view of the fact that several scholars have found the
origin of the name "Teacher of Righteousness" in Joel 2:23,
immediately before the prophecy of the Spirit.[9]

---

[9] Cf. among others, Dupont-Sommer, *The Essene Writings from Qumran*, p. 228 n. 1; and W. H. Brownlee, *The Meaning of the Qumran Scrolls
for the Bible* (New York: Oxford, 1964), p. 138. The word *môrê* can mean
"early rain" as well as "teacher." In Joel the expression is *hammôrè
liṣedāqā*, translated "the early rain for (your) vindication," but capable of
translation as "the teacher for (or of) righteousness."

The members of the early Church believed they were "filled" with the Holy Spirit, that He "fell" on them, and they "received" Him (Acts 6:3; 11:15; 10:47). They believed that the Spirit spoke to them, sent them forth, or forbade them to go (Acts 10:19; 13:2; 16:6). They believed that it was possible to "lie to" the Holy Spirit, and to "tempt" Him (Acts 5:3, 9). In short, the Spirit to them was a person: God Himself. It is not a question of historicity at this point; it is a matter of records. It would have been just as easy for the Qumranians to fabricate stories like these, if they are mere fabrications. The point we insist upon stressing is simply this: the Qumran record does not contain anything comparable to the Christian record in this area of thought.

But I think it is also more than a matter of records. There is such a thing as the verdict of history. Cullmann expresses it as follows:

> It is not sufficient that the Qumran sect had a Teacher of Righteousness and wrote about the Spirit: the Teacher and the Spirit do not dominate all the thought and life of the community as Jesus and the Spirit which is given to those who believe in him dominate Christianity. This driving impulse is lacking in the Qumran sect, and that is the reason that the Essenes ceased to exist after the Jewish wars in A.D. 70, whereas Christianity could survive that crisis, and from then on even more effectively spread over the world.[10]

## Summary

The closest parallels between the Qumran Community and the early Church are in the area of the "church idea" or the elect, redemptive, end-time society, and in the area of organization. These are perhaps the least distinctive elements, or the areas in which similarity has the least significance.

The most significant differences are found in the areas of worship and the doctrine of the Spirit. In the preaching of the gospel, the redemptive symbolism of the Lord's Supper, and the personality and deity of the Spirit, the Church presents unique elements not found in Qumran.

[10] Oscar Cullmann, "The Significance of the Qumran Texts for Research into the Beginnings of Christianity," in *The Scrolls and the New Testament*, p. 32.

These points in themselves do not necessarily indicate complete independence of the two sectarian movements. It would have been possible for the Church to have developed out of Qumran sectarianism (if other factors permitted or demonstrated such a thesis) and still have produced these distinctive characteristics. Whether it did so develop must be determined from other evidence.

## CHAPTER THIRTEEN

# THE PAULINE WRITINGS AND QUMRAN

The striking similarity between certain points in Qumran theology and characteristic points in Paul's epistles has been noted by several scholars. Millar Burrows called attention to it in both of his general works on the Scrolls, and also recorded some of the observations of other scholars.[1] W. D. Davies published an important study of one phase of the subject, Kuhn another, and S. E. Johnson still another.[2] Jerome Murphy-O'Connor has gathered together nine articles previously published in various journals, and put them out under the title *Paul and Qumran*.[3] We can only scan some of the highlights here.

## *Justification by Faith*

Perhaps the most characteristic of all the Pauline doctrines is the teaching that man is "justified" before God, not on the basis of his works but on the basis of his faith in the redeeming work of Christ. Protestants and Catholics differ in their interpretation of the word "justify," but that need not detain

[1] M. Burrows, *The Dead Sea Scrolls* (New York: Viking, 1956), pp. 333-336; *More Light on the Dead Sea Scrolls*, p. 119.

[2] W. D. Davies, "Paul and the Dead Sea Scrolls: Flesh and Spirit," in *The Scrolls and the New Testament*, pp. 157-182; K. G. Kuhn, "New Light on Temptation, Sin and Flesh in the New Testament," in *ibid.*, pp. 94-113, especially pp. 102-108; and S. E. Johnson, "Paul and the Manual of Discipline," *Harvard Theological Review* 48 (1955), pp. 157-165.

[3] J. Murphy-O'Connor, *Paul and Qumran: Studies in New Testament Exegesis* (Chicago: Priory, 1968; 254 pp.).

us here. Paul sets forth his teaching in detail in his Epistle to the Galatians (chs. 3 and 4) and in his Epistle to the Romans (chs. 3 — 5).

To support his doctrine, Paul quotes a verse from Habakkuk, "The righteous shall live by faith" (Hab. 2:4) — the passage is explicitly quoted twice (Rom. 1:17; Gal. 3:11), and paraphrased or adapted in several other places (cf. Rom. 3:28; Eph. 2:8; Phil. 3:9; and Col. 2:12).

In the Qumran Commentary on Habakkuk, this verse is interpreted as follows:

> Its interpretation, concerning all the doers of the Law in the house of Judah whom God will deliver from the house of judgment for the sake of their toil and their faith in the Teacher of Righteousness. (1QpHab 8:1-3)

The obvious parallel between Paul's idea of salvation through faith in Jesus Christ and the Qumranian teaching of salvation through faith in the Teacher of Righteousness has often been pointed out.[1] However, the whole subject is more complex than may seem obvious on the surface, and it deserves fuller study.

*The Component Parts.* The doctrine of justification by faith rests on two basic assumptions: first, the perfect *righteousness of God,* who is too holy to have any contact with any person or thing that is not holy; and second, the utter *sinfulness of man,* who can never by his own efforts achieve the holiness he must have if he is to enjoy life with God (or "salvation"). Around these two basic assumptions cluster several other teachings that are integral with the total doctrine of justification by faith. The most significant are: *grace,* or the willingness of God to provide for sinful man the righteousness that he cannot achieve for himself; *election,* or the sovereign choice by which God confers this righteousness on some while withholding it from others; *faith,* or the human act of trusting God by recognizing that salvation is only possible through God's grace; and the presence of God's Spirit in the man of

---

4 Cf. M. Burrows, *The Dead Sea Scrolls,* pp. 333-336; *More Light on the Dead Sea Scrolls,* pp. 119f.; Walter Grundmann, "The Teacher of Righteousness of Qumran and the Question of Justification by Faith in the Theology of the Apostle Paul," in *Paul and Qumran,* pp. 85-114.

faith, by which Spirit man is able to gain the ultimate victory over sinfulness.[5]

*The Righteousness of God.* The righteousness of God is presented alongside the sinfulness of man in Paul's doctrinal writings in such a way that the two doctrines seem like two sides of a coin. For example, the wickedness of man is spelled out in ugly detail in Romans 1:18-32; then Paul proceeds to argue *ad hominem* that when we momentarily judge these wicked deeds of other men we sit in judgment upon ourselves (Rom. 2:1). All therefore are under condemnation (Rom. 2:12-13). All have sinned (Rom. 3:23). God's forebearance and long-suffering with sinful humanity, His refusal to blot out the sinner from the face of the earth, was a manifestation of His righteousness (Rom. 3:25). Specifically the righteousness of God is revealed by His gift of righteousness — in other words, by His justifying the man who has faith in Jesus (Rom. 3:26).

The righteousness of God is also set forth in Qumran writings in a similar way. Throughout the Thanksgiving Hymns there are expressions of this doctrine, but perhaps the most sustained note is found in the psalm at the end of the Manual of Discipline (1QS 9:24—11:22). The more significant portions are quoted:

> For with God is (the) judgment of all life, and He will repay to man his recompense. . . . As for me, to God is my judgment, and in His hand is the perfection of my way; with Him the strength of my heart, and by His righteousness shall my rebellion be wiped out. . . .

> As for me, to man is wickedness and to the secret council of flesh is unrighteousness; my iniquities, my rebellions, my sins, along with the perversions of my heart (belong) to the secret council of vermin and those who walk in darkness. For to man is his way, and the frail being cannot establish his steps; but to God is judgment, and from His hand is perfection of the way. . . .

---

[5] I have deliberately tried not to couch these ideas in Christian or Pauline terminology in order that the Qumran parallels might not be excluded at the outset. In doing so, I recognize that important differences have been eliminated or obscured, but we shall return to these. I recognize also that it is almost impossible for one who has lived in Pauline or Biblical thought for all his life to avoid a Pauline coloring, try as he may.

As for me, if I stagger, the mercies of God are my salvation for ever. And if I stumble by the iniquity of flesh, my judgment is in the righteousness of God: it shall stand perpetually. . . . By His tender mercies He has caused me to approach, and by His covenant love He will bring in my judgment. By His true righteousness [He] will judge me, and in the abundance of His goodness He will make atonement on behalf of all my iniquities, and by His righteousness He will cleanse me from the impurity of man and the sin of humankind, to give thanks to God (for) His righteousness and to the Most High (for) His majesty. . . . Prepare in righteousness all His works and establish < —?— >[6] to the son of Thy hand-maid, even as Thou hast willed the elect of mankind to take his place before Thee for ever. (1QS 10:19—11:17)

The ideas of the righteousness of God, the sinfulness of man, grace, election, and faith are all found in this passage.

*Human Inability to Please God.* Long before the discovery of the Dead Sea Scrolls, scholars had noted that Paul's sense of human inability to please God was almost unique. There was nothing like it in Judaism except in the work known as Fourth Ezra (or Second Esdras), and the complementary teaching that righteousness is the gift of a righteous God is not even found in Fourth Ezra. This makes the similarity between Paul and Qumran at this point all the more striking. It might be added that Fourth Ezra is generally dated about the time of the final destruction of Qumran, and no fragments of the work have turned up at Qumran.

How Paul came to this sense of frustration before the demands of a righteous God is not entirely clear to us. Much depends on the interpretation of the seventh chapter of Romans. If this describes Paul's preconversion experience, as seems probable to me, then he certainly had come to this position before his visit to Damascus — and accordingly this would make impossible the suggestion that he had derived his ideas from Qumranians in Damascus. Moreover, if he was the rigid Pharisee described in the New Testament, including his own portrait of himself — and there is no reason sufficient to compel us to deny this — then it seems impossible that he could

---

[6] It seems that a word such as "Thy favor" has fallen out.

have been influenced by a schismatic movement such as the Qumran Sect.[7]

Still, we are faced with the fact that similarities exist, and we know nothing else quite like them. Perhaps the link is to be found in what Cullmann has labelled "Hellenism,"[8] or the Judaism of the Diaspora which had been almost severed from the Temple and therefore was no longer closely tied to the sacrificial system. With the separation from the sacrificial system there may have come a realization that human sin cannot easily be blotted out, that the slaughtering of an animal in the sacred Temple precinct in Jerusalem could not take away human sin, that this repulsive act was only designed to show how utterly repulsive sin must be to a holy God. The study of the Old Testament Scriptures, particularly the Prophets and the Psalms, would support this line of thought.

It seems certain that Paul has to be placed within the main stream of the development of early Christianity, and can no longer be looked upon as a strong individual who dominated, shaped, and even altered Christian faith and practice. It is also true that Paul has to be placed within the development of early Judaism. But Paul was always a strange complex of a personality, both before and after conversion. According to the New Testament records, Paul was both a "Hellenist" (i.e. a Jew of the Diaspora, from the strong gentile center of Tarsus) and a strict Pharisee with the viewpoint of the Temple Jews. He was trained by the great Rabbin Gamaliel (Acts 22:3), who was himself a strange combination of the liberalizing Hellenizing forces in Judaism and at the same time the ardent champion of Pharisaism. But these things alone will not explain Paul.

According to the consistent and oft-repeated account in Acts and in Paul's own writings, the discrete particles in his life became fused into the new creature when he was con-

[7] We might ask with similar cogency how it was that only Martin Luther of all the Romanist monks was moved to protest the sale of indulgences on the basis of studies in Galatians and Romans. But who can ever completely explain the great creative geniuses of history or those who act out of an overwhelming conviction that God has spoken to them? We who are little spend our time trying to explain them, hoping that when we have unlocked their secret we too may become great — but greatness never comes this way!

[8] I still think the term was an unfortunate choice; cf. my *Amazing Dead Sea Scrolls,* pp. 148f. and 237.

fronted by the risen Christ while he was on his way to Damascus. This great crisis in his religious experience becomes the single and sufficient explanation of Paul's doctrine — as Paul himself argues most strenuously in his letter to the Galatians:

> I would have you know, brethren, that the gospel which was preached by me is not man's gospel. For I did not receive it from man, nor was I taught it, but it came through a revelation of Jesus Christ. (Gal. 1:11-12)

This fact is an integral part of his doctrine of justification by faith, and this fact differentiates his doctrine from that of Qumran. According to Paul's gospel, the righteousness of God is given to the man of faith in the person of Jesus Christ. In Galatians, the dominant note is not "justification by faith," but rather "justified by faith in Christ" (cf. Gal. 2:16, 17, 20; 3:14, 26). Likewise in Romans, Paul stresses faith in Jesus Christ (cf. Rom. 2:22, 24, 26; 4:24; 5:1, 17, 21, and many other passages). This faith in Christ is set over against human works: it is the work of Christ that has saving merit; human works can never save. "For we hold that a man is justified by faith apart from works of law" (Rom. 3:28).

In Qumran doctrine, on the other hand, "justification by faith" as spelled out in the Habakkuk Commentary includes the works of the law (1QpHab 8:1-3). If this passage by itself does not make clear the necessity of works of the law, certainly a study of the Qumran literature will make abundantly clear the binding nature of the Law (cf. pp. 63-66, 88f. above).

## The Flesh and the Spirit

The discussion of the sinfulness of man in Qumran and in Pauline thought leads to a consideration of the conflict between the "flesh" and the "spirit."

Before the discovery of the Scrolls, W. D. Davies had already rejected the idea that Paul's concept of the "flesh" had to be explained as the result of Hellenistic influences, but he also admitted that Rabbinic Judaism offered no parallel. The discovery of the Dead Sea Scrolls led him to reopen the study.[9] In the Scrolls, "flesh" is used, but not in the Hellenistic sense,

[9] Cf. W. D. Davies, art. cit., The Scrolls and the New Testament, pp. 157-182.

as K. G. Kuhn had demonstrated;[10] and Davies follows this up to show that "flesh" has two usages: with and without moral connotation. Then Davies lists Paul's use of the term and shows not only that the same twofold usage occurs but also that the moral connotation is found principally in Romans and Galatians, with other references in Second Corinthians, Ephesians, and Colossians.

The passages in Romans are principally in chapters 7 and 8 where Paul describes his personal struggle with the flesh. He does not use the term where he discusses sin in the broader sense (chs. 1, 2, and 5). Similarly, in Qumran "flesh" is not used when discussing sin in the broad sense.

The term "flesh" occurs in a passage in Colossians (2:11-23), which has been studied on other grounds for points of contact with Qumran. The expression, "the body of the flesh," is used both in Colossians (2:11) and in the Habakkuk Commentary (1QpHab 9:2) to mean the physical body. In the former passage, Paul speaks of the reconciliation accomplished by Christ "in his body of flesh by his death." In the latter, the passage follows a break in the manuscript, and reads, "they smote with judgments of wickedness, and scandals of evil diseases they wrought in him, and vengeance on the body of his flesh" (1QpHab 9:1-2). Some scholars believe the passage referred to the Teacher of Righteousness, and have therefore seen a parallel with the statement about Jesus. The preceding context, however, makes it more likely that the Wicked Priest is the one intended.

In this same passage from Colossians there are references to the calendar (cf. CD 3:13-16; 1QS 1:14; 10:1-9), to the Sabbath (cf. CD 10:14 — 11:18), to meat and drink (cf. CD 6:18), to wisdom and knowledge (cf. 1QS 3:13-15), and to angels (cf. 1QM 10:10f.). At one time a Gnostic milieu was argued for Colossians, and a late date was proposed for its composition. It now appears that the objective of Colossians was this early so-called Jewish Gnosticism.

In Ephesians, Paul refers to "principalities and powers," "every name that is named," to "the prince of the power of the air," to the "spirit that is now at work in the sons of disobedience" — terms that are reminiscent of the language of the Scrolls, particularly with reference to Belial (who is men-

10 K. G. Kuhn, art. cit., The Scrolls and the New Testament, pp. 101f.

tioned in the New Testament, incidentally, only by Paul in 2 Cor. 6:15), and the passage in the Manual of Discipline (1QS 3:13 – 4:26).[11]

This does not imply that Paul was engaging in a veiled attack on Qumranism or that he had borrowed terminology from Qumran.[12] It is entirely possible that the thoughts and terminology that had penetrated Qumran theology were in current usage in a stream of sectarian Judaism which also reached Asia Minor, and that Paul was using the thought-molds of that group. In the absence of objective evidence, however, this must remain only a hypothesis.

A long passage in Galatians (5:13-21) is compared with the passage concerning the "two spirits" in the Manual of Discipline (1QS 3:13–4:26). Davies tabularizes his observations for the latter passage. We have already considered this section of the Manual of Discipline in connection with the concept of Dualism in Qumran theology (pp. 78-81 above). The "works of the flesh" in Galatians are:

> immorality, impurity, licentiousness, idolatry, sorcery, enmity, strife, jealousy, anger, selfishness, dissension, party spirit, envy, drunkenness, carousing, and the like.

In the Qumran text, "to the spirit of unrighteousness" the following works belong:

> greediness and negligence in the work of righteousness, wickedness and falsehood, pride and haughty heart, lying and deceit, cruelty and much hypocrisy, quickness of anger and much stupidity and presumptuous zeal, loathsome works in the spirit of fornication and ways of impurity in deeds of uncleanness, and a tongue of insults, blindness of eyes and heaviness of ear, stiffness of neck and hardness of heart, to walk in all the ways of darkness and the cunningness of wickedness. (1QS 4:9-11)

The parallel would be even more impressive if I deliberately tried to use parallel translations of terms in cases where they are justified.

11 For fuller discussions, cf. K. G. Kuhn, "The Epistle to the Ephesians in the Light of the Qumran Texts," in *Paul and Qumran*, pp. 115-131; and J. Murphy-O'Connor, "Truth: Paul and Qumran," in *ibid.*, pp. 207-213.

12 Murphy-O'Connor inclines to the view that "those who penned epistles (under his [Paul's] aegis but with varying degrees of freedom) [were] influenced by different applications of the Essenian concept" (*art. cit.*, p. 230).

Davies points out, however, that there is a similar list of evils proceeding from the heart of man in Mark 7:20-23. The Marcan list emphasizes principally the sins of the flesh and of the selfish nature; the list in Galatians is directed more at evils which create disunity. The Qumran list, on the other hand, is more concerned with immorality in the Community.

Obviously the problem cannot be reduced to similarities in lists of terms. In Paul the conflict is between flesh and Spirit. In Qumran it is between the spirit of truth and the spirit of unrighteousness (or error). Flesh, in Qumran, is not the spirit of unrighteousness, but the sphere in which the spirit works. In Paul, the Spirit is the Spirit of God, and not just the spirit in man, nor even a created spirit influencing man. In other words, when man has come to God in faith — justifying faith, as Paul describes it in Galatians — the Spirit of God begins to combat the flesh, the old nature of man. The Spirit enables man to fulfill the Law. In Qumran, two spirits struggle within man, and the law continues to make demands which are never fulfilled.

Davies concludes that Paul is therefore more in the stream of the Old Testament and rabbinic Judaism than in that of Qumran. That there have been influences at work upon Paul, whether from Qumran or from antecedents of Qumran, is not denied.

## Other Suggested Parallels

Parallels between Pauline writings and Qumran texts in the area of Baptism, Communion, and the concept of the New Covenant have been suggested. These subjects have been considered above,[13] and there seems to be no special or peculiar emphasis in Paul to require further consideration.

The suggestion has been made that Paul's use of Scripture is similar to that of the Qumran Sect. In my opinion this is obvious only in one place, namely, the allegory of the two covenants, where Paul says, "Now Hagar is Mount Sinai in Arabia; she corresponds to the present Jerusalem, for she is in slavery with her children" (Gal. 4:25). Paul's use of Scripture is comparable to the rabbinical method at more points, but in general his own originality dominates.

13On Baptism, cf. pp. 149-151; on Communion or the Lord's Supper, cf. pp. 163-165; on the New Covenant, cf. pp. 155-156.

Paul's use of the expression, "to deliver this man to Satan" (1 Cor. 5:5), and "whom I have delivered to Satan" (1 Tim. 1:20), has been compared to the Qumran statement "so [that they might be sei]zed by Belial in the error of t[heir iniqui]ty" (4QFlor 1:9). Because of the broken text, some have read this, "to d[eliver] his [so]ul to Belial" — a possibility, if we do not consider context. But there is no antecedent for the singular suffix "his"; the entire context is in the plural.

The reference to "Jannes and his brother" in the Damascus Document (CD 5:19) has been compared to Paul's mention of "Jannes and Jambres" (2 Tim. 3:8). The context is not similar; and the names of Jannes and Jambres are known in Jewish traditions. It is therefore unnecessary, if not misleading, to find any connection between Paul and Qumran at this point.

The expression "the mysteries of rebellion (or, transgression)" (1QH 5:36) has been compared to Paul's expression "the mystery of iniquity" (2 Thess. 2:7). The word "mystery" is found also in other places in Paul's writings,[14] and some scholars have pointed out that this word is used frequently in the Qumran texts.[15]

Likewise the expression "sons of light" is found in Paul's writings (Rom. 13:12; Eph. 5:8, 11; 6:12; 1 Thess. 5:4f.) and is characteristic in Qumran writings.

Dupont-Sommer says that the Qumran Psalmist means "my body" when he uses the word "fabric" (*mabniti*, 1QH 7:9), and suggests that it was "easy to slip from one idea to the other, from that of the body to that of the Church." He then

14 The word "mystery" occurs 27 times in the New Testament, 3x (representing one usage) in a parallel passage in the Synoptics, 4x in Revelation, the balance in "Paul." The distribution in the last group is very significant: 2x in Rom., 5x in 1 Cor., 6x in Eph., 4x in Col., 1x in 2 Thess., 2x in 1 Tim. Critical scholars have always granted Pauline authorship of Romans and First Corinthians, and generally also of Second Thessalonians; Pauline authorship of Ephesians, Colossians, and First Timothy has generally been seriously questioned or flatly denied. Repeatedly, it should be noted, the "Qumran parallels" pointed out by some of these same scholars have involved Ephesians and Colossians, and to a lesser extent the Pastoral Epistles, along with the "assuredly Pauline" writings. One cannot but question a methodology which finds it convenient to forget its own critical canons!

15 J. Coppens, " 'Mystery' in the Theology of Saint Paul and Its Parallels at Qumran," in *Paul and Qumran*, pp. 132-158.

offers as comparable passages Ephesians 1:23; 4:12, 16, etc.[16]
The word is closer in meaning to "structure" but in 1QH 7:4
it clearly is used as a figure of the body — less clearly in 1QH
7:9 where it has more of the significance of "my self, my very
being." Dupont-Sommer says the "same metaphor" is used in
1QH 6:26 and 7:8 to describe the Community which the
Psalmist has built. But the word does not occur in 6:26, and
the context of 7:8 (the word is found actually in 7:9) has
nothing to do with the Community. The reference to Ephesians seems to be dragged into the discussion without basis
in fact.

## Summary

There are many surface similarities between Pauline and
Qumran texts. Some of these disappear as soon as they are
examined in the light of context. Some of them remain until
we reach the deepest level of analysis. There seems to be no
reason to suppose that Paul was directly influenced by Qumran thought. It is possible that he was influenced by a stream
of Judaism that also touched Qumran. It seems quite reasonable to suppose that in some cases, notably in the writings to
the Church in Asia Minor, he was attempting to combat ideas
which were remarkably similar to and may have had a common
origin with certain Qumranian beliefs.[17]

This last observation shows the importance of the Qumran texts for understanding and interpreting the letters to
the Ephesians and the Colossians. It now seems clear that
Paul was in reaction not against Greek thought, but against
Jewish thought which had its origin in, or at least its close
relationship with, sectarian Judaism in Palestine.

---

[16] Dupont-Sommer, *The Essene Writings from Qumran*, p. 222 n. 1 and
n. 4.

[17] Murphy-O'Connor points out, "It has been suggested more than
once that it was at Ephesus that Paul came into contact with influences
emanating from Qumran" (*art. cit.*, pp. 197f.). Leaving aside the question
of authorship of Ephesians, we would note that Murphy-O'Connor treats
the Pastorals as clearly Pauline, and makes the following point: "Is it a
pure coincidence that, although Timothy and Titus were in almost identical circumstances in having to contend with opposition, 'truth' appears
far more frequently in the Epistles addressed to the former — in Ephesus?"
(pp. 199f.). He had been making the point that "truth" was used in a
characteristically Qumranian way.

## CHAPTER FOURTEEN

# THE EPISTLE TO THE HEBREWS AND THE QUMRAN WRITINGS

Among the first questions to be answered when we study any literary work are the simple matters of Introduction: Who wrote it? When? To whom was it addressed? Why was it written? The answers to these and related questions help us better to understand and interpret the document. In the case of the Epistle to the Hebrews, scholars have long been baffled by these simple questions.

The Epistle to the Hebrews contains no author's name. Traditionally it has often been attributed to Paul, but there are strong arguments against this. For one thing, the language is quite unlike Paul's. Again, when Paul's letters were first arranged in order in the New Testament, they were put, not in chronological sequence, but in the order of decreasing length: the longest first and the shortest last. Hebrews obviously does not fit in this arrangement, suggesting that even at that early date it was not definitively attributed to Paul. Further, the tradition that Paul wrote the book developed gradually: not earlier than the late second century in Alexandria, and not until the fourth or fifth century in the West.

Equally enigmatic is the address of Hebrews: scholars are divided on the identification of the group to whom the epistle was written. The subscription, "Written to the Hebrews from Italy by Timothy," at the end of the epistle, has no manuscript support of any merit. The closing verses (Heb. 13:22-25) seem as though they may have become attached to Hebrews from another document, for Hebrews can hardly be described as "a letter . . . in few words." Some scholars feel, with sound reason, that the description of Judaism in the Epistle to the Hebrews is not that of Judaism of the Dispersion, and hence the document could hardy have been written to Jews. Other scholars, also with sound logic, point out that the long and sustained argument involving the Levitical sacrifices and Temple cultus could hardly have been written to Gentiles.[1] But, if not to Jews and if not to Gentiles, then to whom was the work written?

## Hebrews Addressed to Former Qumranians?

Professor Yigael Yadin, in a stimulating article, has put forth the suggestion that Hebrews was written to "a group of Jews originally belonging to the [Dead Sea Scrolls] Sect who were converted to Christianity, carrying with them some of their previous beliefs."[2] He suggests that the reason why scholars have objected to a Jewish address for the Epistle is simply "the fact that the only type of Judaism of which we have had any thorough knowledge up till now was the so-called normative Judaism." Now, with the available Qumran material, we have a basis for analyzing Hebrews in the light of a development of sectarian Judaism.

Yadin's theory is not unique, for several scholars have made similar suggestions. Daniélou, for example, devoted a chapter to the thesis that Hebrews was addressed to the Essenes.[3] F. F. Bruce was more cautious, suggesting that "The recipients of the epistle were probably Jewish believers in

[1] Details can be found in the introductory portion of any good commentary on Hebrews. The suggestion that there was some relationship between the Essenes, the Therapeutae, and the "Hebrews" of this Epistle is found 150 years before the discovery of the Scrolls (David Schulz, Der Brief an die Hebräer [Breslau: Holäufer, 1818]); cf. also M. Friedlaender, "La secte de Melchisédec et l'Épître aux Hébreux," Revue des Études Juives 5 (1882), pp. 1-26, 188-198; 6 (1883), pp. 187-199. I am indebted to J. Carmignac for these references.

[2] Y. Yadin, "The Scrolls and the Epistle to the Hebrews," in Aspects of the Dead Sea Scrolls, ed. Ch. Rabin and Y. Yadin (Scripta Hierosolymitana, IV; Jerusalem: Magnes, 1958), p. 38. The material in this chapter is drawn largely from the article, which extends from p. 36 to p. 55 in the publication cited. This blanket acknowledgment of my indebtedness to Prof. Yadin's article will take the place of continuous documentation.

[3] J. Daniélou, The Dead Sea Scrolls and Primitive Christianity, pp. 111-114.

Jesus whose background was not so much the normative Judaism represented by rabbinical tradition as the nonconformist Judaism of which the Essenes and the Qumran Community are outstanding representatives, but not the only representatives."[4] C. Spicq suggested that Hebrews was addressed by Apollos to Esseno-christians, Jewish priests, among whom were a number of ex-Qumranians.[5] However, Yadin's theory is developed more fully than any of the others, so we shall use it as a basis for our study.

*Analysis of the Epistle.* The treatise under consideration—it can hardly be called an "epistle" — is devoted to proving that Jesus is superior to the prophets (1:1-2), to the angels (1:3—2:18), to Moses (3:1—4:13), and to the Aaronic priesthood (4:14—10:18). Therefore the readers are urged to hold on to their faith in Jesus (10:19—12:29). Yadin reasons from this that the readers were inclined either to look upon these creatures as superior to Jesus in certain functions or to substitute one or another of these creatures in roles that rightly belonged to Jesus. Before the discovery of the Dead Sea Scrolls, scholars had noted the sudden transition to the subject of angels, and had concluded that the addressees tended to exalt angels to a place that was either above or equal to that which belonged to Christ.[6]

In the opening statement of Hebrews, in which Jesus is set over against the prophets, Yadin notes two points: Jesus the Son is the only agent of God's revelation at this time, and this time is designated as "these days at the end" (Heb. 1:1-2; *art. cit.*, p. 39). Therefore, the readers must have belonged to an eschatological movement and believed that there was another prophet who either had appeared or was about to appear. The argument in Hebrews then takes the following line: Jesus is the Son; angels are not sons, but are only servants (1:3-14). Jesus was made lower than the angels only tempo-

---

[4] F. F. Bruce, *Commentary on the Epistle to the Hebrews* (Grand Rapids: Eerdmans, 1964), p. xxix. Earlier, Bruce had written that to call the addressees of Hebrews "Essenes" would be "outstripping the evidence" (cf. "'To the Hebrews' or 'To the Essenes'?" in *New Testament Studies* 9 (1962-63), p. 232.

[5] C. Spicq, "*L'Épître aux Hébreux*, Apollos, Jean-Baptiste, les Hellénistes et Qumrân," in *Revue de Qumrân* 1,3 (Feb. 1959), p. 388.

[6] Cf. A. B. Bruce, "Hebrews," in Hastings' *Dictionary of the Bible* (New York: Scribner, 1900), vol. 2, p. 328.

rarily to suffer death, but was perfected through death to become the originator of salvation (2:9-10). The world to come
was put not under the authority of angels, but (by inference)
under Jesus (2:5).

Passing to the next point — the superiority over Moses —
Yadin reasons that it is not merely Moses' office as mediator
of the Law that is under discussion, but in addition an eschatological role that Moses was to play. This is supported by
Hebrews 8:1-13, which Yadin takes to imply that Moses was
believed to be also the mediator of the New Covenant.

The most important point, however — judging from the
amount of space devoted to it — is the superiority of Jesus over
the Aaronic priesthood. Yadin notes that nearly half of the
Epistle is devoted to this and subsidiary points (Heb. 4:14—10:
23; *art. cit.*, p. 41), and that the author interrupts his flow of
arguments to try to impress his readers with the importance
of the subject (Heb. 5:11-12). Yadin asks, "Why did the
writer focus his arguments on this concept of Jesus as the
priest? Why did he go to such length to compare Jesus to
Aaron?" His reply is significant: " . . . because of his readers'
belief that the eschatological priest, belonging to the House
of Aaron, was also to be of a Messianic character." To argue
against this view, the writer of Hebrews makes three points:
(1) Jesus is a High Priest; (2) His priesthood is of an order
superior to that of Aaron; (3) He is a royal priest, in other
words, both Messiah-King and Messiah-Priest. In the footnote
Yadin compares the play on the name Melchizedek ("king of
righteousness") in Hebrews with the Qumran title *môrè haṣṣédeq* ("teacher of righteousness") (*art. cit.*, p. 44 n. 15).

Yadin then pauses to emphasize the attitude toward sacrifices in the Epistle to the Hebrews, concluding that the readers believed that in the end of days the full sacrificial system
would be resumed and continued forever.

*Melchizedek.* With the discovery of thirteen fragments of
a manuscript about Melchizedek (11QMelch)[7] theories rele-

---

[7] Cf. A. S. van der Woude, "Melchisedek als himmlische Erlösergestalt
in den neugefundenen eschatologischen Midraschim aus Qumran Höhle
XI," *Oudtestamentische Studiën* 14 (Leiden: Brill, 1965), pp. 354-373; M.
de Jonge and A. S. van der Woude, "11Q Melchizedek and the New Testament," *New Testament Studies* 12 (1965-66), pp. 301-326; and J. A. Fitzmyer, "Further Light on Melchizedek from Qumran Cave 11," *Journal of
Biblical Literature* 86 (1967), pp. 25-41.

vant to the Epistle to the Hebrews and its reference to Melchizedek began to multiply.[8]

It would lead us far afield to trace in detail the developed theories concerning the Qumran Melchizedek. Carmignac points out that there are at least four possible ways of interpreting the figure: as a historical Melchizedek, as a heavenly Melchizedek, as a symbolic Melchizedek, or as an etymological Melchizedek. He rules out the first since it is contradicted by the Qumran interpretations. Van der Woude, de Jonge, and (with caution) Fitzmyer find a heavenly Melchizedek in the Qumran text. After pointing out the difficulties with this view, Carmignac inclines to the other views, "those which see in this Malkî-Ṣèdèq an earthly personage, whose coming is predicted and who would reproduce the figure of the biblical Melchizedek, or who would simply bear his name."[9]

De Jonge and van der Woude make the astonishing statement, "On the evidence of 11QMelch the most plausible inference is that he [the author of the Epistle to the Hebrews] regarded Melchizedek as an angel, who appeared to Abraham long ago."[10] However, careful reading of the passage in Hebrews (5:1—7:28) brings out the following facts. (1) The author of Hebrews is dealing with the historical Melchizedek (7:1-2) to whom Abraham paid tithes (Gen. 14:17-20). (2) The author of Hebrews has also drawn upon Psalm 110:4, "Thou art a priest for ever after the order of Melchizedek" (Heb. 5:6, 10; 6:20; 7:11, 15, 17, 21, 28). (3) The superiority of the priestly order of Melchizedek is not attributed to the proposition that he is a heavenly or angelic being. Rather it is due to the fact that Abraham paid tithes to him, and by virtue of that fact, Levi paid tithes to Melchizedek: "One might even say that Levi himself, who received tithes, paid tithes through Abraham, for he was still in the loins of his ancestor when Melchizedek met him" (Heb. 7:9-10). The Aaronic priesthood, which descended from the Levitical priesthood, was therefore likewise inferior to Melchizedek.

This line of reasoning may appear strange to us, but it is not unlike much rabbinic logic. Carmignac is right in seeing

---

[8] For a survey, see J. Carmignac, "Le document de Qumrân sur Melchisédeq," *Revue de Qumrân* 7,27 (Dec. 1970), pp. 343-378.

[9] Carmignac, *art. cit.*, p. 369.

[10] M. de Jonge and A. S. van der Woude, *art. cit.*, pp. 321f.

either a symbolic or etymological figure in the Qumran Melchizedek, but I feel he is not warranted in finding "a new
argument in favor or those who see in the addressees of this
epistle Judeo-Christians influenced by the community of Qumran."[11] The Biblical treatment springs from the historical Melchizedek. The author of Hebrews, by a process of rabbinical
exegesis including etymological developments from "Mechiz-
edek" and "king of Salem" producing "king of righteousness"
and "king of peace," and by developing the fact that Melchizedek is without genealogy (Heb. 7:2-3), makes the point
that the priestly office of Christ is of the order of Melchizedek. All of this the author of Hebrews could have developed
from the Old Testament, using rabbinical exegesis, without
any contact whatever with Qumran. At the same time it is
possible that the author of Hebrews was reacting against an
emphasis on the Aaronic priesthood, such as that of Qumran,
by stressing the superiority of the "Melchizedek" priesthood
of Christ.

*The Messianic Beliefs of the "Hebrews": Angels.* Following
this analysis of the Epistle to the Hebrews, Yadin proceeds to
compare the messianic beliefs of the "Hebrews" with those of
the Qumran Sect.

The eschatological role of the angels as deduced from the
Epistle is summarized in three points:   (1) They operate under
the direct order of God, and not as servants to any other messianic personage.   (2) In the world to come they have a certain
control over other eschatological figures.   (3) Qualities of sonship are implied.   On these points Yadin offers the following
quotations from Qumran for comparison:[12]

> Thou [O God] didst redeem us for Thyself as an eternal peo-
> ple, and into the Lot of Light Thou didst cause us to fall,
> through Thy truth. Thou didst appoint from of old the Prince
> of Light (i.e., the archangel Michael) to assist us, and [all the
> Sons of Righteousness are in his] lot and all Spirits of Truth
> in his dominion. (1QM 13:9-10)

> Within the hand of the Prince of Light the dominion over all
> the Sons of Righteousness — in the ways of Light they shall
> walk. (1QS 3:20)

> Today in His appointed time to subdue and bring low the
> Prince of the Dominion of Wickedness. And He will send

11 Carmignac, *art. cit.,* p. 373.
12 The translations in this section are Yadin's.

> eternal assistance to the lot to-be-redeemed-by-Him, through the might of an angel; He hath magnified the authority of Michael through eternal light to light up in joy the [House] of Israel, peace and blessing for the lot of God, so as to raise among the angels (lit., gods) the authority of Michael, and the dominion of Israel amongst all flesh. And righteousness shall rejoice in Heavens, and all sons of His truth shall be glad in eternal knowledge. (1QM 17:6-8)

> Lo, Thou art the Prince of angels (lit., gods) and the king of all the glorious ones and the Lord of every spirit. (1QH 10:8)

> To stand firm with a host of angels (lit., saints) and to enter unto the community together with the angels (lit., sons of heavens). (1QH 3:21-22)

> And He hath caused them to share the lot of angels (lit., saints) He associated their assembly to form a Council of Community. (1QS 11:7-8)

In the Qumran Sect, Michael the Angel of Light, with his heavenly subordinates, is to have not only eschatological functions but also control over the world to come. Yadin sets in contrast with this two quotations from Hebrews: "For to what angel did God ever say. Thou art my son, today have I become thy father," and "For the world to come, of which I am speaking, was not put under the control of angels."

*Two Messiahs.* The reconstruction of the messianic idea of the "Hebrews" is presented under four points: (1) There was to be a priestly Messiah as well as a lay Messiah. (2) The priestly Messiah was to be superior. (3) He was to be of the House of Aaron. (4) In the messianic era, the ritual of the Law including the sacrifices was to be resumed under the priestly Messiah.

Quotations from the Dead Sea Scrolls setting forth the doctrine of the two Messiahs, the priestly Messiah (or Messiah of Aaron) and the lay Messiah (or Messiah of Israel), have already been discussed (pp. 93-103 above). Yadin cites CD 12:22—13:1; 14:19; 20:1; and 1QS 9:11.

To repudiate this doctrine, the author of the Epistle to the Hebrews, frankly admitting that he cannot identify Jesus as descended from Aaron (Heb. 7:14), argues that Jesus is a priest of a higher order, an order older than that of Aaron, and to which order Aaron's ancestors paid tithes. Yadin adds in a footnote that in the Genesis Apocryphon (1QApGen 22:

14-17) "the story of Melchizedek is told in a manner which does not imply Melchizedek's superiority over Abraham."

The most detailed description of the role of the two Messiahs in the eschatological war, according to Yadin, is found in the War Scroll. There the conduct of the entire war is entrusted to the Archangel Michael; the leading person in the conduct of the earthly war is the Chief Priest (identified by Yadin as the priestly Messiah), and the one associated with him but subservient to him is the "Prince of the Whole Congregation." Of this last-named person, Yadin makes two important points in a footnote: First, he is mentioned only once in the entire scroll; second, "there is no doubt that he is identical with the royal Messiah." The second point he supports by the quotation of CD 7:18-21 and 1QSb 3:20-21. We shall return to this later.

In addition to these passages, Yadin believes that the doctrine of two Messiahs, including the priority of the priestly Messiah, is found in The Order of the Congregation (1QSa) and The Benedictions (1QSb). Moreover, the resumption of the sacrifices and the Levitical ritual is, according to Yadin, implied in the War Scroll (1QM 2:1-6).

To reply to this doctrine, the author of the Epistle to the Hebrews stresses that Jesus offered one sacrifice which does not need to be repeated (Heb. 9:25-26).

*The Eschatological Prophet.* From the portions of the Epistle that deal with the prophets and with Moses, Yadin concludes that the "Hebrews" must have believed that "in the eschatological era a prophet should appear — a prophet who is not to be identified with the Messiah himself" (*art. cit.,* p. 53).

That a similar belief was found in the Qumran Sect, Yadin deduces from 1QS 9:11, "Until the coming of a prophet and of the Messiahs from Aaron and Israel." This is supported by the document known as 4Q Testimonia, in which quotations from Deuteronomy 18:18ff., Numbers 24:15-17, and Deuteronomy 33:8-11 bring together the Moses-like prophet, the Star of Jacob, and the blessing on Levi. We have already seen that other scholars identify these as three "messianic" or "eschatological" persons (pp. 104f. above).

One other point is added to the discussion of the subject, namely the considerable amount of Pentateuchal material used in the Epistle to the Hebrews. Yadin thinks that this is no accident, but is connected with the particular persons to whom the writing was addressed. He then points out that the Qumran group organized itself "in as exact as possible a replica of the life of the tribes of Israel in the wilderness." With this in the back of his mind, the author of the Epistle drew on the same metaphors and allusions, which would have a very strong appeal to the hearts and minds of people descending from the Qumran Sect.[13]

## An Examination of Yadin's Thesis

This interesting thesis has been presented in considerable detail for several reasons. It is, to the best of my knowledge, the most fully detailed study of the possible relationship between the Epistle to the Hebrews and the Qumran literature. It is, moreover, a very thorough study which deserves careful consideration. If more need be said, it is stimulating, and on first reading at least cogent.

However attractive the theory may be — and I confess that I find it extremely so, from the viewpoint of Biblical interpretation — there are certain fundamental weaknesses that should be pointed out.

*The Analysis Is Slanted.* First, the analysis of the Epistle to the Hebrews which Yadin presents has been slanted in such a way as to make the parallels with Qumran material more obvious. In other words, Yadin has read into the Epistle more than he has read out of it. This is not necessarily a fatal step in methodology, and for a work as difficult to place in its proper milieu as the Epistle every attempt of this nature should be made and should receive serious attention. Still the basic methodology must be recognized for its inherent dangers.

*The Doctrine of Angels.* Yadin's treatment of angels suffers from reading into Hebrews too much material from Qum-

[13] Spicq observes that Hebrews, the Damascus Document, and the Habakkuk Commentary all conceive of the religious life on the pattern of the Exodus from Egypt to Canaan as a migration and an exile. He goes on to suggest that the title "To the Hebrews" may therefore designate a homogeneous group, not only of Judeo-Christians, but of wanderers and fugitives bound together by their common heavenly calling. His footnote, which brings in the relationship of *'ibri* and *Habiru,* however, has no relevance; did the author of Hebrews know about the *Habiru?* Cf. "*L'Épître aux Hébreux* . . . et Qumrân," in *Revue de Qumrân* 1,3 (Feb. 1959), pp. 371f. and n. 44.

ran. Careful study of the section in Hebrews fails to uncover any implication that the readers looked upon angels either as sons of God or as exercising any authority in the world to come.

In fact, the author of the Epistle makes his arguments by pointing out just the reverse: "To which of the angels did he say at any time, 'Thou art my Son'?" "To which of the angels did he say at any time, 'Sit on my right hand . . .'?" (Heb. 1:5,13). If there had been any such doctrine among the "Hebrews" the author could hardly have refuted it by this method. His approach would only be convincing if his readers could find no answer to these questions.

*The Two Messiahs.* Yadin's discussion of the priestly Messiah, and the argument concerning Aaron in the Epistle, is subject to question on an entirely different basis. Here the material in the Epistle seems more clearly to support Yadin's analysis, although we should be aware of the fact that he has read into it certain concepts which were not at all obvious to students of Hebrews prior to the discovery of the Scrolls.

The main objection to his theory, in my opinion, arises from his complete acceptance of the two-Messiah doctrine. We have already discussed this subject (pp. 100-103 above), and seen that there is no Qumran textual evidence to support the theory of a "Messiah of Aaron." The Chief Priest performs no messianic function as commonly defined. He is present in two possibly eschatological passages: in the Order of the Congregation and in the battle described in the War Scroll. In neither case is he called "Messiah," and there is no textual indication that he had but recently appeared. The "coming" of the Messiah, whenever it is mentioned, applies to the Davidic person, with one possible exception, namely 1QS 9:11, where the "Messiah of Aaron" is commonly understood by most scholars. I have presented reasons for rejecting it elsewhere, and have summarized them in a previous chapter in this work (see pp. 100-103).

But if the author of the Epistle is not attempting to refute a Messiah-of-Aaron doctrine, what was he attempting to do in this extended argument? The classical answer has been to this effect: Writing at a time when the Temple had been destroyed and the sacrificial system abolished, the author was attempting to show that these were, after all, no longer necessary.

The sacrifice of Jesus has a finality that has rendered all other sacrifices unnecessary. The heavenly High Priesthood of Jesus makes any earthly priesthood superfluous.

This explanation is self-consistent, and does not need the support of any exterior literature. It is not contradicted by the Qumran documents. Whether it is more satisfactory than Yadin's thesis, or less so, each of us must decide for himself.

*The Eschatological Moses.* The analysis of the Epistle with reference to the prophet to come, or the new "Moses," in my opinion, lacks sufficient support to bear the weight of the argument. Repeated reading of the indicated passages has not convinced me that any connection between Moses or a second Moses and the New Covenant is intended. The opening contrast between Jesus and the prophets is best explained, and commentators have always explained it, as the effort of the author to present Jesus as the culmination of the prophets of the Old Testament.

That the Qumran group may have had some belief in an eschatological prophet — based on Deuteronomy 18:18ff. it would seem — has no particular bearing on the Epistle to the Hebrews, if the author of the Epistle was not concerned with this particular doctrine. But since Yadin has raised the subject we must point out a significant fact. Milik also attempted to make such a "prophet" one of the eschatological figures in Qumran doctrine — only to concede that this prophet "seems scarcely to be mentioned elsewhere in the Qumran texts and little further can be said about his functions and person."[14]

At the same time, there was a "prophet" in the Qumran Sect whose function has been compared to that of a second Moses, namely the Teacher of Righteousness, who may or may not be identical with the Interpreter of the Law (who would also fit the qualifications of the second Moses). One difficulty with the identification of the Teacher of Righteousness in such a role is that he was of the priestly line.

The most we can say at present, it seems, is this: It is not certain that the Qumranians looked for an eschatological prophet. When we place alongside this statement a second statement, namely that it is not certain that there is any eschatological significance attached to Moses in the Epistle to the

[14] J. T. Milik, *Ten Years of Discovery in the Wilderness of Judaea,* p. 126.

Hebrews, we must conclude that Yadin's thesis, at this point, is supported by two uncertainties, each of which is used to support the other.

## Summary

Some sectarian Jewish group such as the Qumranians would seem to be in the mind of the author of the Epistle to the Hebrews. The details of Professor Yadin's thesis, however, do not seem to fit either the details of the argument of Hebrews or the details of Qumran eschatology at significant points. Whether the central point of the thesis, namely that the Epistle was addressed to former Qumranians, can be sustained by further rearrangement and realignment of the supporting arguments is not at present clear to me.

## CHAPTER FIFTEEN

# THE JOHANNINE WRITINGS
# AND THE QUMRAN DISCOVERIES

The Gospel of John has been something of an enigma to Bible students. There is an obvious similarity between the Gospels of Matthew, Mark, and Luke; hence the name "Synoptic Gospels" has been given to them. The Gospel of John (the "Fourth Gospel") does not exhibit this similarity. To "harmonize" the Synoptics, i.e. to put the three Gospels into a synchronous single account, is not exceedingly difficult; but to attempt to harmonize the Fourth Gospel with the Synoptics is very difficult, and some would say impossible. The teachings of Jesus in the Synoptics are often described as simple ethical instructions (this is grossly oversimplified, but it will serve to point up the difference); the teachings of Jesus in the Fourth Gospel are more in the nature of theological discourses, so that editors are frequently uncertain where a quotation by Jesus ends and where a comment by John begins. This theological characteristic is also found in the Johannine epistles, particularly First John.

Scholars attempting to account for the Johannine characteristics have advanced various theories. From these theories we may mention here three relevant points: (1) the Gospel was written very late, perhaps as late as the middle of the second century, and was the result of theological developments in the early Church; (2) the Fourth Gospel is strongly "anti-Semitic" or more accurately "anti-Jewish"; and (3) the Gospel and the Epistles have Gnostic tones and overtones. On this point some have suggested that the First Epistle is clearly anti-Gnostic.

With the discovery of the Dead Sea Scrolls, a number of scholars were impressed with the similarities between the Johannine writings and the Qumran materials. This was particularly pointed out with reference to the Dualism of Qumran and the dualistic terminology of the Johannine writings that was part of their "anti-Gnostic" nature. The "anti-Jewish" tendency of the Fourth Gospel could be explained as an echo of the Qumranian attitude toward Jerusalem Judaism, if its author was either an ex-Qumranian or one who had been influenced by Qumran teachings. Further, if these points were sustained, it followed that the Gospel was not a second-century product but an early writing, perhaps the earliest of the Gospels.[1]

These points are interesting and very important, and deserve further examination. A cautionary word, however, is in order. The methodology of scholars working in the area is subject to the same criticism previously expressed, namely the deliberate attempt to find similarities has led sometimes to their "discovery" where they do not exist and sometimes to the obscuring of important differences.

## The Gospel of John

The Gospel of John was written to convince its readers that Jesus (the historical Man of Galilee) is the Christ (the Messiah of Israel) and the Son of God. This is the stated purpose of the author (John 20:30-31), and I can find no reason to set it aside. From beginning to end, in structure and in detail, this is clearly the author's purpose.

He begins with a prologue (John 1:1-18) in which the eternal pre-existence of the "Word" is declared, and in which the identity of this Word with the incarnate One is established: "The Word became flesh and dwelt among us" (1:14). There can be no question that the author is referring to Jesus, for this is established through the identification by John the Baptist (1:6-8, 19-34).

This great truth calls forth a twofold response: faith and

[1] Cf. W. F. Albright, "Recent Discoveries in Palestine and the Gospel of John," in *The Background of the New Testament and Its Eschatology*, ed. W. D. Davies and D. Daube (Cambridge: Cambridge University Press, 1954), pp. 170f.

unbelief (John 1:11-12), which the author symbolizes by "light" and "darkness." Light has a twofold aspect: the Light that comes into the world (1:4-5, 8); and also the light that shines in men who believe in the Light (1:9).

John then divides his composition into two major parts: the historic manifestation of this Light, the Word incarnate, through His works and His teachings, with the reactions both of faith and of unbelief (John 1:19—11:57); and the culmination of this struggle in the events of the final week, including the teachings, the crucifixion, and the resurrection of Jesus (12:1—20:29). Chapter 12 may be looked upon as belonging to either portion, since it is essentially a transition. The purpose of the writing is expressed in 20:30-31.

Chapter 21 is in the nature of a postscript, written, some believe, by one of John's disciples; others believe by John himself as a personal authentication.

Obviously in this type of presentation the author has occasion to use a kind of "dualism": the dualism of two worlds (Heaven and earth), the dualism of two natures (Word or spirit and flesh), the dualism of two attitudes (faith and unbelief), the dualism of two results (life and death), etc. Essentially this becomes a dualism of two forces (light and darkness), which upon examination becomes the struggle of two spiritual beings (the incarnate Word and the Devil).

"Satan" is named only once (John 13:27) — which may be significant in view of the theory that Satan is supposed to be an Iranian or Zoroastrian element and part of the Dualism supposedly found in the Old Testament, in Qumran, and in the Johannine writings. The "devil" (*diábolos*) is mentioned twice in connection with Judas (6:70; 13:2 — Satan was likewise mentioned in connection with Judas) and once in a passage dealing with unbelieving Pharisees or "Jews" (8:44). The word "demon" is used six times, three times in the already mentioned passage in chapter 8, which is one of the strongly "anti-Jewish" chapters of the Gospel. In each instance the demon is mentioned either in citing an allegation that Jesus was possessed by a demon or in a denial of the allegation.

Even though the Fourth Gospel is unlike the Synoptics and its recorded events are difficult of harmonization (perhaps even to impossibility), one fact must be stated beyond question: John has presented his entire work against the background of a flesh-and-blood Jesus. Whether we accept the historicity of the events in the Fourth Gospel or not, it is undeniable that John has presented his story in a historic or quasi-historic form.

From the time that the Word became flesh and dwelt among men on earth until the time that the risen Jesus was handled by them and ate with them He was Jesus the Son of man. The men and women among whom He walked are named. The chief priests Annas and Caiaphas are named, as is the Roman Pilate. Geographical locations are given — so carefully that some have argued that the author must have been a Palestinian. The feasts of Judaism are used to date events. If this Gospel is not "historical" in a sense that would satisfy modern historians, we must at least grant that the author intended it to be "historical" rather than "philosophical." He is not dealing with general principles and philosophical speculations as such; he has set all of his theories and principles in persons and places, in life situations, or what must be called the elements of history.

If John were merely attempting to set forth a spiritual dualism, then we must ask, Why did he choose to make of Jesus a mortal man? Why did he not mention (except perhaps in the most veiled way in 1:14) the Transfiguration? Why did he not record the Virgin Birth or the Ascension? Why did he go into such elaborate detail in his account of the trial and crucifixion and death of Jesus? Why did he include the "physical" characteristics of the resurrection body of Jesus?

The teachings concerning the Spirit in the Fourth Gospel have often been pointed out. God is Spirit (John 4:24). The sign of the Spirit descending on Jesus at the Baptism was the sign for which John the Baptist had waited (1:33). Man must be born anew, born of the Spirit, if he would enter into the Kingdom of God (3:5). The Spirit makes men to live (6:63). Above all, the Spirit is to be sent to take Jesus' place after His departure (chs. 14—16). But the Spirit is clearly presented as a heavenly, personal being. In the Fourth Gospel, Jesus is a being of earth who had been sent from Heaven; the Spirit is a being of Heaven who was to be sent to earth after Jesus returned to Heaven (14:16-17: and especially 16:7).

## The Epistles of John

John wrote the epistles to combat error and to assure those who "believe" that they have "eternal life" (1 John 5:13). The error was the spirit of antichrist which was already in the world (2:12; 4:3).

The spirit of antichrist affects three areas of Christian life: holiness or righteousness (which is man's intrinsic character), love (which is the expression of that holiness, particularly to one's fellow man), and faith (which is the response to God and to the truth revealed in Christ Jesus). The author, in what seems to me to have no clear outline, returns to these dominant notes repeatedly throughout the First Epistle.

Holiness, or righteousness, is expressed also as fellowship (with God and with one another, 1 John 1:6-7), or as a "walk." We walk "in the light" or we walk "in darkness." Our ideal example is Christ (2:6). If we do the works of righteousness we are sons of God (2:29; 3:2); if we sin we are of the devil (3:8). Our way of life, then, declares whether we belong to God or to the devil (3:10).

Love is the identifying characteristic of the Christian in his outward expression — but love and righteousness are so interrelated that John passes easily from one to the other. Love is inspired by God's love (1 John 3:1; 4:10), therefore we ought to love one another (4:11). It is impossible to love God and hate our brother (4:20). In fact, if we do not love, we do not know God (4:8). He who hates his brother is in darkness (2:11).

The source of holiness and love is faith in Jesus Christ, who cleanses from sin (I John 1:7). To know Him is to keep His commandments (2:3-4), and to abide in Him is to walk as He walked (2:6). The spirit of antichrist is, after all, the denial of Jesus: specifically, the denial that Jesus is the Christ, and the denial of the Father-Son relationship of God and Jesus (2:22-23). The Son of God was revealed to destroy the works of the devil (3:8), but if we do not believe this we are not of God; in fact we are of antichrist (4:3). If we believe this we are born of God (5:1) — but if we are born of God we will keep His commandments, we will love Him and His children, we will overcome the world (5:2-5).

The Second Epistle, although very brief, seems to be concerned with the same error (cf. 2 John 4-7). The Third Epistle contains a hint of the same (3 John 11).

Once again the "dualistic" nature of John's writing is obvious. To make his point he avoids shades of gray: everything is either light or darkness, truth or error, spirit of Christ or spirit of antichrist. The error against which John writes seems quite clearly to be a system denying the incarnation of God in Jesus Christ, and probably also including some kind of "liberty" or libertinism which in essence denied sin. John's repeated use of the expression "we know" or "hereby we know" suggests that he is reacting against some type of "Gnosticism" incorporating these other elements.

With this bit of background perhaps we are in a little better position to compare the Johannine literature with the Qumran writings.

## Dualism in John and in Qumran

An excellent study has been prepared by Raymond E. Brown[2] and will be the principal basis for our study. He undertakes an analysis of what he terms "modified dualism," which he defines as follows:

> By dualism we mean the doctrine that the universe is under the dominion of two opposing principles, one good and the other evil. Modified dualism adds the corrective that these principles are not uncreated, but are both dependent on God the Creator.[3]

*Creation.*   We have already considered the dualism of Qumran (pp. 78-81 above). We have compared it briefly with the Zoroastrian concept of Dualism: the latter considers both spirits as coeval, i.e. without a created beginning; Qumran follows the Biblical teaching that God is the Creator of all beings including the spirits of evil (1QS 3:15; 11:11).[4] It is this point

---

[2] R. E. Brown, "The Qumran Scrolls and the Johannine Gospel and Epistles," in *The Scrolls and the New Testament,* pp. 183-207.

[3] *Ibid.,* p. 184.

[4] J. Pryke is certainly correct when he defines Qumran dualism as moral and not metaphysical, and in pointing out that "in Zoroastrianism, the forces of evil are independent of the godhead and coequal with good, while in the Qumran sect, as in Judaism, Yahweh is the Creator of the whole Universe: both good and bad exist only by His divine will" (" 'Spirit' and 'Flesh' in the Qumran Documents and Some New Testament Texts," *Revue de Qumrân* 5,19 [Nov. 1965], p. 351).

that Brown has singled out in his definition of "modified dualism." If there is anything that may properly be called Dualism in the writings of John, it must certainly be placed in this category, for according to John, "All things were made through him, and without him was not anything made that was made" (John 1:3). In Qumran doctrine, however, the spirits of light and darkness were created by God (1QS 3:25). In John there is no such doctrine concerning the spirits of light and darkness. The suggestion has been made that Qumran writings may at this point be reacting against Zoroastrianism, and Miss Mowry suggests that there may be a similar motive in John's Gospel.[5] But, as Brown points out, John does not make much of the point.

*The Two Spirits.* The section on the two spirits in the Qumran Manual of Discipline has been printed in full (1QS 3:13—4:24, pp. 78-81 above). The one is the spirit of truth, the holy spirit, the prince of lights, the angel of His truth; the other is the spirit of unrighteousness, the spirit of impurity, the angel of darkness, elsewhere called Belial and Mastema (or the adversary). In most texts the two spirits seem to be portrayed as beings existing outside and apart from man, but they are also presented as impersonal forces within man (cf. 1QS 4:23-24).

In John the expressions "light" and "truth" occur often. However, the contrasts are not presented as often as we might be led to believe by the published discussions.[6] I find the light-darkness contrast only three times in the Gospel (1:4; 3:19; 12:35) and four times in the First Epistle (1:5; 2:8, 9-11); the truth-error contrast I find only once (1 John 4:6), and the truth-lie contrast three times (John 8:44; 1 John 2:21, 27).

In the Johannine writings, God is light (1 John 1:5) and Christ is light (John 9:5), but there is no "spirit of light." John mentions "the prince of this world" (12:31; 14:30; 16:11), but no "prince (or spirit) of darkness."

On the other hand, there is nothing in Qumran teaching to compare with the teachings about the Spirit found in John:

[5] Lucetta Mowry, "The Dead Sea Scrolls and the Background for the Gospel of John," *Biblical Archaeologist* 17,4 (Dec. 1954), p. 83.

[6] The word "light" occurs 25 times in John, and "truth" 40 times. "Darkness" occurs 12 times (*skotia* 10 times and *skótos* twice); "falsehood" once, and "lie" 3 times. The heaviest concentrations are in John 12 and 1 John 2; with John 1, 3, and 8 also containing significant sections.

the Qumran spirit is not a divine person, there is no indication that the Teacher of Righteousness or anyone else was to
send the Spirit, there is no mention of the Spirit descending
upon the Teacher of Righteousness.

   *The Spirit of Truth.* The term the "Spirit of truth" is
peculiar to John in the New Testament. Three times it refers
to the Holy Spirit and has personal significance (John 14:
16-17; 15:26; 16:13). In First John, however, the term "the
spirit of truth" is used in what appears to be a somewhat lower
sense:

> Beloved, do not believe every spirit, but test the spirits to see
> whether they are of God. . . . Whoever knows God listens to
> us, and he who is not of God does not listen to us. By this we
> know the spirit of truth and the spirit of error. (1 John 4:1-6)

This usage seems remarkably similar to that of Qumran.

   In this same category there are several other expressions
that are found in both the Johannine writings and those of
Qumran. The Qumran texts use the phrase "to do the truth"
(1QS 1:5; 5:3; 8:2), an expression also found in John 3:21.
The Qumran texts speak of "walking in truth" (1QS 4:6, 15);
John uses the expression "walking in truth" in 2 John 4 and in
3 John 3. Qumranians were called "witnesses of truth" (1QS
8:6). This expression is found in the New Testament only in
John, referring both to John the Baptist (John 5:33) and to
Jesus (18:37). In Qumran teaching, men are cleansed through
a holy spirit (1QS 4:20-21). In John the somewhat similar
idea occurs: "Sanctify them through Thy truth" (John 17:
17-19).

   *The Conflict.* In Qumran theology, the two spirits are in
conflict throughout this age (1QS 4:18-19). Only at the end
shall "wickedness depart before righteousness as darkness before light" (1QMyst 6, p. 91 above).

   In John, the conflict has reached its crisis. Christ came into
the world as light, and darkness was not able to overcome it
(John 1:5); darkness is passing away and the true light now
shines (1 John 2:8). Christ has overcome (John 16:33) and
the prince of this world is as though he were already cast out
(12:31).

   We have not included the Revelation (Apocalypse) in the
Johannine literature in this study, but at this point we might
mention an important contrast. In the Qumran War Scroll,

the final battle takes place here on earth; in Revelation, the final battle takes place in Heaven, and only the backlash of that battle is felt upon earth (Rev. 12:7-10).

*Man's Part in the Struggle.* In Qumran theology we are never quite sure whether man is the arena in which the spiritual struggle takes place, or whether he is the hapless pawn played by the spiritual leaders. Thus we are never quite sure whether he is truly free or completely determined in his spiritual lot. Both free will and determinism are expressed side by side in the extended passage to which we have turned on several occasions, in which the doctrine of the two spirits is set forth (1QS 3:13—4:26; note 3:15ff., 4:14 and 24, on the one hand, and 4:2-12 and 23-24 on the other; cf. pp. 78-81 above).

John presents the light as that which reveals the nature of man's deeds (John 3:19-20); but it seems evident that man is responsible for his own choice, and he is urged to walk in the light before the darkness overtakes him with grim finality (12:35). Still the problem is not completely resolved in the Biblical texts, and even in John we find men who seem to be the victims of the spiritual forces of evil. The devil led Judas to betray Jesus (13:2). Those who did not believe in Jesus were children of the devil: if God had been their father, they would have loved Jesus (8:42-47). Of His disciples Jesus said, "You have not chosen me, but I have chosen you" (15:16).

*Sons of Light.* Concerning the question, "What ultimately constitutes a man one of the sons of light?" Brown has provided a very helpful discussion.[7] Refusal to do the will of God makes a man a son of darkness; but the opposite is not exactly true, for there is no discussion of "doing the will of God" except as a member of the Qumran Community. It is this fact, of course, that makes Qumran a "sect"; and we have seen how it applies in the nature of the Sect (pp. 63f.), the ritual of the Sect (pp. 67f.), the secret knowledge of the Sect (pp. 81f.), etc. Of course there are ethical and moral implications, and a member of the Sect was not *ipso facto* brought into salvation: he could indeed be expelled or excommunicated — although even here it seems that sins against the brotherhood were the more reprehensible.

It is equally true that the New Testament, not alone John, restricts doing the will of God to those who are mem-

[7] R. E. Brown, *art. cit.* in *The Scrolls and the New Testament*, p. 192.

bers of the Christian Community. John makes this abundantly clear. "If God were your father, you would love me" (John 8:42). "This is the will of my Father, that every one who sees the Son and believes in him should have eternal life" (6:40). "He who has the Son has life; he who has not the Son has not life" (1 John 5:12).

But even in this exclusive sectarianism expressed in its most severe form we can see the basic difference between Qumran and John. In Qumran, being a "son of light" meant keeping the Law of God as revealed to the Qumran Community. In John's writings, being a son of light or a child of God means believing in Jesus Christ. Personal faith in the incarnate Son of God, personal commitment to Him, personal belief that forgiveness, propitiation for sins, and eternal life come through Him, or in whatever figure he chose to express it — this is the sustained message of John from beginning to end. No such faith in the Teacher of Righteousness, or in any other personage in Qumran, is found.

*Brotherly Love.* In the Qumran texts we find not only the admonition to love good and hate evil (cf. 1QS 1:3-4; CD 3:1), but we find also a passage requiring that the Qumranians hate the sons of darkness (1QS 1:10). Terrible curses are pronounced against them (2:7-8). The Covenanters were to separate themselves from such men (5:10-11), and not to reveal to them the true interpretation of the Law (9:17-18).

Some scholars have tried to soften these passages by pointing out that in two places a less narrow view is presented, one speaking of pursuing a man only with good will (1QS 10:18), and the other referring to a duty to teach those who stray (11:1). Others have pointed out that there is a strong emphasis on love for the members of the Community (1:10; 5:26), while sins against the fellow members are severely punished (7:4-8).

The New Testament at several points stresses love for one's enemies, repaying good for evil, feeding a hungry enemy or giving him to drink, etc. In John's writings, however, as several writers have pointed out, the stress is put on love for the brother in Christ (John 13:34-35; 15:12; 1 John 2:10). The believer is admonished, "Do not love the world," which seems to refer to the people, for the next clause says, "or the things of the world" (1 John 2:15).

Brown's summary is pointed:

> The prevalence of the theme of brotherly love in both the Qumran and the Johannine literature is not a conclusive proof of interrelationship. But it is certainly remarkable that the New Testament writer who shares so many other ideological and terminological peculiarities with Qumran should also stress the particular aspect of charity which is emphasized more at Qumran than anywhere else in Jewish literature before Christ.[8]

## The Last Supper in John and in the Synoptics and the Qumran Calendar

We have seen that the Qumranians followed a different system of calendration from that of official Judaism (pp. 71f. above). Scholars who have attempted to harmonize the Synoptics and the Fourth Gospel have long noted that the date of the Last Supper does not seem to be the same. With the discovery of the Qumran Scrolls, a possible solution to the problem of the Last Supper has been suggested.

In the Synoptics, the Supper is called "the Passover" (Matt. 26:17; Mark 14:12; Luke 22:7). In the Fourth Gospel, the Supper was "before the feast of the Passover" (John 13:1-2), and the trial of Jesus before Pilate was on "the day of Preparation for the Passover" (19:14). The "Preparation" was the name that had come to be used for the day before the Sabbath, which began Friday at sundown (Mark 15:42; Luke 23:54). Matthew also puts the Crucifixion on the Preparation,[9] but he omits the qualifying term "for the Passover."

The Biblical description of the Passover is given in Exodus 12. On the tenth day of the first month (Nisan or Abib) the lamb was to be selected, and on the fourteenth day, the lamb was to be killed "between the evenings" and eaten that night (Exod. 12:3, 6, 8).[10]

---

[8] Ibid., p. 199.

[9] Matthew speaks of the day after the Crucifixion as the day "that followed the day of the Preparation" (Matt. 27:62). It might be added that John puts the anointing in Bethany "six days before the Passover" (John 12:1), whereas Matthew and Mark seem to put it two days before the Passover (Matt. 26:2; Mark 14:1).

[10] According to the regulations in Leviticus the 14th day of the month, "between the evenings," was "the Lord's passover," and the 15th day was "the feast of unleavened bread" (Lev. 23:5-6). Jewish scholars have long debated the meaning of "between the evenings," with two schools of thought: between noon and sunset, or between sunset and dark.

According to the reconstruction of the Qumran calendar, the month of Nisan always began on Wednesday, and the 14th of Nisan therefore always fell on Tuesday.[11] If we assume that Jesus and the Twelve were keeping the "old" solar calendar, while the official calendar at Jerusalem was the "newer" lunar calendar, we can reconstruct the events of Passion Week somewhat as follows:

| Event | Day | Date (solar calendar) | Date (lunar calendar) |
|---|---|---|---|
| Triumphal Entry | Sunday | 12 Nisan | 9 Nisan |
| Arrangements for Last Supper | day of Tuesday | 14 Nisan | 11 Nisan |
| Last Supper | evening of Tuesday | 15 Nisan "Passover" | 12 Nisan |
| Arrest | after midnight | 15 Nisan | 12 Nisan |
| Trial | Wednesday-Thursday | 15-16 Nisan | 12-13 Nisan |
| Crucifixion | Friday | 17 Nisan | 14 Nisan "Preparation" |
| Sabbath | evening of Friday | 18 Nisan | 15 Nisan |
|  |  |  | "Passover" |
| Resurrection | Sunday morning | 19 Nisan | 16 Nisan |

A number of scholars have pointed out that this adjustment of the events of Passion Week makes it possible to expand the trial of Jesus, which traditionally has been compressed into the period between the end of the Last Supper on Thursday night and the Crucifixion on Friday morning.[12] It might also be added that this eliminates the "silent period" of the last week, for harmonists have never been able to account for any record

11 A. Jaubert, "Aperçus sur le calendrier de Qumrân," in *La Secte de Qumrân et les origines du Christianisme*, ed. J. van der Ploeg *et al.* (Bruges: Desclée de Brouwer, 1959), p. 114; *La date de la Cène*, pp. 79-136.

12 Cf. Driver, *The Judaean Scrolls*, pp. 330-335; and Eugen Ruckstuhl, *Chronology of the Last Days of Jesus* (New York: Desclée, 1965), pp. 32-55, among others.

of Tuesday and Wednesday. This is particularly difficult to explain in view of the detailed description of Passion Week found in all four Gospels.

The theory is attractive, the more so since it appears to solve a problem that has long nagged scholars and for which many suggested solutions have failed to find general acceptance.[13] However, there are a number of serious difficulties in the theory.

The calendar of the Book of Jubilees and 1 Enoch, which is generally taken to be that of Qumran, is strictly a 364-day calendar. In periods of three, five, and eight years, there is no evidence of any intercalation to bring the year into synchronism with the true solar year of 365 $\frac{1}{4}$ days.[14] Official Judaism intercalated one month as needed (seven times in nineteen years) to keep the calendar in phase with the seasons. Now since all Jews — whether those who followed a calendar such as that of Jubilees, 1 Enoch, and Qumran, or the priests of Jerusalem — were obligated to observe the annual feasts, and since these feasts are all tied to the agricultural year, we may assume that some method of intercalation was practiced that would achieve this result.[15] At the same time, we must assume that the Sabbath was rigidly observed on a seven-day interval. Any method of intercalation, such as adding an extra day or two every year, that did not observe the seven-day Sabbath, we can

---

[13] Among the numerous theories we might point out that one, at least, has gained some support from the theory of the Qumran calendar. I refer to the suggestion found in H. L. Strack and P. Billerbeck, *Kommentar zum Neuen Testament aus Talmud und Midrasch*, 2te. Band (München: Beck, 1924), pp. 847-853. Billerbeck, following J. Lichtenstein, proposed that the Boethusians were following a different calendar which was one day off that of the official Jerusalem priesthood. However, he lacked historical support for the theory. G. R. Driver has connected the Boethusians with the Qumranians in his elaborate theory (*Judaean Scrolls*, pp. 228-240).

[14] Thus "in eight years there are 2,912 days" (1 Enoch 74:13).

[15] The theory, for example, that 35 days were intercalated every 28 years, faces a severe problem at this point, and the theory of an intercalated "year" of 49 days (the Jubilee year) after 49 years is even more difficult to accept. These and other theories are given briefly in R. T. Beckwith, "The Modern Attempt to Reconcile the Qumran Calendar with the True Solar Year," *Revue de Qumrân* 7,27 (Dec. 1970), pp. 379-387. His own theory, that there was no intercalation at all, but that the year (like the Mohammedan calendar) was allowed to move in planetary manner so that it could be as much as six months off the annual seasons (pp. 391-396), I find impossible to accept.

be certain would not have been acceptable. Therefore, to say that the Qumran calendar always commenced on "Wednesday" is to say that intercalation, if used, must have been in seven-day units or multiples.

Now we can assume as beyond doubt that Jesus and the Twelve observed the same Sabbath as the officials, for when He was accused of breaking the Sabbath, He never used the defense that His critics were mistaken as to the day.[15a] Rather, He set Himself as "Lord of the Sabbath" (Mark 2:28).

We are therefore forced to assume that some method of calendration had just brought the Qumran calendar into phase, if not with the solar year, at least with the official Jewish calendar,[16] so that the two Passovers fell within the same week. This in itself is not fatal to Mlle. Jaubert's theory, but when we add an additional fact, namely that the feasts observed by Jesus and the Twelve, as recorded in the Gospels, apparently coincided with the feasts of official Judaism during the entire period of His ministry, this problem becomes acute.[17]

If we follow Beckwith's theory that the Qumran calendar had no intercalation, and that it was probably about eight months out of phase with the solar calendar,[18] then, of course, the suggestion that the Qumran calendar was used by the Synoptists is completely impossible.

I would raise another, and perhaps more serious problem inherent in the theory of Mlle. Jaubert. According to this theory, as we have seen, the Synoptics use the Qumran calendar, while the Fourth Gospel uses the calendar of official Judaism. Now, it is John who is supposed to have the strongest ties with Qumran. Therefore we should have expected to find the Qumran calendar in John. The Synoptists, on the other hand, would be expected to use the official calendar. Luke, the Gentile, writing to some dignitary named Theophilus, or Mark, traditionally writing to an audience in Rome, would hardly have used the calendar of an obscure sect in

15a Johannes Lehmann, *Rabbi J.* (pp. 79ff.), fails to take this into account.

16 The lunar calendar, having 354 days, is eleven days out of phase with the solar calendar of 365 days.

17 Milik raised this objection, without tying it to the problem of intercalation; cf. *Ten Years of Discovery in the Wilderness of Judaea*, p. 112.

18 Beckwith, *art. cit.*, p. 396.

Palestine. And what would Matthew, the former Roman tax-collector, be doing with the Qumran calendar?[19]

## Summary

The Johannine writings show several points of similarity with the Qumran writings, especially in the so-called dualistic ideas. The similarity, however, seems to be more in the polarity of ideas than in any truly dualistic concepts. The Dualism of Qumran, as we have seen previously, is substantially modified; and the system in the Johannine writings is essentially monistic. The most marked parallel is the use of the light-darkness figures of speech.

The Qumran writings may lend some support to the traditional theory of authorship and date of the Fourth Gospel. The ideas of the Johannine writings, as those in certain Pauline writings, can now be seen in a Jewish framework with origins or early development in Palestine. It is not necessary to look to the Hellenistic or western world to find the thought milieu for these writings. Likewise, it is not necessary to push the writing of the Johannine scriptures into the second century. On the other hand, I find no support in Qumran studies for the theory that John is perhaps the earliest of the Gospels; at the same time I feel that the difference in presentation between the Synoptics and the Qumran writings indicates that the Synoptic sources were considerably earlier than the Fourth Gospel.

The theory that the Qumran calendar may explain the difference between the Synoptics and John with reference to the date of the Passover or Last Supper is not satisfactory in its present form.

---

19 It may be replied that the Synoptic account goes back to an earlier tradition, and hence does not involve the authors. On this same argument, we should be forced to include the Fourth Gospel, since there are several parallels, both in arrangement of events and in the words quoted, between John and the Synoptics just at this point. Why would John, rather than the Synoptists, have altered the tradition to avoid the Qumran details?

CHAPTER SIXTEEN

# THE LIFE OF JESUS CHRIST
# AND THE QUMRAN WRITINGS

"The Galilean Master, as He is presented to us in the writings of the New Testament, appears in many respects as an astonishing reincarnation of the Master of Justice [or Teacher of Righteousness]" — thus wrote Dupont-Sommer.[1] If we did not know who made this statement, we might be inclined to believe that he had never read the New Testament!

It is our purpose to compare the details of the life, the teachings, and the redemptive work of Jesus Christ, as set forth in the New Testament, with what we have learned about the Teacher of Righteousness as set forth in the Qumran material. There is nothing else that can properly be compared. It is improper methodology to compare the life of the Teacher of Righteousness as reconstructed from the Qumran documents plus the interpretation that has been read into them from the New Testament account of Jesus, on the one hand, with the life of Jesus as found in the New Testament, on the other hand. It is equally improper to read into the Qumran account certain details from the life of Jesus which have been rejected by certain critics as later accretions to the Christian tradition, and then suppose that these are historical facts in the life of the Teacher of Righteousness, but nonhistorical myths in the life of Jesus. Yet it is by just such methodology that Jesus has been presented as a pale reflection of the Teacher of Righteousness.

[1] Dupont-Sommer, *The Dead Sea Scrolls*, p. 99.

The New Testament is readily available to all who wish to study for themselves the details recorded there concerning the Galilean Teacher. I shall include here certain points from the New Testament record, not to insist that they are historically factual, but simply to compare what is found in the two sets of writings, the New Testament and Qumran. I shall add scriptural references, not to indicate final authority (as may sometimes seem to be the intention), but to assist those who wish to examine the reference in the light of the context. So far as the material is available, I shall draw from two or more independent traditions or sources, but I shall not cite two Synoptic references that are clearly parallel accounts.

## The Birth of Jesus

The details of Jesus' birth are recorded in Matthew and Luke. His parents were Joseph and Mary (Matt. 1:18; Luke 1:27).[2] The genealogy of Jesus is given in two forms not completely in agreement, but nevertheless agreeing in the significant fact that Jesus was of the house or family of David (Matt. 1:1-16; Luke 3:23-29). Joseph and Mary came from the village of Nazareth in Galilee (Luke 1:26).[3] The date of Jesus' birth can be established within a few years. It was in the days of Herod the Great, king of Judea, not more than two years before the "slaughter of the innocents" and clearly not many years before the death of Herod (Matt. 2:1, 16, 19). On the basis of historical and astronomical data,[4] the death of Herod can be dated in late March or early April, 4 B.C.; hence the birth of Jesus occurred between 7 (or at the earliest 8) and 5 B.C. Jesus was born in Bethlehem of Judea, a small village not far south of Jerusalem. This was occasioned by an imperatorial decree requiring families to register in their ancestral homes (Luke 2:1-7; Matt. 2:1-8).

No such details are known of the Teacher of Righteousness. We do not know his name, his parents' names, his birthplace, or the date of his birth.

2 These accounts are, according to scientific textual criticism, from independent sources, which means we have an early twofold tradition.

3 Matthew records simply that Joseph and Mary went to live in Nazareth after the birth of Jesus (Matt. 2:23).

4 The time is established by an eclipse of the moon and by the Passover. Cf. Josephus *Antiquities* 17.6.4 §167; 17.9.3 §213.

There are in the New Testament two independent accounts of the conception of Jesus, or what has come to be called the "Virgin Birth." According to Matthew's account — which is told from Joseph's side of the story — Mary was found to be pregnant before Joseph and Mary had any marital union (Matt. 1:18). An angelic visitor explained to Joseph that the child was conceived by the Holy Spirit (Matt. 1:20). Luke reports Mary's side of the story: an angelic visitor explained that the child was to be conceived by the Holy Spirit and that He was to be called the Son of God and to occupy the throne of David (Luke 1:31-35). Mary's protest included the simple statement that she had not had relations with any man (Luke 1:34).

Whether we wish to accept these records as factual or not, they can hardly be described as "the virgin birth myth." If there had been a common virgin-birth myth, or myth of the Mother of the Messiah, we should expect to find it more formalized and more extensively used in the New Testament. Scholars have often pointed out, sometimes with the purpose of discrediting the Matthean and Lucan stories, that the Virgin Birth is not known in the rest of the New Testament. It was not found in the sources used by Mark or in the source known as "Q." John and Paul, both of whom might be expected to use such a "myth" to support their "high Christology," make no reference to it.[5] Still the fact remains: there were two independent lines of tradition, one known to Matthew and the other to Luke.

Dupont-Sommer suggests that the myth concerning the Mother of the Messiah "developed, no doubt, from Isa. 7:14, and also from Mic. 5:2; something of it reappears in Rev. 12."[6] The passage in Micah (5:3 in our English Bible) is a vague reference to a woman in travail, following the well-known prophecy about Bethlehem. There is no allusion whatever to a virgin birth. Likewise in Revelation 12 there is nothing at all concerning a virgin birth; the details do perhaps suggest that

[5] Some believe that John refers to the Virgin Birth in John 1:14 and Paul in Galatians 4:4. Both references are so veiled, if they are indeed references to the Virgin Birth, that they would lend little or no support to the Christology of Paul or John. In fact, if the Virgin Birth were not known from Matthew and Luke, it could not be derived from John or Galatians or any other source.

[6] Dupont-Sommer, *The Essene Writings from Qumran*, p. 208 n. 1.

the woman was the mother of the Messiah. As for Isaiah 7:14, it is generally admitted that prior to its use in the New Testament, this passage was never considered to be messianic. No contemporary Jewish writing makes use of it as a messianic prophecy, and the verse taken in its context bears no suggestion of a messianic prophecy.[7]

But regardless of the interpretation we place on these passages, it must be admitted that in the New Testament we have simple, clearly stated accounts of experiences purported to have happened to Mary and Joseph. This is certainly much different in every way from the very obscure passage in the Qumran Hymns (1QH 3:7-18, pp. 128ff. above) which has been offered in support of a supposed Qumran virgin-birth account. In this document there is no clear statement or even any implication of a virgin birth; the messianic implication is inferred from the use of the term "Marvelous Counselor," and there is nothing to connect it with the Teacher of Righteousness.

## The Boyhood of Jesus

There are few details of the boyhood of Jesus given in the New Testament. He was brought up in Nazareth (Luke 4:16). His brothers are named, and there is reference to His sisters (Mark 6:3). He was a normal Jewish boy, attending synagogue (Luke 4:16), visiting Jerusalem for Passover (2:41-42), and displaying keen interest in religious matters (2:46-47). His observations of details of life in the home and of nature outside are scattered throughout His teachings.[8] He worked at the same trade as did Joseph — traditionally carpentry, but possibly stone-masonry (Mark 6:3).[9] There is nothing in the Gospel records to suggest that Jesus' boyhood was in any way unusual, either marvelous or offensive to His fellow townspeople, such as the apocryphal gospels portray Him.

We know nothing of the boyhood of the Teacher of Right-

7 Cf. B. S. Easton, "Virgin," in *International Standard Bible Encyclopaedia* (Grand Rapids: Eerdmans, 1929), vol. 5, p. 3051, "But in NT times the Jews never interpreted the verse as a prediction of a virgin birth...."

8 For illustrations, see my *Great Personalities of the New Testament*, ch. 4, "Jesus the Son of Man."

9 The Greek word *tektōn* means one who creates or fashions something. It can mean any kind of craftsman and can even mean author or physician, but it seems to have been used by classical writers specifically of a carpenter or joiner as over against a smith or a mason.

eousness. So far as the Qumran records are concerned, or any
other documents that we have, we might just as well say that
the "Teacher of Righteousness" was like Melchizedek, "without father, without mother, without genealogy."

## The Manhood of Jesus

Of the adult manhood of Jesus up to the time of His ministry we know next to nothing. He continued to live and work
in Nazareth (Matt. 21:11), and subsequently came to be known
as "Jesus of Nazareth" (John 19:19; Acts 2:22, etc.). There is
no indication that He left Nazareth to live at Qumran or in
any other community; and when John the Baptist was conduct-
ing his ministry at the Jordan, Jesus went, we are told, from
Nazareth to be baptized by John (Mark 1:9).

Whether Jesus was at any time a member of the Essene sect
is a debatable point, with no convincing evidence to support or
refute the theory. Many Christians have been willing to accept
such a view, both before and since the discovery of the Scrolls.
Others have felt that the differences between Jesus' life and
teachings on the one hand and that of the Essenes on the other
make such a theory untenable.[10]

## The Ministry of Jesus

When He was about thirty years of age Jesus began His
ministry[11] (Luke 3:23). This was, if Luke intended to apply his
date-formula to Jesus as well as to John, in the fifteenth year of
Tiberius Caesar, which would be A.D. 27 or 28.[12] The ministry of
Jesus lasted over a year, to judge from the sequence of seasons
represented in the Synoptics, and may have lasted two and a
quarter or even three and a quarter years.[13] In view of the

[10] The fullest treatment prior to the Qumran discoveries was by J. B.
Lightfoot, St. Paul's Epistles to the Colossians and to Philemon (London:
Macmillan, 1875), pp. 82-95, 114-179.

[11] Only bare details for historical and chronological purposes are treated
here. We shall devote the succeeding chapters to the subject in detail.

[12] This would seem to put the birth of Jesus in 3 or 2 B.C., which is
after the death of Herod and inconsistent with Luke's own chronology
(Luke 1:5). There is no reason, however, to force mathematical exactitude
into Luke's statement that "Jesus began to be about thirty."

[13] The problem arises from the feasts mentioned by John: does he
refer to three Passovers or to four? Since we cannot determine whether
the "feast" in John 5:1 was a Passover, we cannot answer this question.

time it would take to develop interest, select disciples, and stir up hostility leading finally to the death sentence, a ministry of at least two and a quarter years is reasonable.

Other chronological data in the Gospels are consistent with what has been set down: the length of time Herod was rebuilding the Temple (John 2:20; Josephus *Antiquities* 15.11.1 §380); the high priesthood of Caiaphas (Matt. 26:3, 57; John 11:49; Josephus *Antiquities* 18.2.2 §95); the tetrarchy of Herod Antipas (Luke 23:7; Josephus *Antiquities* 18.5.1, 3 §§109-112); and the procuratorship of Pilate (Luke 3:1; Josephus *Antiquities* 18.2.2 §35, 3.1-2 §§55-62).

Nothing is known of the ministry of the Teacher of Righteousness beyond the fact that he was a teacher of righteousness, plus indefinite references that imply that he was rebuked, his teaching was rejected, and he was persecuted by an enemy or enemies but revered as the spiritual leader of the Community. There are no chronological details, and there are few if any names that can be clearly correlated with persons known in other historical sources.

## The Death of Jesus

Because of the popular reaction to Jesus, the religious leaders decided to put Him to death, and obtained the decision of the Roman Procurator, Pontius Pilate, to crucify Jesus (Mark 15:1; John 18:29; Acts 3:13, etc.). Pilate was the Roman Procurator in Syria (Palestine), according to Josephus, from A.D. 26 to 36.[14] Jesus was crucified between two thieves on a hill just outside the city of Jerusalem, the death being effected by Roman officials and witnessed by Romans and Jews (Mark 15:25-39; John 19:13-34).

The so-called crucifixion of the Teacher of Righteousness can be found in the Qumran writings only with the aid of a gifted imagination (cf. pp. 122-125 above).

## The Resurrection of Jesus

One other set of data about Jesus is included in the Gospels as historical material: the Gospel writers present the resurrec-

[14] Josephus *Antiquities* 18.2.2 §35, 4.2 §89. Tacitus (*Annals* 15.44.2) refers to the execution of Christ in the reign of Tiberius by the Procurator of Judea, Pontius Pilate.

tion of Jesus in the same way as they present the other events of His life.

His body was taken from the cross by friends, prepared for burial, and buried in a cave-tomb. The friends are named: Joseph of Arimathea and Nicodemus. It is stated that Joseph obtained permission from Pilate. The tomb is identified as belonging to Joseph. It is recorded that women witnessed the burial.[15] One tradition reports that a guard was obtained from Pilate to keep the disciples from stealing the body (Matt. 27:62-66).

On the third day, early in the morning following the Sabbath, women visited the tomb to care for the body that had been hastily buried on the evening before the Sabbath, and they returned with the report that they found the tomb empty and that an angel or angels had told them that Jesus was risen.[16] They also reported that Jesus had appeared to them (Matt. 28:9-10; John 20:11-18); and somewhere in the confusion and excitement of the morning are to be placed the reports that Peter and John also visited the tomb and found it empty (Luke 24:12; John 20:3-10), and that the guards at the tomb likewise reported that it was empty (Matt. 28:11-15).

Later in the day two disciples reported that Jesus had joined them while they were walking to their home in Emmaus (Luke 24:13-33). The excited disciples, who with the exception of Thomas had meanwhile regathered in Jerusalem, heard the reports, including one that Jesus had appeared to Peter (Luke 24:33-34; cf. 1 Cor. 15:5). At this moment Jesus appeared in their midst (Luke 24:36-44; John 20:19-23).

Other appearances are recorded, including one to the disciples when Thomas was present (John 20:24-29), at least one to the disciples in Galilee (Matt. 28:16-18), and possibly another Galilean appearance (John 21:1-14). Paul reports in a carefully worded argument concerning the historicity of the resurrection of Jesus (1 Cor. 15:1-20) that Jesus also appeared to five hundred followers on one occasion (15:6), to James (15:7), and of course—for this was Paul's only claim to apostleship (1 Cor. 9:1) — to Paul himself (15:8).

Forty days later the resurrection appearances of Jesus ceased as suddenly as they had begun. Jesus led His disciples to

15 Mark 15:42-47; John 19:38-42.
16 Mark 16:1-9; John 20:1.

Bethany, east of the Mount of Olives, near Jerusalem, and after blessing them was taken up to Heaven in their sight (Luke 24:50-51; Acts 1:4-9).[17]

Nothing whatever like this is found of the Teacher of Righteousness. The supposition that he rose from the dead is based on a curious distortion of a text by which he is made to "appear" in the Temple (1QpHab 11:4-8, see pp. 125f. above), and by taking passages that refer to the Teacher in past time and a passage that refers to a teacher in the future and concluding therefrom that there must have been a doctrine of resurrection and second coming. (See pp. 125-128 above.)

Little wonder that Allegro had to admit that "Jesus is much more of a flesh-and-blood character than the Qumran teacher could ever be."[18] To suggest that Jesus is only a reincarnation of the Teacher of Righteousness, in the light of the vast amount of material we have on Jesus as compared with the almost complete absence of anything even purporting to be historical in the Qumran writings, could be branded as ridiculous. This would mean that either Jesus or the authors of the Gospel traditions had access to detailed accounts of the Teacher of Righteousness which are not known to us, that either Jesus or the tradition-maker reworked this material to form the life of Christ as we now know it, and then destroyed all traces of the material. Such a method of constructing history must be repudiated by every serious scholar.

History can only be written from existing documents. To attempt it on any other basis can result only in fantasy.

---

[17] While specific reference to the Ascension is omitted from many ancient MSS of Luke, its presence in p75 BAC, among others, in my opinion indicates its presence in the original Gospel.

[18] Allegro, *The Dead Sea Scrolls*, p. 159.

## CHAPTER SEVENTEEN

# THE TEACHINGS OF JESUS CHRIST AND THE QUMRAN WRITINGS

If, because of the sketchy nature of details of the life of Jesus, scholars despair of writing His biography, it certainly cannot be said that we are faced with a similar problem regarding His teachings. The Gospel writers, who it would seem only sought to give such historical details as were necessary to authenticate the outlines of His life, concentrated on those items which set forth His redemptive ministry, namely His teachings and His sacrificial death. In this chapter we shall consider the teachings of Jesus, in order that we may have a basis for comparison with the teachings found in the Dead Sea Scrolls.

## The Selection and Training of Disciples

An essential element of the teaching of Jesus was the selection and training of disciples. In fact, this was so much an integral part of His ministry that we fail to understand what Jesus was doing if we fail to take it into account. It is obvious that Jesus was not attempting to educate or indoctrinate the entire nation, or even an entire city. He was training and preparing a chosen few to continue His work after His removal from their midst. This is implicit in the place given to the disciples in the New Testament, both in the Gospels and in Acts, and it is explicitly stated there also.

For example, Matthew presents the Sermon on the Mount in a setting designed for the disciples (Matt. 5:1-2). Likewise in the chapter of parables (Matt. 13) he distinguishes between the general teachings given to the multitudes (13:2) and the explanation given to the disciples (13:36). That this is not merely an editorial technique of Matthew is clear from Mark's inclusion of the same (cf. Mark 4:10; 8:1-21). Luke also includes teachings specifically designated for the disciples (Luke 16:1; 17:1), and John devotes a large portion of his Gospel to private teachings (John 13:1—18:1).

In fact, Mark includes a statement defining the purpose of the Twelve in these words: "And he appointed twelve, to be with him, and to be sent out to preach" (Mark 3:14). Possibly the same purpose lay behind Peter's suggestion for the selection of a successor to Judas Iscariot: "So one of these men who have accompanied us during all the time that the Lord Jesus went in and out among us, beginning from the baptism of John until the day when he was taken up from us — one of these men must become with us a witness to his resurrection (Acts 1:21-22).

*The Church.* Whether Jesus intended to found a "church," specifically whether He planned a church such as that which has developed historically, may be a debatable point. The sole reference we have in the Gospels is found in the words to Peter, "You are Peter, and on this rock I will build my church; and the gates of Hades will not prevail against it" (Matt. 16:18, RSV margin).[1] The figure does not seem to be that of a cloistered ecclesiasticism but rather of a determined effort to storm the very gates of Hell. The dominant characteristic of the band of disciples was to be sacrificial love: "By this will all men know that you are my disciples, if you have love for one another" (John 13:35). In the early Church the apostles sought to be free from administrative responsibilities in order to preach the word (Acts 6:2). In fact we might best characterize the Church as a body of "witnesses" seeking only to present the truth as they knew it, hoping thereby to bring others to the same truth (4:20; cf. 1:8).

*Community of Wealth.* Whether Jesus established a voluntary community of wealth in the apostolic band is not known. He emphasized the danger of riches (Mark 10:23-25), and told at least one rich man to sell what he had and give to the poor (Matt. 19:21). On the other hand, Jesus built several of His

---

[1] The church is also mentioned in Matt. 18:17, but in such an incidental way that it may simply mean "congregation" or "assembly."

parables around the principle of private ownership (cf. Matt. 20:1-15; 25:14-30; cf. Luke 19:12-26), never indicating that there was anything inherently wrong about such individualism. Certainly His own example would serve to underscore the principle of unselfish, sacrificial love — which is thoroughly consonant with His teachings, and also consonant with private ownership when dominated by the spirit of love.

*Admission.* There is no indication in the Gospels that men seeking to enter the circle of discipleship were put through any process of examination or indoctrination, or that any were "excommunicated" for violation of rules. They came voluntarily, and they left voluntarily if they were dissatisfied with Jesus' teaching or program (cf. John 1:37-46; 6:66-68). On the other hand, Jesus personally chose the Twelve (Mark 3:13-14; John 6:70; 15:16) after they had been with Him for some time as His disciples.[2] But even Judas Iscariot, who was one of the Twelve, made his decision voluntarily and was not dropped by disciplinary action (cf. John 13:21-30; Matt. 26:21-25).

*Rank or Precedence.* There is no indication of rank or precedence among the disciples or the apostles.[3] On the contrary, Jesus made it clear that such ideas belonged to the world, but were entirely out of place among His followers (Matt. 20:20-28, especially 26). When they disputed about who should be greatest in the Kingdom, Jesus said, "If any one would be first, he must be last of all and servant of all" (Mark 9:33-35).

*The "Inner Circle."* It is common to speak of Peter, James, and John as the "Inner Circle," and to look upon them as the privileged few among the disciples. A further study of the occasions on which these three were singled out, however, will indicate that it was for the purpose of special instruction — as, for example, on the Mount of Transfiguration (Luke 9:28-35) or in the Garden of Gethsemane (Matt. 26:36-46). That no special privilege belonged to James and John is clearly indi-

---

[2] It is necessary to keep in mind the distinction between "disciples" and "apostles." See my *Great Personalities of the New Testament*, pp. 50-56.

[3] The reference to sitting "by ranks, by hundreds and by fifties," in connection with the feeding of the 5,000 (Mark 6:40), has been mentioned in at least one publication on the Dead Sea Scrolls. But only by a distorted exegesis could anyone find anything like Qumran rank in this statement. After all, the Qumranians held no patent on the words "rank," "hundreds," or "fifties"!

cated by the fact that Jesus refused to promise them the places of honor they requested in His Kingdom (Mark 10:35-40). Similarly, Jesus' rebuke of Peter following the great confession at Caesarea-Philippi (Matt. 16:23) and at the time of the foot-washing (John 13:6-9), and, above all, Jesus' searching examination of Peter's boasted fidelity and the subsequent denials (Luke 22:31-34; cf. Matt. 26:33-35) show that Peter had no special privilege. On no occasion did these three exhibit any kind of authority over the other apostles or over the larger group of disciples.

*Comparison with Qumran.* In the Qumran fellowship there is no indication of anything like the twofold position of disciple-apostle. The council of twelve (1QS 8:1) is not described as having been selected by action of the Teacher of Righteousness, nor is there any indication that they were the recipients of special instruction. Theirs was an administrative function (8:3), and it would be in keeping with the provisions set forth in general in the Scrolls if they advanced to their position through merit and promotion (8:1-2; 5:24). The "three" in the Qumran Community are most probably to be regarded as three priests in addition to the twelve laymen, and therefore they form no true parallel to the "Inner Circle" of Peter, James, and John. Above all, there is clearly absent from the Dead Sea Scrolls any indication of close fellowship with the Teacher of Righteousness like that which obtained between Jesus and His disciples.

## The Teachings of Jesus

To attempt to summarize the teachings of Jesus in a few paragraphs is next to impossible. One could, if he wished to demonstrate parallels with Qumran teachings, select from the teachings of Jesus that which is most similar. Contrariwise, if he wished to show dissimilarity, it would be possible to select material from the Gospels to accomplish this purpose. We have already made it clear that we repudiate such methodology. We shall therefore attempt a broad summary, with the warning that there will of necessity be serious gaps and more serious points at which differences of interpretation could yield different conclusions.

*The Kingdom of God.* The subject of Jesus' teaching can be stated, I think, in a word: the Kingdom of God. He came to proclaim the Kingdom (Mark 1:15). This Kingdom is "near" or "at hand" — it is "in your midst" or possibly "within you" (Luke 17:21) — and yet it is not "of this world," and Jesus repudiated the use of force by His Kingdom (John 18:36). The Kingdom "is not coming with signs to be observed" (Luke 17:20); in fact, its development is a mystery like the growth of a seed (Mark 4:26-32) or the leavening of dough (Matt. 13:33). Yet there is another sense in which men will see the Son of Man coming in His Kingdom (16:28), and at the end of the age there will be a process of judgment and separation integral with the establishment of the Kingdom (Matt. 13:47-49; cf. 25:31-46).

In other words, there are two aspects or phases of the Kingdom: an immediate, spiritual Kingdom in this present age, which develops or grows but which does not completely triumph; and an ultimate, final Kingdom which is universal only after a process of judgment. This dual nature of the Kingdom has baffled many scholars, and there have been various attempts to explain it or simplify it. The fact remains that the New Testament contains the complex or two-phase representation of the Kingdom of God, both in the teachings of Jesus and in the preaching of the early Church.

The Qumran materials contain no reference to the "Kingdom of God." The Community, as we have seen, resembles somewhat the Kingdom in its present aspect,[4] and various ideas and expressions can readily be located in the Qumran texts to demonstrate the similarity. The distinction between the "Kingdom" and the "world," for example, is essentially similar to the distinction between "light" and "darkness."

Likewise the final phase of the Kingdom finds a parallel in the Qumran materials, particularly in the War Scroll. This final conflict in Qumran theology is admittedly difficult to interpret — as indeed it is in the New Testament! — and scholars are not in agreement. Will it be a war, or is it a spiritual conflict? As in the case of the eschatological Kingdom of Jesus' teachings, we can only analyze what the texts contain and leave

[4] It has been pointed out that the Qumran belief in an existing union between the Community and Heaven "worked against a futurist eschatology and in favour of an eschatology of the present"; see Franz Mussner, "Contributions Made by Qumran to the Understanding of the Epistle to the Ephesians," in *Paul and Qumran*, pp. 165f. Cf. J. Maier, *Die Texte vom Toten Meer, II. Anmerkungen* (München: Reinhardt, 1960), pp. 77-79.

the interpretation to others. Jesus portrays the final conflict as one conducted by angels; His disciples take no part in the action. Moreover, it is a process of judgment, not of war.[5] In the Qumran scroll, the members of the Community take part, as well as the angels (1QM 12:6-9), and particularly Michael (1QM 17:6). Both the teachings of Jesus and the Qumran materials are rooted in the Old Testament, and there is no need to try to explain the similarities at this point by any theory of dependence.

*The Fatherhood of God.* In the teachings of Jesus, the Kingdom is "the Kingdom of God." God is "Father," "Heavenly Father," or "our Father who art in Heaven." The term is not used in a comparable way in the Old Testament, although God is called Father (Deut. 32:6; Isa. 63:16), Israel is called His son (cf. Exod. 4:22; Hos. 11:1, etc.), and God declares that He will be the father of David's son (2 Sam. 7:14).

God is also represented as Father in rabbinical literature, and in the Jewish prayer book.[6] The concept also occurs in Sirach (Ecclesiasticus), but these portions are not listed among the Qumran discoveries and they were not in the Cairo Genizah fragments of Sirach.[7]

The word "father" does not occur many times in the Qumran writings. The Examiner was to have pity on the Many as a father toward his children (CD 13:9). The Psalmist was made a father to the sons of grace (1QH 7:20), and in one Hymn God is called "a father to all the sons of Thy truth" (1QH 9:35). There is no other reference I can find that contains the same or a similar concept. Coppens says, "We seek in vain a text recalling the one where St. Paul asserts the presence of the Spirit in the heart of the believers, inviting and urging them to speak to God as their Father with a note of the intimacy of family relations."[8] The difference between Jesus and Qumran at this point seems to be significant.

[5] In the Book of Revelation, on the other hand, the picture is one of war (cf. Rev. 19:11-21).

[6] Cf. *Tanná debî 'Eliyáhú* 10. The expressions, "Our Father, our King," and "merciful Father," occur often. The prayer of the Chief Rabbinate for Israel begins with the words, "Our Father who art in Heaven."

[7] Sir. 23:1, "O Lord, Father and Ruler of my life"; 23:4, "O Lord, Father and God of my life." Cf. Burrows, *More Light on the Dead Sea Scrolls*, p. 92.

[8] J. Coppens, "Les Documents du Désert de Juda et les Origines du Christianisme," *Cahiers du Libre Examen* (1953), p. 32. Not having access to this, I am indebted to R. E. Brown, *art. cit.* in *The Scrolls and the New Testament*, p. 288 n. 72, for this quotation.

*The Sonship of Jesus.* Jesus referred to Himself as "son," usually in the expression "son of man." The exact meaning and significance of this term is not clear. In the apocalyptic literature of the period, "Son of Man" was a title used of the one who was to come from Heaven to rule over this world. In the common Aramaic of a slightly later period, and therefore possibly also at the time of Jesus, "son of man" usually meant merely "human being." In some passages it seems that Jesus is using the expression simply as the equivalent of "I" or "myself" (cf. Mark 2:10; John 1:51). In other passages He clearly intends an apocalyptic or eschatological significance (cf. Matt. 16:28). At still other times His use of the term "son" (e.g. Luke 10:22; John 5:19-31) almost certainly implies a special relationship to the Father, as does His use of the expression "My Father" (cf. Matt. 7:21; 10:32f.).

According to the Gospel of John, Jesus stirred up the wrath of the religious leaders by His use of expressions such as these (cf. John 5:18; 10:31-36). Something of the same nature must have been behind the question of the High Priest, "Tell us if you are the Christ, the Son of God" (Matt. 26:63; cf. Luke 22:70), and the mocking taunt while Jesus hung on the cross (Matt. 27:40). This multiple tradition cannot be easily dismissed by textual criticism.

Nothing remotely resembling such teaching or such claims is found in the Qumran literature.

*The Kingdom of Satan.* This Kingdom of God, also called (in Matthew) the "Kingdom of Heaven," is opposed by another kingdom: the Kingdom of Satan (Matt. 12:26), which is perhaps the same as the kingdom "of this world" (John 18:36).

The "evil one" — doubtless Satan — snatches away the seed (the word of the Kingdom) which is sown in the heart (Matt. 13:19). He sows weeds in the field of good seed, which is God's Kingdom (13:24-25, explained in vv. 37-39). This same devil or Satan attempted to divert Jesus from His ministry at the very beginning (4:1-11), was responsible for the downfall of Judas Iscariot (Luke 22:3; John 13:27), and sought to destroy Simon Peter as well (Luke 22:31). In the "Lord's Prayer" (the *Pater Noster*) Jesus taught His disciples to say, "Deliver us from the evil one" (Matt. 6:13). The word "devil" is derived from the Greek and means a "slanderer." The word "Satan" in Hebrew and Aramaic has the meaning "adversary." It is obvious that these names were used because they described the activity of the personage. The devil, according to one statement of Jesus, has a body of "angels" to assist him in his diabolical work (25:41). The name "Beelzebub" or "Beelzebul" is sometimes used of Satan, and he is described as "the prince of the devils" (12:24). According to the Fourth Gospel, Jesus said to those who opposed Him, "You are of your father the devil," and went on to brand the devil as a murderer and a liar (John 8:44).

In many ways this body of teaching is strikingly similar to Qumran doctrine. The "angel of darkness" or spirit of "unrighteousness" opposes the "prince of lights" or spirit of truth (1QS 3:18-21). The angel of darkness controls the "sons of righteousness" (3:21) and is responsible for leading astray the sons of righteousness and causing the sons of light to stumble (3:22, 24). In the Damascus Document the "prince of lights" is opposed by "Belial" (CD 5:18), and in the War Scroll Belial is described as the "angel of hostility" (1QM 13:10-11). We have found close parallels in the teachings of Paul, but similar terms are not found in the teachings of Jesus.

There is one significant difference that should be noted. In the teachings of Jesus, Satan is already judged. "The ruler of this world is coming. He has no power over me" (John 14:30). "The ruler of this world is judged" (16:11). "I saw Satan fall like lightning from heaven. Behold, I have given you authority . . . over all the power of the enemy" (Luke 10:18-19).

*The Human Implication.* It would be a mistake, however, to think that Jesus stressed the conflict of two kingdoms in a way that did not involve men. Far more emphasis is devoted to the personal implications of the coming of the Kingdom than to the nature of Satan, etc. Entrance into the Kingdom is set forth in the talk with Nicodemus (John 3:1-12). The difficulty of entering the Kingdom when dominated by the importance of wealth is pointed out (Matt. 19:23-26). The ethic of the Kingdom is set forth in great detail in the "Sermon on the Mount" (chs. 5—7). The mysterious development of the Kingdom is described in the parables of the Kingdom (ch. 13). The throbbing heartbeat of God the Father over the lost sinner and the joy over one who repents are set forth in the parables of the sheep, the coin, and the sons (Luke 15). The awful permanence of separation from the Kingdom for one who rejects it is told in the story of the rich man and Lazarus (16:19-31).

This emphasis, particularly the religion of the heart, is lacking in Qumran writings. There are of course expressions of God's goodness and mercy, particularly in the Thanksgiving Hymns. The idea of repentance underlies the nature of the Sect. But we search in vain for any indication that any Qumranian heart was broken over the sheep that had gone astray or rejoiced over the prodigal son who returned. We search in vain, too, for an ethic that extends into principles in the heart and does not stop with the mere letter of the law.

## The Parables

One of the remarkable methods of teaching used by Jesus was the parable. The presentation of truth concerning the Kingdom of God in the form of a parable served to do two things simultaneously: it made truth unusually clear and easy to remember; at the same time, it obscured certain truths from those who were not sufficiently interested to search for the deeper meanings. Jesus pointed out this second aspect in reply to a question from the disciples: " 'Why do you speak to them in parables?' And he answered them, 'To you it has been given to know the secrets of the kingdom of heaven, but to them it has not been given' " (Matt. 13:10-11; cf. 13:36-43).

Esoteric teaching, i.e. teaching to be hidden from nonmembers, was known at Qumran (1QS 5:7-20), but there is nothing similar to the parables. In fact, this method of teaching seems to have been developed by Jesus to an extent not found anywhere else in the world of religious literature.

## The Miracles

Even more remarkable was Jesus' use of mighty works or "miracles" to demonstrate the power of the Kingdom of God over Satan and over the natural forces of this world.

That this was Jesus' intention is clear from two statements in the Gospels. When John the Baptist was in prison, he sent disciples to Jesus to ask, "Are you he who is to come, or shall we look for another?" Jesus sent this reply: "Go and tell John what you have seen and heard: the blind receive their sight, the lame walk, lepers are cleansed, and the deaf hear, the dead are raised up, the poor have the good news preached to them. And blessed is he who takes no offense at me" (Luke 7:20-23).

On another occasion, the Pharisees said, "It is only by Beelzebul, the prince of demons, that this man casts out demons." Jesus replied: " . . . if Satan casts out Satan, he is divided against himself; how then will his kingdom stand? . . . But if it is by the Spirit of God that I cast out demons, then the kingdom of God has come upon you" (Matt. 12:24-28).

It must be added, however, that Jesus performed His mighty works for the benefit of humanity, because His heart was touched by their sufferings. He steadfastly refused to perform any miracle to satisfy the demand to "see a sign" from Him (cf. Matt. 12:38-39), or to provide for His personal needs (cf. 4:2-3), or to protect His own life (cf. 26:52-53).

No miracles of any kind are recorded in the Qumran documents.

There is, of course, the modern tendency to discredit the references to miracles on the so-called scientific basis that they are contrary to natural law, cannot occur, therefore never did occur. At present we are not concerned with debating the credibility of the records — we are only concerned with the records themselves.

If the early Church wrote into the Gospels fantastic accounts of miracles (so stated merely for the sake of argument), the Qumran Community could just as easily have written into their documents miracles at the hand of the Teacher of Righteousness. The objective fact is clear: there are miracles in the New Testament; there are none in the Dead Sea Scrolls.

If someone wishes to add a further objection, that it takes time for legends to develop, let it be pointed out that there was more time between the estimated date of the Teacher of Righteousness and the latest Qumran document than there was between Jesus and the earliest Gospel — and the miracles are plainly in the sources of the Gospels, which must be still earlier.

## The Example

A discussion of the teachings of Jesus should not omit the most influential of all teachings: the power of example. Jesus surrounded Himself with disciples in order that He might teach them — and every minute of the time, whether by word or by silence, whether by action or by meekness, He was teaching His followers.

The power of His example can be clearly seen in the writings of the early Church. The author of the Fourth Gospel remembered that Jesus once said, "I have given you an example, that you also should do as I have done to you" (John 13:15). John passed that on to his own disciples: "He who says he abides in him ought so to walk in the same way in which he walked" (1 John 2:6). Peter declared, "Christ also suffered for you, leaving you an example, that you should follow in his steps" (1 Pet. 2:21). Paul transmitted the idea of example to the Thessalonians, and then wrote with satisfaction, "You became imitators of us and of the Lord . . . so that you became an example to all the believers in Macedonia and Achaia" (1 Thess. 1:6-7).

Without desiring to minimize in any way the character of the Teacher of Righteousness, and willingly acknowledging that he left his imprint on the Qumran Community, we are forced to note that there is no indication that others were seeking to reflect his life in theirs. His suffering and martyrdom, if such there was, did not inspire others to die as, for example, Stephen died (Acts 7:59-60). The "resurrection" of the Teacher of Righteousness, if indeed we find any such idea in the Scrolls, never became a pledge of the resurrection of his followers (cf. 1 Cor. 15:20-23). The unselfish generosity of the Teacher of Righteousness never inspired sacrificial giving such as we find at several places in the early Church (cf. Phil. 4:16-19; 1 Cor. 16:1-3). At least there is no record of such influence in the Qumran writings.

## CHAPTER EIGHTEEN

# THE REDEMPTIVE WORK OF JESUS CHRIST AND THE QUMRAN WRITINGS

According to the teachings of Jesus as set down in the Gospels, the central and indeed the sole purpose of Jesus' presence here on earth was to save men from their sins. There is no possible means by which this central fact can be removed from the records, for it is found in all of the earliest strands in the New Testament: in the earliest sources of the Gospels, in the earliest portions of Acts, and in the earliest and most definitely authentic of the Pauline writings. This unanimous early testimony can only be explained in one way: Jesus Himself was the source of the teaching.

Because of the centrality of this doctrine in early Christian documents, we must consider it in detail, and then compare and contrast the details with whatever may correspond in the Qumran documents.

## The Incarnation

Basic to the redemptive work is the doctrine of the Incarnation, namely that God took upon Himself human form in the person of Jesus in an absolutely unique way, so that Jesus in this respect was unlike every other human being.[1]

Whether Jesus was the author of statements found in the Fourth Gospel, or whether John put the words in Jesus' mouth, has been zealously debated by scholars on both sides. In the

[1] For a brief historical résumé of this doctrine in the formulation of the creedal statements of the Church, see my *Great Personalities of the New Testament*, pp. 41f.

Gospel of John we find such statements as these: "And now, Father, glorify thou me in thy own presence with the glory which I had with thee before the world was made" (John 17:5); and "Before Abraham was, I am" (8:58). John has given us the classical statement of the Incarnation: "In the beginning was the Word, and the Word was with God, and the Word was God. . . . And the Word became flesh and dwelt among us" (1:1, 14).

But the writers of the Synoptic Gospels also included statements implying or teaching the Incarnation. The birth narrative accounts contain reference to "the Son of God" (Luke 1:35) and "Emmanuel (which means, God with us)" (Matt. 1:23). In the boyhood narrative, Jesus seems to correct Mary's reference to Joseph as His father with the words, "Did you not know that I must be in my Father's house?" (Luke 2:49). At the Baptism, a voice from heaven declares, "Thou art my beloved Son" (Mark 1:11); and in the temptations, Satan addresses Jesus as "Son of God" (Matt. 4:3). The demons address Jesus as "the Holy One of God" (Mark 1:27) and "Son of the Most High God" (5:7).[2]

It was out of keeping with Jesus' declared and implied purpose to make claims concerning His person, but even so we find occasional statements on His lips that are consistent only with the Incarnation. For example, He said, "All things have been delivered to me by my Father; and no one knows the Son except the Father, and no one knows the Father except the Son and any one to whom the Son chooses to reveal him" (Matt. 11:27). Again, after the Pharisees had raised the question, "Who can forgive sins but God only?" Jesus said pointedly, "That you may know that the Son of man has authority on earth to forgive sins . . . I say to you, rise, take up your bed and go home" (Luke 5:21-24). And certainly there is more than mere human authority implicit in the striking words, "You have heard that it was said . . . but I say to you . . . ";[3] or the casual reference to sitting on His "glorious throne" in the new world (Matt. 19:28); or the claim that something "greater than Solomon," "greater than Jonah," and "greater than the Temple" is here (see Luke 11:31, 32; Matt. 12:6). Per-

[2] Hence it would seem that "Q," Mark, and the other sources of Matthew and Luke, all knew a "Son of God" tradition.
[3] Matt. 5:21ff., 27ff., 31f., 33ff., 38ff., 43ff.

haps beyond any of these claims is the determined way in which Jesus exalted His authority above that of the Sabbath itself, not once but repeatedly, in a way that could be set forth in a sentence: "The Son of man is lord of the sabbath" (Matt. 12:8; Mark 2:28; Luke 6:5).[4]

The miracles in the Synoptic Gospels, no less than in the Fourth Gospel, likewise testify to the Incarnation. Miracles such as the stilling of the storm (cf. Mark 4:41), the walking on the sea (cf. Matt. 14:33), and the healing of the demoniac son (cf. Luke 9:43) were included as evidence of the power of God Himself in Jesus.

Many more illustrations could be given, but these are sufficient to show that only by completely destroying the Gospel account can the record of the Incarnation of Jesus be removed.

Nothing like an incarnation is found in the Qumran materials. Once again I would raise the question of methodology. To determine that an incarnation is "incredible" and therefore to remove it from the Gospel records or classify it as a theological explanation of a later generation of Christians is questionable methodology. But to read back this same material into the Qumran documents from Christian writings, and then to suggest that the Qumran ideas were responsible for the theological developments in the early Church is highly objectionable. Such methodology disregards the existing records, both Qumranian and Christian. But further, it leaves no sufficient explanation for the development of the concept of incarnation. The Christian record, if not "credible," is at least consistent. The Incarnation became part of the early faith because of the angelic annunciations of the Birth, the heavenly pronouncements at the Baptism and the Transfiguration, the miraculous works of Jesus, and above all the Resurrection. In the Qumran records there is no trace of any event that would give rise to a doctrine of incarnation. Dupont-Sommer once suggested that the expression "body of flesh" (1QpHab 9:2) implied the incarnation of a preexistent divine person;[5] but his later work makes no such suggestion, and his translation shows that "body of flesh" simply means "body."[6]

[4] Cf. A. G. Hebert, *The Throne of David* (London: Faber and Faber, 1951), pp. 143-163.

[5] Dupont-Sommer, *The Dead Sea Scrolls*, p. 34.

[6] Dupont-Sommer, *The Essene Writings from Qumran*, p. 264.

The Teacher of Righteousness is never referred to as "the Son of God" or in any other way that would imply deity. He made no claims of authority and performed no works that would lead men to attribute deity to him. Fritsch's statement that he "must have been regarded as more than human"[7] is gratuitous. Even if it could possibly be demonstrated that the Teacher of Righteousness, or any other living character in the Qumran Community, was regarded as the Messiah, this by itself would still not indicate Incarnation, for the concept of a divine or incarnate Messiah is totally unknown in Judaism.[8]

## Obedience

Basic also to the New Testament doctrine of the redemptive work is the concept of perfect obedience. The absolute perfection of God is taught throughout Scripture. Man's lack of perfection, in other words his sin, is the cause of separation from God. Perfection is often expressed by the word "holy" or "holiness," and sin is expressed by a word that means "to miss the mark."[9] If Jesus had fallen short of perfect holiness in any way, in other words if He had sinned in thought, word, or deed, He could not have accomplished the salvation of other sinners. Accordingly the perfect obedience of Jesus is recorded at several points in the Gospel.

God's "pleasure" with Jesus' life is expressed at the time of the Baptism, i.e. at the beginning of Jesus' ministry (Mark 1:11), and on the Mount of Transfiguration when Jesus openly declared His determination to go to Jerusalem to be crucified (Matt. 17:5). Jesus could say before God His Father, "I always do what is pleasing to him" (John 8:29); and He could challenge His fellow men with the words, "Which of you convicts me of sin?" (8:46).

Not only is there no similar statement made about the

[7] C. T. Fritsch, *The Qumran Community: Its History and Its Scrolls* (New York: Macmillan, 1956), p. 82.

[8] Cf. J. Klausner, *The Messianic Idea in Israel* (New York: Macmillan, 1955), p. 523: "He is a human being, flesh and blood, like all mortals." The appendix, pp. 519-531, "The Jewish and the Christian Messiah," is well worth reading in this connection.

[9] An interesting illustration of this was found in the Israeli news reports of the failure of the American astronaut, Carpenter, to land in the designated area; in order to say "he missed the mark," the newspapers used a form of the Hebrew word which in the Bible means "he sinned."

Teacher of Righteousness in the Dead Sea Scrolls, but if we are to accept the Thanksgiving Hymns as autobiographical there is even a confession of the sinfulness of the Teacher (1QH 4:35; 1:22).[10]

At the same time, along with the record of Jesus' perfect obedience, the Gospels at numerous points record behavior that was in direct violation of the traditional laws of ritual purity. We have already mentioned His repeated and deliberate breaking of the Sabbath laws. Of similar nature was His willingness to eat, drink, and have intimate fellowship with tax collectors and sinners (cf. Matt. 9:11 and 11:19; Luke 7:38). We might note in particular the dinner in the home of Simon the Pharisee (Luke 7:36ff.), at which time the sinful woman anointed Jesus' feet. Commenting on it, Daniélou well observes, "Now if this gesture scandalized the Pharisees, it was even more scandalous in the eyes of the Essenes."[11] The distinction between the Law of God, which Jesus scrupulously obeyed, and the traditions of the fathers, which He violated at many points, certainly must be recognized as a major difference between the New Testament and the Dead Sea Scrolls.

## The Sacrificial Death

Central in the New Testament doctrine of redemption is the death of Jesus. This is so obvious as to need no lengthy argument. However, the statement is sometimes found that the doctrine of the atonement, or the death of Christ as sacrifice for the sins of men, is a "Pauline doctrine" imposed on the simple ethical preaching of the Galilean Carpenter. Such a position can only be supported by complete violation of all the laws of Textual Criticism and historical record.[12]

---

10 If we admit that only part of the Hymns are autobiographical, the passage in 4:35 would generally fall in that category; cf. G. Jeremias, *Der Lehrer der Gerechtigkeit*, p. 171. Holm-Nielson, however, is inclined to see the *Hôdāyôt* as not autobiographical; cf. Svend Holm-Nielsen, *Hodayot: Psalms from Qumran* (Aarhus: Universitetsforlaget, 1960), pp. 347f.

11 J. Daniélou, *The Dead Sea Scrolls and Primitive Christianity*, p. 37.

12 After nearly a century of "scientific" textual criticism, the conclusion of scholars, expressed by Albert Schweitzer, was that it was impossible by that means to get back to the "historical Jesus." In other words, Textual Criticism demonstrated that the Gospel record as we have it today is, on the basis of a critical study of the texts, the same as it was in the earliest form of the documents.

In the first place, the concept of sacrificial atonement by a savior, specifically the Messiah or the Son of God, seems to be unknown in pre-Christian literature, Jewish or pagan. The so-called "dying-rising nature-god myth," which some scholars seem to be able to find everywhere, is in reality not a parallel, since the idea of personal salvation from sin through substitutionary atonement is not part of the myth.

The disciples of Jesus, according to the Gospel record, found the concept of atoning death a most difficult teaching to accept (cf. Matt. 16:21-22; John 6:53-66), hence they could hardly have invented the idea. The Servant-of-the-Lord songs in Isaiah have been suggested as a possible origin of the teaching, particularly Isaiah 53:3-12; but even today Jewish exegetes find no such teaching in the Servant Songs, and Klausner selects the vicarious and atoning death of Jesus as a characteristic point of difference from the Jewish view of the Messiah.[13] Paul, trained in rabbinical Judaism, would have rejected the idea before his conversion, and he afterwards stated that the cross was a stumbling block and an offense to both Jews and Greeks (cf. 1 Cor. 1:23).

In the second place, the doctrine is inextricably woven into the earliest records of Christianity: Paul's earliest letters (1 Thessalonians, Galatians, Romans), the sources of Acts 1—12, the sources of Mark, and the sources of Matthew and Luke other than Mark.[14]

It has often been pointed out that it was not the death of Jesus that was unique, nor even the crucifixion: after all, two other men were crucified on the same hill on the same day. It is the total New Testament teaching that is unique: that the incarnate Son of God died voluntarily as a sacrifice for the sins of men. Nothing like this teaching is found in the Dead Sea Scrolls, nor, for that matter, in any rabbinic literature, nor in any other religious literature.

Allegro, who startled the world with a claim (later modified) that he had found a statement in the Qumran fragments

---

[13] Klausner, *The Messianic Idea in Israel,* p. 527.

[14] In Paul: 1 Thess. 5:9-10; Gal. 2:20; Rom. 5:8-11; in the early sources of Acts: 4:10-12; 8:32-35; in the Marcan source of Matthew: Matt. 20:28 = Mark 10:45; in the independent source of Luke: Luke 19:10; 22:37; in a complex which seems to include "M" and "L" as well as "Mk": Mark 14:22ff.; Matt. 26:26ff.; Luke 22:19ff. I do not find any clear reference to the doctrine in "Q."

indicating that the Teacher of Righteousness was crucified, never associated atoning merit with the act. Dupont-Sommer admits that the Teacher's sufferings are never presented as "serving to atone for the sins of others."[15] This is particularly significant since, according to Dupont-Sommer, the doctrine of atonement was fundamental to the Sect. According to 1QS 8:6-10 the duty of the Council of the Community was "to make atonement on behalf of the earth" by making "offerings of sweet savor." In context this seems to say that their witness to truth will be acceptable to God in lieu of the Levitical animal sacrifices. In the Sayings of Moses (1QDibMos 3:11; 4:3), which Dupont-Sommer cites to support his position, there is reference to the Day of Atonement. But in neither passage is there any personal sacrifice for atonement. The most that can be established is that the Community, by sacrificial obedience, was accomplishing atonement for the "earth" (cf. 1QSa 1:3). But this doctrine is also found in similar form in Judaism, and is a commonly held interpretation of the Servant Songs in Isaiah. It is not the same as the Christian doctrine of the atonement — as Jewish writers clearly recognize.[16]

Some writers think they have found a doctrine of the atonement in a portion of the Damascus Document (CD 14:18). The text at this point is considerably damaged. The words "[ . . . ]h of Aaron and Israel" can be read, suggesting that "[Messia]h" should be restored. Then follow the words, "and he shall make atonement for our iniquity"; then the text is broken again. It is impossible to say definitively what the subject of the verb is or where the sentence ends. Six other times the expression "God shall make atonement on their behalf" or a similar expression is found in the Damascus Document; the subject is

---

15 Dupont-Sommer, *The Essene Writings from Qumran*, p. 366 n. 1.

16 Cf. T. Gaster, *The Dead Sea Scriptures*, pp. vi, 12, and especially 19. Klausner is particularly to the point: "The Jewish Messiah is the redeemer of his people and the redeemer of mankind. But he does not redeem them by his blood; instead, he lends aid to their redemption by his great abilities and deeds. Even Messiah ben Joseph, who is slain, affords no atonement by his blood and his sufferings are not vicarious. . . . Each man is responsible for himself, and through his good deeds he must find atonement for his sins. He cannot lean upon the Messiah or upon the Messiah's suffering and death" (*Messianic Ideal in Israel*, p. 530). For further support Klausner refers to A. Büchler, *Studies in Sin and Atonement* (Oxford: Rosenthall, 1928), pp. 375-461.

always God.[17] It is therefore questionable methodology to find a radically different concept of atonement in the damaged text of 14:18.[18]

## The Resurrection

In the New Testament doctrine of redemption accomplished by Jesus Christ, the resurrection of Jesus is as important as the death on the cross. In fact, in the preaching of the early Church and in the writings of Paul, the two are almost invariably mentioned together. Paul goes so far as to say that if Christ did not rise from the dead, there is no atoning value in His death and our faith is in vain (see 1 Cor. 15:17). Peter likewise placed stress on the significance of the resurrection in his first sermon (Acts 2:24-36).

In considering the details of the life of Jesus we have already discussed the witness to the resurrection (pp. 211-213 above). Here it is only necessary to add that the resurrection was looked upon as the seal of God's approval placed on the life and death of Jesus — which seems to be the point Peter was making (Acts 2:36), and certainly was the thrust of Paul's statement, "designated (or, declared to be) Son of God in power . . . by his resurrection from the dead" (Rom. 1:4).

We have previously seen that there is no clear reference, and probably no inference, to a resurrection of the Teacher of Righteousness (pp. 125f. above). If the Qumran Sect believed in a general resurrection at the end of the age, this would of course include the Teacher's resurrection. But this is not in any way similar to the teaching that God placed a seal of approval on the work of His Son incarnate in the person of Jesus by raising Him from the dead.

On this point, Burrows has well stated the case:

> No objective historian, whatever may be his personal belief about the resurrection of Jesus, can fail to see the decisive

[17] CD 2:5; 3:18; 4:6, 9, 10; 20:34. In 2:5 the subject is not stated in the immediate context; nevertheless there can be no question that the same subject as expressed two lines earlier is intended.

[18] To give the full picture it should be added that the concept of atonement by the Community is found in 1QS (5:6; 8:6, 10; 9:4), 1QSa (1:3); by the priests in 1QM 2:5; by the spirit in 1QS 3:6, 8; and by man through the spirit in 1QS 3:11. All of these expressions are consistent with the Old Testament concept of atonement.

difference here in the beliefs of the two groups. What for the community of Qumran was at most a hope was for the Christians an accomplished fact, the guarantee of all their hopes.[19]

## The Gift of the Holy Spirit

The New Testament doctrine of redemption does not end with the death and resurrection of Jesus; it includes the complete redemption of the life of the believer and the ultimate redemption of the whole creation. To accomplish the redemption of the believer, Jesus sent the Holy Spirit into the world. To complete the redemption of the world, Jesus will return from Heaven. These are essential parts of the New Testament teaching concerning the work of Christ and must not be omitted from an objective study of the significant details. We therefore turn to a consideration of them.

According to teachings of Jesus recorded principally in the Fourth Gospel, Jesus promised to send His Spirit after His own departure from the earth (cf. John 14:16-17, 26; 15:26-27; 16:7-11). That this doctrine was not created by the author of the Fourth Gospel should be clear from two facts: the early sources of Acts place strong emphasis on the gift of the Holy Spirit;[20] and the doctrine is plainly present in Paul's early writings.[21]

The work of the Spirit in the believer is complex, and to set it forth in detail would require much space. The principal redemptive work of the Spirit is known technically as "sanctification," or the accomplishment of holiness in the life of the believer. Paul speaks of this as "the fruit of the Spirit" (Gal. 5:22-23), and urges his readers to "walk by the Spirit" (Gal. 5:16, 25). In this present life "we sigh with anxiety," but God has prepared us for something better and "has given us the Spirit as a guarantee" (2 Cor. 5:1-5). In Romans, Paul contrasts the "mind that is set on the flesh" with the mind set "on the Spirit" (Rom. 8:5-7), and develops the contrast in an extended passage.

This doctrine, incidentally, frees Christianity from the charge sometimes made that it offers a "cheap" salvation. While salvation is freely offered to men, according to the New

19 Burrows, *More Light on the Dead Sea Scrolls*, pp. 66f.
20 Cf. Acts 1:8; 2:4; 8:17; 10:44, and many other references.
21 Cf. Gal. 3:2; 5:16-25; Rom. 8:9-27; 1 Cor. 12:4-11.

Testament, the ultimate goal of salvation is complete redemption from sin, from its bondage as well as from its penalty. The work of the Spirit is to redeem men from the bondage of sin (cf. Gal. 3:2-3; 5:13-17).

In the Dead Sea Scrolls there is considerable emphasis on the spirit, and points of comparison have been noted by many writers. The warfare between the flesh and the Spirit in the New Testament has been compared to the struggle between the spirit of darkness and the spirit of light in the Qumran texts. The specific doctrine that the Spirit has been given to aid men in the way of righteousness is set forth at length in the Manual of Discipline (1QS 3:18 — 4:26). A careful reading will show, I am convinced, that two spirits struggle in man, and that God and His "Angel of Truth" (who is distinct from either of these spirits) aid the sons of light (3:24-25). This is not the same as the Christian doctrine of the sanctifying work of the Holy Spirit. The two spirits in Qumran continue their struggle within man until the end of the age (4:16-17), and there is no indication that the presence of God's Spirit is a pledge or guarantee of ultimate triumph over sin. Still, when we have pointed out these differences, we must go on to note that the stress on the Spirit in the Qumran writings is significant, and that it may indicate a preparatory stage for the New Testament doctrine, whether directly or indirectly.

The doctrine of the Holy Spirit is not unknown in the Old Testament, and the moral purity of man is related to the Spirit (cf. Ps. 143:10; Isa. 32:15-17; Ezek. 36:26-27).[22] In the intertestamental period, emphasis on the Spirit is found in the Testaments of the Twelve Patriarchs (TestBenj 8; TestLevi 18), the Wisdom of Solomon (7:22-30), and particularly in Philo (*Allegories* 13, *inter alia*). We therefore cannot say that the New Testament derived its doctrine of the Spirit directly from Qumran; both may have been developments of a growing con-

---

[22] G. Graystone points out that the expression "the (Holy) Spirit of God" is not used in a personal sense in Qumran texts, but "in the sense in which it is commonly employed in the Old Testament, of an active attribute of God whereby he gives life, raises up and equips for their tasks judges, kings, prophets and psalmists, sanctifies and purifies." He also points out that the Spirit, according to Qumran doctrine, is to be communicated to the Sectarians only at the end of time to purify and sanctify them completely. Cf. *The Dead Sea Scrolls and the Originality of Christ* (London: Sheed & Ward, 1956), p. 73.

cept in Judaism at the time. At the same time we must include the creative genius of Jesus in the New Testament development of the doctrine if we are to take the New Testament record seriously.

There is of course no Qumran parallel to the Christian concept of the Trinity.

## The Second Coming

The final stage in the redemption of the world, according to the New Testament, is connected with the return of Jesus Christ to earth — commonly known as the Second Coming — and the last judgment. This is clearly taught in various ways by Jesus, and is consistently presented in all parts of the New Testament and at all stages of development of apostolic preaching.

For example, using the figure of wheat growing with weeds Jesus presented the work of the Kingdom as developing alongside, in fact even intermixed with, the work of the Satanic kingdom until the final separation (Matt. 13:24-30, explained by Jesus in 37-43). In an extended passage Jesus spoke of His return to earth and the end of the age (Matt. 24:3-51), and followed it with the parables of the maidens and the talents, and with a picture of the judgment scene (Matt. 25; cf. Mark 13). Incidental statements implying or specifically teaching His return to earth can be found scattered throughout the teachings of Jesus.

In the early part of Acts the same doctrine is found. The angelic visitors proclaimed it at the time of the Ascension (Acts 1:11). Peter referred to the Second Coming in his sermon by Solomon's portico (Acts 3:19-21). Paul's earliest letters are devoted in part to clarifying certain misunderstandings about the doctrine of the Return of Christ (1 Thess. 4:13 — 5:11; 2 Thess. 2:1-15). Comparing the sufferings of this present time and the glory to be revealed, Paul writes, "We know that the whole creation has been groaning in travail together until now; and not only the creation, but we ourselves, who have the first fruits of the Spirit, groan inwardly as we wait for adoption as sons, the redemption of our bodies" (Rom. 8:22-23). In the light of his discussion of the body in 2 Corinthians 5:1-10, it is clear that Paul is referring to the Second Coming as the time of the redemption of the body.

It would be tedious and pointless to list all the references to the Second Coming in the New Testament. So clearly was this doctrine set forth[23] that all creeds of the Christian Church include a statement of the Second Coming of Christ. Modern scholars are inclined to find it an aberration of the early Church, forgotten in later generations — but they still admit thereby that it was taught in the early Church.

That a person who has died should rise, go to Heaven, and at some future time return to earth, is a teaching that borders on the fantastic. Accordingly, it is repudiated by some. Yet it is clearly taught in the New Testament. No such teaching is found in the Qumran literature. There is no statement that the Teacher of Righteousness was "taken up to Heaven"; there is no statement that "he shall so come" or that he "shall come on the clouds in power and great glory"; there is no statement that his followers waited for him in groaning and travail or in hope; there is no indication that the last judgment is connected with his return.

The Qumranians did look for the coming of the Messiah, and they did look for the end of the age and the judgment of God. These items they had in common with other groups within Judaism, although there are differences in detail.

## Summary

For the Christian, atonement for sin is an accomplished fact, achieved by the death of the Son of God on the cross, attested by the resurrection of the crucified One; the presence of the Spirit is an experience with sanctifying value; the coming again of Jesus is a glorious hope; the final judgment will be a time of fearsome punishment only for the ungodly, but for believers it will be the beginning of the new and glorious age.

These doctrines are unique — there is nothing like them in Qumran writings.

---

[23] The broad outlines are clear; the details are often obscure, leading to all sorts of speculation. Some of the more significant passages are: Matt. 13:36-50; 19:28 — 20:28; chs. 24 — 25; Luke 17:20-37; 19:12-27; Acts 1:6-11; 1 Cor. 15:20-28; 1 Thess. 4:13-17; 2 Thess. 2:1-8; Heb. 9:11-28; and the Book of Revelation. On the last, see my *Great Personalities of the New Testament*, pp. 175-184.

## CHAPTER NINETEEN

# SPECIFIC POINTS OF COMPARISON BETWEEN JESUS AND QUMRAN

It is of course possible that in our general handling of the life and teachings of Jesus we have avoided specific parallels with the Qumran materials. Therefore we shall take up a number of significant similarities, pointed out by several scholars, that have not been included in our previous study.

## "To Men of Good Will"

In the birth narrative in Luke, the angelic hosts sing, "Glory to God in the highest, and on earth peace, good will toward men" (Luke 2:14, KJV). The exact meaning of the last phrase has been discussed many times. The Revised Standard Version translates it, " . . . peace among men with whom he is pleased!" Other translators have suggested, " . . . peace to men of good will."

In the Qumran literature an expression occurs several times which, in the opinion of some scholars, helps to clarify this phrase. In the Thanksgiving Hymns we find these passages:

> . . . by the spirit (which) God created for him, to perfect a way for the sons of men in order that they might know all His works in the might of His power and multitude of His mercies unto all the sons of His pleasure (or good will, $re\dot{s}\acute{o}n\acute{o}$). (1QH 4:31-33)
>
> . . . and Thy mercies to all the sons of Thy pleasure. (1QH 11:9)

A similar expression is found in the Manual of Discipline,

. . . the witnesses of truth for justice and the chosen ones of
(His) will to make atonement on behalf of the earth . . . .
(1QS 8:6)

In the light of the Qumran expression Vogt concludes that
the New Testament passage "refers more naturally to the will
of God to confer grace on those he has chosen, than to God's
delighting in and approving of the goodness in men's lives,"
which supports the translation "peace among men of God's
good pleasure."[1]

However, Vogt's argument turns on the application of the
basic theology of Qumran, which is strongly electionistic. This
raises the question whether we have any right to use a passage
from Qumran, interpreted by Qumran theology, to help us
understand a New Testament passage. Are we not thereby imposing Qumran theology on the New Testament quotation?
Unless positive relationship between the two movements is
clearly demonstrated, specifically on the point of theology involved, this methodology is open to serious question.

## The Sermon on the Mount

The Sermon on the Mount (Matt. 5–7), in the minds of
several scholars, discloses remarkable parallels with the Dead
Sea Scrolls.

*The Beatitudes.* According to a report mentioned by Burrows,[2] there is a text from Cave 4 that contains a series of
beatitudes beginning with the word "blessed." The only text
resembling this early and indefinite description is the "angelic
liturgy" published by Strugnell.[3] In each stanza the formula
"he shall bless" occurs, but neither this word (contrasted with
"Blessed is . . . " in the Beatitudes) nor the context of the
stanzas bears any similarity to the Beatitudes in Matthew or
Luke.

Kurt Schubert finds help in understanding Jesus' words,
"Blessed are the poor in spirit" (Matt. 5:3), by a study of the

[1] Ernest Vogt, " 'Peace Among Men of God's Good Pleasure' Lk. 2:14,"
in *The Scrolls and the New Testament,* p. 117.

[2] Burrows, *More Light on the Dead Sea Scrolls,* p. 95.

[3] Cf. J. Strugnell, "The Angelic Liturgy at Qumran (4Q Serek *Šîrôt
'ôlat haššabbāt),*" in *Supplements to Vetus Testamentum* 7 (Leiden: Brill,
1960), pp. 318-345. The translation can be seen in Dupont-Sommer, *The
Essene Writings from Qumran,* pp. 330f., or in G. Vermès, *The Dead Sea
Scrolls in English* (Baltimore: Penguin Books, 1962), pp. 211f.

words "poor" and "spirit" in the Qumran texts. We have discussed the term "poor" (pp. 60f. above) as a possible name of the Sect. Schubert says, "The very first of the beatitudes indicates a conscious awareness of Essene thought and an intention of Jesus to make clear his stand against their sect."[4] He supports this supposition by showing that the word translated "spirit" in its Hebrew original could also mean "will, agreement," and that the beatitude could be rendered, "Blessed are the poor in will, poor in inward agreement, voluntarily poor." He goes on to argue that by thus referring to people "to whom worldly goods were nothing," Jesus aligned Himself with one of the basic tenets of the Essenes. "Probably the Essenes took this name because they practiced full community of goods in their settlements and because contempt for money was one of their chief principles."[5]

This argument is a succession of non sequitur's. That the Hebrew word (even if it could be positively identified) could be translated "will" does not affect the meaning of the Greek word in the New Testament, and our exegesis of a New Testament text must necessarily begin with the text before us. Nor does it follow that because $rú^uh$ can be translated "will," the expression here must be translated "poor in will" — it could still mean "poor in spirit." Nor does it follow that "poor in will" means "voluntarily poor" — it could and probably would more likely mean "feeble in will or self-assertion." Nor does it follow that even if we translate it "voluntarily poor" this was a name for the Sect. Our previous study leaves this point still in doubt. Nor does it follow, even if it happened to be the name of the Qumran Sect, that Jesus was deliberately speaking to men who belonged to or had come out of or were in some way related to the Qumranians — much less the Essenes.

The concluding beatitude (Matt. 5:11-12), according to Schubert, fits in with this theory that Jesus was addressing Essenes. The word "prophets" was used of the Essenes themselves. But even if Christ did not intend this word to apply to His listeners, Schubert tells us, the mention of "persecution" still suggests the Essenes. Thereupon Schubert goes into a study

---

[4] K. Schubert, "The Sermon on the Mount and the Qumran Texts," in *The Scrolls and the New Testament*, pp. 121f.

[5] *Ibid.*, p. 122.

of the development of the legend that Isaiah was martyred by Manasseh.[6]

This is curious scholarship indeed. Were not the Biblical prophets persecuted? Is there any reason why Jesus could not have been referring to them? Were the Essenes the only Jews who knew what persecution meant? And how did the martyrdom of Isaiah get into the Sermon on the Mount? Schubert does not tell us. Burrows comments, "This is an astonishing example of reckless leaping from one conjecture to another."[7]

"*Hate Your Enemy.*" The commandment to love our neighbor is found in the Law of Moses (Lev. 19:18), but nowhere in the Old Testament or in Judaism is there any command to hate our enemy such as Jesus referred to in Matthew 5:43. With the discovery of the Scrolls, some scholars have suggested, we have found the origin of this saying. In the Scrolls we read,

> to love all the sons of light, each according to his lot in the Council of God, and to hate all the sons of darkness, each according to his guilt in the vengeance of God. (1QS 1:9-11)

This is not an isolated reference in Qumran literature. The same admonition is found in less personal form a few lines earlier (1QS 1:3-4); the Levites were to curse the men of Belial's lot (1QS 2:4-9); and the Community was "to make atonement on behalf of the earth and to return to the wicked their recompense" (1QS 8:6-7). Details concerning what the Qumranians should love and hate are spelled out, somewhat impersonally, but including the words, "Eternal hatred with the men of the pit" (cf. 1QS 9:21-26).[8] We have considered some of the discussion of this point in connection with the chapter on the Johannine writings (cf. pp. 200f. above).

Schubert feels that Jesus was "aiming at a very specific point of his auditor's eschatology" and wanted to "soften" it. According to Schubert, the Essenes believed that they could

---

[6] *Ibid.*, pp. 122-124.

[7] Burrows, *More Light on the Dead Sea Scrolls*, p. 97.

[8] Dupont-Sommer reminds us that, according to Josephus, the Essene took an oath "to hate the wicked always and to fight together with the good" (Josephus *War* 2.8.7 §139); cf. *The Essene Writings from Qumran*, p. 73 n. 3. Hippolytus, on the other hand, reports this as "to hate no man, neither the wicked nor the enemy, but to pray for them and to fight together with the good" (*Refutation of All Heresies* 9.18).

hasten the End of Days by making the Mosaic Law more strict; Jesus was trying to show that this great event was not dependent upon human effort alone, and that man was not the instrument of God's vengeance.[9] This assumes that Jesus was talking to Essenes and that He was talking about the End of Days. Nothing in the Sermon on the Mount requires either assumption. That Jesus was attempting to "soften" the keeping of the Law stands in contradiction with the fact that in the Sermon on the Mount Jesus was seemingly making the Law more binding and more difficult to keep by spiritualizing it. The righteousness He was demanding had to exceed that of the Pharisees (cf. Matt. 5:17-20) — and if He were talking to Essenes whose legalistic "righteousness" already exceeded that of the Pharisees, the words would have had little point.

Schubert deals with the passage just cited (Matt. 5:17-20), and says "judging from the context given in v. 19, the original meaning of the passage seems to be that one must be more scrupulous with the Law, i.e., more ascetic and pious — as far as the spirit if not the letter of the Law is concerned — than the Pharisees."[10] The best way, however, to determine "the original meaning of the passage" is to study it in the light of Jesus' words and actions as contained in the New Testament. It is difficult to find justification for Schubert's statement if we use this methodology. Jesus was criticized because He was not sufficiently ascetic and pious and because He had not taught His disciples to be scrupulous in such matters (cf. Matt. 11:18-19; 15:1-2; Luke 5:30).

*Adultery and Divorce.* Jesus' discussion of adultery and lust (Matt. 5:27-30) and divorce (5:31-32) has been compared to the Qumran teachings on these subjects. Proposed parallels are found in Jesus' words, "every one who looks at a woman lustfully has already committed adultery with her in his heart" (5:28), and such Qumran expressions as "eyes of fornication" (1QS 1:6), "a spirit of fornication" (4:10), "who did not commit fornication after their eyes" (1QpHab 5:7), and "thoughts of guilty impulse and e[y]es of fornication" (CD 2:16). The parallels are not sufficiently unusual to justify any theory of dependence.

Jesus said, "Every one who divorces his wife, except on the

---

[9] Schubert, *art. cit.* in *The Scrolls and the New Testament*, pp. 120f.
[10] *Ibid.*, p. 125.

ground of unchastity, makes her an adulteress; and whoever marries a divorced woman commits adultery" (Matt. 5:31-32). When the Damascus Document was first published (as the "Zadokite Fragments") scholars noted the similarity between the teaching of Jesus on divorce and the "Zadokite" doctrine. One of the charges against the Jerusalem priesthood was "in fornication [they] take two women in their lifetime, and ( = but, although) the foundation of creation, 'Male and female created He them,' and those entering the ark, 'Two by two they entered into the ark' " (CD 4:20—5:1).

The passage has been repeatedly discussed, particularly in view of a grammatical peculiarity that makes interpretation difficult.[11] If it pertains to divorce, then, we are reminded, it is based on the same argument that Jesus used on another occasion when He spoke of divorce (Matt. 19:3-6). But to say that the Damascus Document and Jesus both make use of Genesis 1:27 when discussing divorce hardly comes to the heart of the matter. The use of the creation and flood scriptures in the Damascus Document is in the line of rabbinical citation of Scripture or previous rabbinical authority, and strongly resembles the use commonly found in rabbinical writings. Jesus, on the other hand, not only cited a passage of Scripture, but He also pointed out the consequent implication.

Moreover, it is not yet clear — and without other evidence to help us will probably never be clear — that the Damascus Document is talking about the same problem. Three different interpretations are possible: (1) marrying a second woman, regardless of whether the first had died or had been divorced; (2) marrying a second woman while the divorced woman was still alive; or (3) marrying a second woman without divorcing the first.[12] In the New Testament passage Jesus is talking about divorce and remarriage. There is no problem of interpreta-

---

[11] The word translated "in their lifetime" has a masculine suffixial ending suggesting that the sin consisted in marrying two women successively, not simultaneously. Some scholars therefore concluded that it referred to divorce. On the other hand it is possible that this is a grammatical slip, since the preceding word "women" has a masculine plural ending in Hebrew and easily attracts a masculine suffix to a modifier. If so, the interpretation would be bigamy.

[12] For a post-Dead Sea Scrolls discussion of the problem, cf. P. Winter, "Sadoqite Fragments IV 20, 21 and the Exegesis of Genesis 1:27 in Late Judaism," *Zeitschrift für die Alttestamentliche Wissenschaft* 68 (1956), pp. 71-84.

tion: what He says is clear. Some have felt that in this matter Jesus stands closer to the strict school of Shammai than to the more tolerant school of Hillel — although in other matters Jesus is usually closer to Hillel.

*Oaths.* Jesus said in part, "Do not swear at all, either by heaven, for it is the throne of God, or by the earth, for it is his footstool, or by Jerusalem, for it is the city of the great King" (Matt. 5:34-35). In the Damascus Document we read, "[Do not swea]r, either by aleph and lamed or by aleph and daled, but an oath of the [covenant or] by the curses of the covenant" (CD 15:1-2). These sayings have been compared, and several scholars have quoted Josephus on the Essene refusal to take an oath (*War* 2.8.6 §135; cf. *Antiquities* 15.10.4 §§368, 371).

To bring Josephus into the discussion is to assume that Josephus was talking about the Qumranians — which, as I have tried to show (Ch. 10), is not beyond question. If we limit our discussion to the Qumran texts, we have the following facts: (1) The long and detailed list of ordinances and punishments for infractions thereof contains no proscription of oaths other than mention of the "name which is honored above all" (1QS 6:27 — 7:1). (2) The Damascus Document contains provision for oaths (CD 9:8-12). (3) The section that forbids the use of "aleph and lamed" and "aleph and daled" — which are almost certainly abbreviations of the words *'ĕlôhîm* (God) and *'ădônay* (Lord) — continues with a discussion of various kinds of oaths and the penalties for breaking them (cf. CD 15:1 — 16:19). Hence it seems to be beyond question that the Qumranians were opposed not to oaths in general but to the irreverant and profane use of the divine name.[13]

*Perfection.* Jesus summarized the first part of the Sermon on the Mount in the words, "You, therefore, must be perfect, as your heavenly Father is perfect" (Matt. 5:48). Some scholars have found a parallel to this saying in the Manual of Discipline, particularly in the expression "in perfection of way" (1QS 8:10, 18, 21, 25). But the use of the word translated "perfection" in the Dead Sea Scrolls is fully in accord with Old Testament usage,[14] and certainly Jesus was conversant with

[13] The difference between the Essenes and the Qumranians in the matter of oaths is only one of several reasons why the two sects cannot be easily identified as one and the same.

[14] Cf. Ezek. 28:15; Prov. 11:20; Ps. 119:1; 2 Sam. 22:33; Ps. 101:6, etc.

Biblical expressions. Moreover, the thrust of Jesus' words taken in context is quite different from that of the Manual of Discipline. In the latter, the expression describes the members of the Community. They are men who enter "into the Council of Holiness, who walk in perfection of way" (1QS 8:21). They have already walked in perfection of way "in the Establishment of the Community two years of days" (8:10). They have been forbidden to touch the "Purity" of the Men of Holiness until they walked in perfection of way (8:18). In the words of Jesus, the attainment of perfection is a goal to strive after, and the preceding teachings make it clear that the striving will be far more difficult than "the men of old time" had ever imagined.

## Other Parallels

Schubert says, "Outside of Matthew 5 we find only occasional Essene parallels." He and others have suggested some, to which we now turn our attention.

*Sabbath Laws.* Referring to the curing of the man with a withered hand, Schubert finds Jesus and also His opponents the Pharisees versed in Essene rules. When they asked, "Is it lawful to heal on the sabbath," Jesus replied, "What man of you, if he has one sheep and it falls into a pit on the sabbath, will not lay hold of it and lift it out? Of how much more value is a man than a sheep!" (Matt. 12:10-12). In the Manual of Discipline, Schubert reminds us, this would have been forbidden: "Let not a man assist an animal in bearing on the Sabbath Day, and if it fall into a cistern or into a pit, let him not raise it on the Sabbath" (CD 11:13-14).

I find it difficult to follow Schubert's logic. Jesus is using the familiar *qal vāḥómer* argument of the rabbis, which He used on many occasions, and which the rabbis loved to use. The argument *qal vāḥómer* ("light and heavy") is the argument *a fortiori,* or from the lesser to the greater: If it is allowed to help an animal in need on the Sabbath, how much more is it allowed to help a man in need. There is no reason to bring Essene or Qumran rules into the discussion.

*Mammon.* The use of the word "Mammon" in Matthew 6:24 has been compared with the use of the same word in the Manual of Discipline (1QS 6:2). However, this was a common word for "wealth," and the contexts cited are not at all similar.

*Corban.* Jesus' discussion of "Corban" or dedicated things (Mark 7:9-13) has been compared with a sentence in the Damascus Document: "Let [no] man dedicate the food of his mouth [to Go]d" (CD 16:14-15). Burrows says this comparison is "far-fetched and very doubtful."[15]

*The "Time of Visitation."* Jesus' use of the expression "the time of your visitation" (Luke 19:44) has been compared to the expression "the season of his visitation" in the Manual of Discipline (1QS 3:14, 18; 4:6, 11, 19, 26). Jesus was referring to the time of His own advent, already an accomplished fact. The Qumran expression refers to a future time and has to do with the final judgment. The expression is well known from the Old Testament (cf. Isa. 10:3; Hos. 9:7; Mic. 7:4, etc.).

*The "Sons of This World."* Some scholars have pointed out that the "closest parallel of all" between the sayings of Jesus recorded in the Synoptic Gospels and the Qumran literature is Luke 16:8, "The sons of this world are wiser in their own generation than the sons of light." The terms "sons of this world" and "sons of light" are strongly reminiscent of the dualistic concepts of the Qumran Scrolls. "Sons of light" is found several times in the Dead Sea Scrolls, principally in the Manual of Discipline (1QS 1:9; 2:16; 3:13, 24, 25) and in the War Scroll (1QM 1:3, 9, 11, 13, 16). I have not been able to locate a single usage of the expression "the sons of this world" in Qumran literature, the closest equivalent being "[the sons of the] world" (1QH 1:8) in a broken text.

An examination of the extensive literature written about Qumran will disclose many other alleged similarities between the teachings of Jesus and the Dead Sea Scrolls. In my opinion I have presented the most striking. It is of course possible that I have overlooked some that should be given consideration; it is also true that my judgment as to what is significant is fallible. But the Scrolls are available in translation, as are the sayings of Jesus, and anyone who will can read and decide for himself the extent of the parallels.

## Significant Contrasts

Not all scholars have been concerned with parallels; many have pointed out important contrasts. Again I shall try to select the more significant.

---

[15] Burrows, *More Light on the Dead Sea Scrolls,* p. 103.

Qumran was a closed sect. Admission was by a stern process of judgment. It had no message for the world. Jesus extended a gracious invitation to all and built into His disciples the concept of the universal spread of the Gospel (Matt. 11:28-30; 8:11-12; 28:19-20).

Qumran was strongly legalistic. Jesus set aside the legalism of the Pharisees and deliberately broke the Sabbath day as they interpreted it (cf. Matt. 23:1-28; 12:11-14; Mark 2:23-28).

Qumran was a way of life, a regimen of ritual activity and ritual purity. Jesus sought to instill spiritual principles rather than mere formality (Matt. 5:21-48; 12:1-8; Mark 7:1-23; John 4:21-24).

Qumran was in some ways a monastery. While there is no indication that celibacy was required (and indeed some evidence to the contrary), yet the desert location, the enforced community of goods, the emphasis on poverty, and the attitude toward the world can correctly be called asceticism. Possibly we can reconstruct the virtues of Qumran by noting the vices as specified under the term "the three nets of Belial": lust, riches, and defilement of the Sanctuary (CD 4:17-18). It will not, of course, be accurate to say that Jesus was opposed to these virtues. Yet He did set Himself in a different category from that of John the Baptist (Matt. 11:18-19). He made celibacy a personal and voluntary matter (Matt. 19:10-12). And while He underscored the perils of riches (Matt. 19:23-24), He did not enforce poverty or community of property as a condition of discipleship.

Other contrasts have been noted in passing, in our previous studies of specific matters.

## Summary

A quotation of Edmund Wilson provides an apt summary:

Anyone who goes to the Gospels from the literature of the intertestamental apocrypha and the literature of the Dead Sea Sect must feel at once the special genius of Jesus and be struck by the impossibility of falling in with one of the worst tendencies of insensitive modern scholarship and accounting for everything in the Gospels in terms of analogies and precedents.[16]

16 Wilson, *The Dead Sea Scrolls*, p. 102.

## CHAPTER TWENTY

# SUMMARY AND CONCLUSIONS

Perhaps it will help us better to compare the two bodies of material if we set down the data in parallel columns, rather than merely recapitulating what we have already written.

## *Summary*

| THE DEAD SEA SCROLLS | THE NEW TESTAMENT |
|---|---|
| *Sources* | |
| The Dead Sea Scrolls, written during first century B.C. and early first century A.D. | The New Testament, written during the latter half of first century A.D. |
| Discovered 1947-1956 | In use continuously since original composition. |
| Original texts extant. | Copies of copies from the fourth century, and fragments from second century, but no original texts extant. |
| In Hebrew and some in Aramaic; a few fragments of Greek papyri. | In Greek; a small portion possibly from an Aramaic original. |
| *The Communities* | |
| "Qumran" Community; name not known. | Came to be known as Christians. |
| Originated probably in middle of second century B.C. | Originated about A.D. 30. |

| | |
|---|---|
| A Jewish sectarian movement. | A Jewish sectarian movement. |
| No record of beginnings. | Began in Jerusalem, on the Feast of Pentecost (Shavu-'ot), when the Holy Spirit came on the Apostles with visible and audible signs. |
| Origin of movement unknown. Early development was apparently shaped by Teacher of Righteousness. | Originated by Jesus Christ, who called His first followers, trained them, and commissioned them to evangelize the world after they had received the Spirit. |
| Devoted to the Law of the Old Testament. | Accepted Old Testament as Word of God, but refused to enforce Law upon converts. |
| Composed of priests and laymen, with priority to priests, and primary authority in priesthood. | No distinction between priests and laymen. |
| Admission only after two-year probationary period. | Immediate admission upon profession of faith in Jesus Christ. |
| Arrangement according to rank or precedence, determined by obedience to Law and to rules of the Community. | No indication of rank or precedence. Such would be contrary to expressed principles. |
| Community of goods enforced on all coming into Sect. | Community of goods practiced voluntarily by some members, but only after coming into the Church. |
| Experienced poverty and perhaps looked on it as the Lord's blessing. | Experienced poverty, at least in the Jerusalem area. No indication that it was considered charismatic. |

| | |
|---|---|
| Provisions for married members; most probably a quasi-monastic group. | Marriage considered normal; celibacy considered unusual but not prohibited. |
| The Priest (or Chief Priest) seems to have been the primary person in authority. | No single human authority; apostolic office authoritative. |
| The "Examiner" or Superintendent had supervisorial responsibilities. | James the brother of the Lord acted as president or moderator of Jerusalem Conference. Paul asserted authority of a kind over churches he founded. |
| Council of "Twelve and Three" had some administrative function in Community. | Twelve Apostles trained by Jesus and sent out; no indication that they functioned as an administrative body. |
| Other organizational details centered about the priestly system. | The Seven handled administration of relief for the poor at Jerusalem. No provision for priestly system. |
| Devoted to study of the Law. Interpreted it in peculiar way, centering about the Community. | Studied Scriptures, it would seem, mostly to find prophecies fulfilled in Jesus. Also studied words and acts of Jesus as reflected in the *kerygma* of early Church. |
| Rigid Sabbatarians. | Observed Sabbath; Jesus deliberately broke traditional Sabbatarian laws. |
| No indication of local sacrificial system; they may have sent offerings to Jerusalem. | Jewish members at Jerusalem participated in Temple services. Jesus went to Jerusalem for the feasts. |

| | |
|---|---|
| Definitely repudiated Jerusalem priesthood and would have no part in it. | Jesus was openly critical of Pharisaism. Apostles were critical of officials for rejecting Jesus, but continued to testify to them. Paul "turned to the Gentiles," but did not cease to participate in the Temple worship. |
| Recognized value of spiritual sacrifices. | Stressed true worth of spiritual sacrifices, ultimately rejecting animal sacrifices (cf. Epistle to Hebrews). |
| Practiced ritual washing for members in good standing; denied to those seeking admission. | Administered baptism to new members upon confession of faith in Jesus and repentance. |
| Had some cult object or meal known as the "purity." | Nothing similar known; Lord's Supper only vaguely parallel. |
| Observed a calendar other than the official calendar. | No indication of special calendration. |
| Observed the holy days and feasts of Judaism but according to their own calendration. | Jewish members observed the holy days. In principle, Church insisted that no day was holy above another. Soon observed the first day of the week as the Lord's Day. |
| Prescribed fines and punishments for specified offenses; temporary or permanent exclusion for more serious offenses. | Enforced discipline in some recorded cases. No specified system of fines and punishments recorded. |
| Worshipped the God of the Jews. | Worshipped the God of the Jews and Christ as the Son equal with God in honor. |

Had a modified system of dualism, stressing the place of good and evil spirits in deterining the ways of men. Ultimately monistic, however.

Had a purely monistic system; God creator of all. Doctrine of Satan and demons brought under the doctrine of God.

Elaborate system of angelology.

Somewhat less elaborate system of angelology.

Man essentially sinful and unable to please God.

Man essentially sinful and unable to please God.

Salvation by grace of God, to those who keep the Law according to the interpretation of the Community.

Salvation by grace of God, to those who trust Christ, apart from the works of the Law. Good works are the evidence of salvation.

Esoteric knowledge concerning the interpretation of the Law and the place of the Community in the end-time.

No esoteric knowledge, except in the parabolic teaching; even here anyone who will seek to understand can do so.

A Community living in the end of days, expecting the final judgment of God. No provision for coming generations.

The "last days," which at times seems to indicate the proximate end of the age, was upon them. However, the program included evangelization and training of coming generations.

Judgment is described principally upon those outside the Community.

Judgment begins with the House of God; salvation from punishment, however, is promised to those who trust in Christ.

Reward for the blessed is peace, security, and earthly existence.

Reward for the saved is blessed fellowship with God in Heaven.

Looked for the Davidic Messiah. Some scholars hold that they also looked for a priestly Messiah.

Believed that Jesus was the Davidic Messiah who had come, the royal High Priest, who would come again at the end of the age.

| | |
|---|---|
| No doctrine of a heavenly Son of Man is found in the texts. | Believed that Jesus was also the heavenly Son of Man who had come veiled in humanity and who would come again in power and glory. |

### The Religious Leaders

| | |
|---|---|
| The Teacher of Righteousness. | Jesus of Nazareth called the Christ. |
| Date of birth unknown. | Born about 7 to 5 B.C. |
| Place of birth unknown. | Born in Bethlehem of Judah. |
| Parents not recorded. | Son of Mary; legal son of Joseph of Nazareth. |
| No record of unusual birth. | Records of Mary and Joseph indicate no marital union between them; child named as Son of God by the Holy Spirit. |
| Early life and training not recorded. | Few details of early life and training given; a carpenter in Nazareth. |
| Probably grew up under influence of early movement of sectarianism. | Seems to have grown up in normal Jewish home and community. |
| Probably was a priest. | Was not a priest. Was called "Rabbi." |
| Date of beginning of ministry unknown; perhaps c. 177 B.C. | Began His ministry about A.D. 26/27. |
| Details of beginning of ministry unknown. | Baptized by John and announced by John as the "One who was to come." |
| No indication that he called or trained disciples. No indication that there were disciples or apostles. | Called disciples and, after a period, appointed Twelve to be apostles. Concentrated His training on them. |

No record of miracles or indication that he was a supernatural person.

Performed many mighty works; His followers believed He was more than human.

No records of teaching.

Taught by parables and by example.

If Hymns are autobiographical, confessed his own sin.

Not conscious of any sin; declared His perfection of character; record includes a similar declaration heard from heaven.

Was not called a prophet, but interpreted the prophets.

Called a prophet by Church; set His own authority over that of earlier teachers; claimed to fulfill the prophets.

Died; manner not definitely known. Was persecuted, possibly put to death. No record of any crucifixion.

Was tried by Jewish officials; convicted and sentenced to death by Roman Procurator Pontius Pilate; crucified on hill near Jerusalem before many witnesses.

No record of burial.

Buried in tomb of Joseph of Arimathea. Burial place witnessed by followers and placed under guard of soldiers.

No record of resurrection or of further appearances.

The tomb was found empty on the third day. Jesus was seen alive by many, on several occasions during period of forty days.

No record of ascension.

Ascended into Heaven from Mount of Olives in sight of His followers.

No record of promise of return.

Promised to return to earth visibly, in power and glory, at end of age.

No record of promise of Spirit.     Promised to send the Spirit on
                                     His followers, to be with them
                                     throughout the age.

## Conclusions

Certain conclusions of an objective nature can be made.

First, the two bodies of material are essentially different in historical perspectives. There is little or no historical material in the Qumran texts. There is much historical material in the Gospels. In using the word "historical" I am not implying that it is credible. I am simply designating its nature. The persons and places are named, the chronological details are indicated. They may be right or wrong — that is to be determined by the laws of testimony — but they are present nevertheless.

In historical matters, therefore, we are not faced with the question, Do the Dead Sea Scrolls confirm the New Testament? The two bodies of material are moving in different orbits. Not a single person, date, or event is mentioned in common in both sets of documents, hence there is no occasion for either to confirm or deny the other. The orbits simply do not intersect.

Second, the two bodies of material are essentially similar in religious perspectives. Both have arisen from sectarian movements in Judaism under influence of eschatological expectations. There will therefore be many points of similarity, as we have noted repeatedly. There will also be characteristic points of difference, as we have likewise noted.

Third, it seems reasonable to conclude that the two movements were independent beyond the initial origins in Judaism. The similarities have been examined, and can be explained in nearly all cases by the Jewish origin of the movements. The differences are such that they seem to require independent development of the two movements.

Fourth, the Dead Sea Scrolls furnish valuable material for the study of sectarian Judaism. This has important values for the study of Christianity as a sectarian movement, the more so since both are eschatological or end-time movements. In this area we may point out specific subjects for which the Dead Sea Scrolls provide valuable background materials.

The eschatological teachings of Jesus and the early Church can be seen in perspective against the eschatology of Qumran.

This does not mean that we must attempt to conform the one to the other. Certainly the element of originality in the teachings of Jesus must be accepted as a possibility. But in understanding and interpreting the thought-forms that are used in the New Testament we can profitably study the Qumran writings.

The so-called dualistic and pre-Gnostic elements of the New Testament can be seen against the background of the Qumran writings. The developing doctrines of Satan (under whatever name used), of Satanic or demonic spiritual beings, of the spiritual struggle not only in man but even above man in "heavenly places," the "mystery" of this ungodliness, the dualism of light and darkness, of truth and error — all of this can be opened up for restudy with advantage in the light of the Dead Sea Scrolls. This will apply particularly to studies in the Johannine writings and certain portions of the Pauline writings, but not to these exclusively.

The development of the "church idea," or the concept of the true "election" within Israel, which is in effect an expansion of the "remnant" concept of the Old Testament prophets, can now be examined in a non-Christian setting. This is not to suggest that we were unable to study it previously; but many times our judgments are so preconditioned by our own loyalties that it is difficult almost to impossibility to be objective. We now are able to study the Christian Church as a "true Israel" alongside the Qumran Community in a similar capacity, with mutual advantages to both sides of the study. It is possible that this may also help us to understand modern Christian "remnant" movements a little better.

The rise of legalism and the development of halakic elements (oral tradition) in interpretation of the Law, and the opposition to these movements both in the teachings of Jesus and in the writings of Paul, can now be seen against the background of sectarian Judaism and not merely against that of normative Judaism. This is not suggested as an either-or alternative. The Qumranians seem to have been in opposition to the "Builders of the wall" but they were developing their own characteristic kind of legalism. It would not be correct to suppose that Christianity resembles Qumran in opposition to the legalism of normative Judaism. We are simply suggesting that *both* Qumran *and* normative Judaism can now be used as background for the study of the New Testament teaching of grace "apart from the works of the Law."

But what of the Teacher of Righteousness? We seem to have lost him completely in our conclusions. Perhaps this is as it should be: certainly the mere records of Qumran preserve very little about him. History otherwise preserves nothing at all. But somehow we feel that this can hardly be a true verdict. If we have been led to expect too much by the fantastic myths of the Teacher of Righteousness that have been spun by a few scholars, with no textual or historical support, certainly the opposite extreme of eliminating him entirely is not the corrective.

The Teacher of Righteousness must take his place as a reformer, a man committed to the Scriptures of the Old Testament and to the conviction that God had given him understanding in interpreting them, a man filled with a deep sense of gratitude and election for the high calling that was his, a man who seems to have sparked the Community to live according to principles which he or others near him had set forth, and a man who left them with the hope that God would raise up in the end of days a teacher of righteousness — whether himself or another like him is not clear to us at present.

Was he a forerunner of Christ? This is perhaps a matter of interpretation. Those who have a strong sense of divine activity in history will probably say that he was one of several factors by which God was preparing the world, and particularly the people of God, for the advent of His Son. Others will scoff at such a notion. He was a reformer, a visionary, with strange ideas about withdrawing from the world and waiting for the judgment of God to fall. History generally ignores such fanatics, and moves on, leaving little or no trace of them. But that is a matter of personal conviction, and that sacred precinct I will not invade.

# THE DEAD SEA SCROLLS, THE NEW TESTAMENT, AND HISTORICAL METHOD

We have considered the Dead Sea Scrolls, and we have considered those portions of the New Testament where there are possible or potential parallels with the Scrolls. We have repeatedly insisted upon correct methodology, and we have been severely critical of improper methodology. The pointed question will be asked, What about your own methodology? We must be prepared to answer it.

## *The Texts We Have Used*

We have used the original Dead Sea Scrolls. By that I mean, we have the actual texts of the Qumran Community, recovered from the caves at Qumran where they were hidden, almost beyond doubt, by the members of the Sect. We may not have the original copy or first edition of all of these texts: it is certain in the case of Biblical Scriptures that we have only later copies; it is possible in the case of other documents such as the Manual of Discipline, the Damascus Document, and any other text that was found in multiple copies, that we have copies of the original. But in some cases, perhaps in most cases where only one copy of a text was recovered (the Biblical commentaries, for example), we very likely have in our possession the original document from the hand of its author or his scribe.

In the case of the New Testament, we do not have the original Scriptures. In fact, we are working with a text that is dated in the early part of the fourth century — at least 200 or 250 years after the writing of the original Scriptures. This means that we are working with texts that are removed by several generations from their ancestors — copies of copies, etc. — and there has been the possibility of alteration, elimination, and addition, in each generation of the text.

Are we not therefore guilty of an initial mistake in methodology when we compare text with text?

First, let it be said that we are fully aware of the problem. But what is the alternative? To emend the New Testament text by using the Dead Sea Scrolls, and then to use the emended text for comparative purposes, is the use of circular argument. It cannot be tolerated by sound historical method. To attempt to control the New Testament text by other existing historical documents would be sound methodology — but where are these other documents? For centuries historians have longed for historical materials by which to control the New Testament statements of historical nature. Here and there we find a brief reference in Josephus, or Tacitus, or Suetonius. But there just are no other texts in existence. To distort the New Testament record on the basis of subjective scholarly opinion, without any documentary support whatever, is to open the door to the admission of every sort of fantasy. Libraries are full of books with such theories, and each one remains in vogue only until a newer theory destroys it. History has passed its own verdict on this methodology.

In the second place, let us not forget that there are available to us the accumulated results of two centuries and more of Textual Criticism. No book in the world, literary, religious, or historical, has been subjected to the searching analysis of Textual Criticism in the way that the Bible has been. No book in the world has the same number of ancient copies of the text extant for comparative study. No book in the world has the scholarly "tools" readily available for use: word counts, dictionaries, concordances, grammatical studies, comparative studies and references to other historical, literary, and religious works, translations into hundreds of languages ancient and modern. Whatever is needed for any type of study is available — or if it is not available, as soon as scholars recognize the need for such a tool it will be made available. In fact, in the comparative study of the Dead Sea Scrolls and the New Testament, it has not been the lack of Biblical materials but, quite the contrary, it has been the lack of scholarly tools for the Qumran materials that has handicapped scholarship. Some of the questionable statements that got into print in the early days of Qumraniana might never have been made if a concordance, an index of words with word counts, and a grammar of Qumran Hebrew had been then available.

We might follow up this second point a bit further and point out that textual scholars assure us that the results of Textual Criticism have provided us with a New Testament text that is for all purposes the equivalent of the original text. These results can be found in any standard work on New Testament Textual Criticism or New Testament Introduction. This means, in other words, that if we had the original copies of the works written by Matthew, or John, or Paul, and made our comparative study of the Dead Sea Scrolls by using the original New Testament texts, our results would not be substantially altered in any significant way.

## History and the Scientific Method

Modern problems of New Testament scholarship do not develop from a questionable text of the New Testament. That was made crystal clear when the "Quest for the Historical Jesus" led right back to the Jesus of the New Testament text. Our problem is with "scientific method."

We live in a "scientific age," and we have learned to apply the methodology of science to all areas of life. We have even tried to apply it to history.

Science—and I mean chiefly the physical sciences—is based on repeatable or verifiable data. The scientist not only makes observations; he also controls these observations by repeating them. In the laboratory he is able to perform the experiment several times, controlling the various factors that influence the process he is observing, until he can establish a "formula" or a "law." This formula or law can then be repeated by other scientists. Or in the world of nature the scientist can make multiple observations. He can control the cross-fertilization of the plant, or he can repeat observations of the stars, or he can study the sequence of tree-rings or varves in various locations. This is scientific method.

The historian, on the other hand, is not dealing with repeatable phenomena. He cannot ask Caesar to run through his Gallic wars again in order that the historian can check his observations. There is an element of once-for-all-ness in every historical event. The historian therefore can work only from the records of past events, and those records are based on the testimony of eyewitnesses or accounts gathered ultimately from witnesses.

The "scientific" historian is trying to impose objective controls upon the records. And since he cannot repeat the event and he cannot cross-examine the witnesses, he is left with only one control: the application of his own experience. One historian in my hearing stated it as follows: "If it cannot happen today, it never happened; unless we impose this rigid control, we open the door to all sorts of legends, rumors, and fairy tales." The scientific historian, then, is imposing a judgment — a value-judgment, based upon his own experience — on records of the past.

## The New Testament and Historical Method

The New Testament contains accounts of events and deeds which "cannot happen today." "Miracle" — the very word shocks the sensitivity of the modern scientific mind, for does it not mean an event or effect which cannot be explained by any known natural law? The entire story about Jesus is filled with such accounts, from the angelic annunciations of His birth to the angelic annunciation of His ascension and second coming. Likewise the record of the early Church, while more in the nature of ordinary history, contains accounts of instantaneous healing, walking out of prison in spite of chains and gates and guards, raising of the dead, and other things that do not happen today.

The historian asks, "Why should the New Testament be treated any differently from any other book?" He wants to know why, for example, he should accept the accounts of the miracles performed by Jesus, and rule out the accounts of miracles performed by Buddha. Why should he accept as historical the statement that Paul was bitten by a poisonous serpent and was unharmed, and reject a similar statement by some witch doctor in Africa or some hillbilly preacher in the Bible belt. And he is perfectly right in asking the question. The Bible, as a historical book, must be subjected to exactly the same rules as any other history.

The "Bible-believing" Christian, especially, must accept this statement wholeheartedly, for if he is not willing to subject the Bible to the rigid laws of historical methodology on the grounds that "it is a religious book," he must grant exactly the same right to the followers of Buddha, Mohammed, Joseph Smith, or any other religious leader. He thereby loses the only means by which he can establish the unique authority of his own Bible.

It is at this point that the central problem of comparing the Dead Sea Scrolls with the New Testament takes on a peculiar characteristic. In the New Testament we have a number of "supernatural" or "miraculous" details connected with the person and work of Jesus and with some members of the early Church. No such details are found in the Qumran materials. But certain scholars, by a process of removing such details from the New Testament record as "nonhistorical," or by the reverse process of reading them into the Qumran writings, have been able to construct a remarkable parallel between Jesus and the Teacher of Righteousness and between the Church and the Qumranian Community.

How can we handle these two bodies of religious literature while maintaining "scientific historical methodology"? This is the basic problem.

## The Man from Outer Space

The "scientific" historian, we have said, attempts to impose objective controls upon the records — but these objective controls turn out in some ways to be quite subjective. They are based upon his own limited experience or that of his fellow men. The weakness of this can be demonstrated by the following illustration.

Let us suppose that a visitor from outer space, who had never seen water in any of its forms, were to return to his planet and report his observations made here on Earth. Scientists assure us that it is entirely possible, even probable, that life exists on other planets, and that life could have developed to an advanced stage without being adapted to the need of water — therefore this illustration cannot be dismissed as pure fantasy. But in any event, the details in it are otherwise beyond objection.

The visitor from space, among other observations, would report what he observed concerning water: when its temperature is lowered, its density increases to a certain point in "natural" fashion; but when its temperature is lowered still further, its density suddenly decreases, so that water in its solid form (we call it "ice") floats on water in its liquid form.

Now, let us suppose that two thousand years later on that planet in another galaxy, a historian tries to evaluate the record. Being a "scientific" historian, and attempting to impose objective controls upon his materials, he questions the statement about floating solid water. He knows that there is no known case in which a solid has a lower density than its own liquid (except water, of course, which he has never seen). He therefore concludes "scientifically" that this part of the report is erroneous. Thereupon he tries to explain away the statement that solid water floats on liquid water. Perhaps it was a hallucination of the Earth-people. Perhaps it was a deliberate attempt on the part of Earth-people to add some mysterious or "divine" quality to the substance they revere so highly and without which they think they cannot live. Perhaps it was the accumulation of myths. Perhaps the Earthlings saw a mass of water-vapor — "clouds" — at sea and thought it was "ice," or some other deviation from "scientific truth." We smile at such ideas — but the fact remains that *this space historian is using, within his framework of knowledge, true scientific method.* His error was to suppose that there could be no reality outside his own system.

In much the same way some modern historians report that many of the elements in the New Testament cannot be historical. That the record of the life of Jesus from beginning to end is filled with reports of the miraculous or supernatural everyone must admit. That these portions cannot be removed by Textual Criticism is the verdict of critics: the search for the "historical Jesus" — i.e. a nonsupernatural person who could be handled as "historical" — led back to the Jesus of the Gospels including all the supernatural elements.

But suppose Jesus is indeed from "outer space." If in fact He is the Creator of the Universe who has taken upon Himself the form of an Earthling, coming to our planet as the Babe of

Bethlehem, living here for a brief period of Earth-time to give us a glimpse of what the Kingdom of Heaven is like, dying for our salvation, rising because such a One cannot be held by death, and returning to His own home with the promise that He will come to see us again — then do not all the pieces of the historical puzzle fall into place?

How can we subject the non-Earthly to the limitations of our Earth-bound experience? Perhaps the visitor from space did see ice floating on water when he was on the planet Earth. Perhaps the scientific incredulity where he lived was due to their lack of experience beyond their own planet. Perhaps the Visitor from Heaven did walk on water, change water into wine, and raise the dead. Who can say that such things are "impossible" for the Son of God?

## What Are the Controls on Historical Method?

The "scientific" historian says, "If it cannot happen today, it never happened. If it is not known in the accumulated experience of our system, it must be rejected as nonhistorical." We have demonstrated that this criterion is false. History is not science, and the data of history are of necessity nonverifiable. It is impossible to repeat a historical event of past time, or to set up a duplicate event for new observations.

Are we then left without controls? How can we distinguish historical fact from legend, myth, and fantasy? The answer, in my opinion, is to be found in the laws of testimony.

In any case which can be supported only by the evidence of witnesses, the laws of testimony apply. These include such items as the following: Was the witness in fact a witness — did he see and hear the things about which he testifies? Was he in his right mind? Was he competent to judge what he saw and heard? (A man with no knowledge of medical terminology could not testify about the learned conversation of two doctors; nor could a person knowing no French testify concerning a conversation held in French.) Is his witness corroborated by other witnesses? Do they agree in essential details? (Agreement in all points is not required.) Is he of good character? Is his testimony self-consistent?

These and similar laws are applied every day by all of us. They are applied not only in courts of law — alongside scientific method, or analysis of material evidence — but they are applied by each of us in daily life. We mentally apply such judgments when someone tells us a story. Fathers and mothers apply them when the child comes home with a tale. The scientist applies the same laws when he hears or reads the reports of other scientists.

These are the laws that govern historical method. When the historian writes about Alexander's conquest of the world, he gathers the reports, and then applies the judgments that have been time-tested. Was this reported by someone who was there? Was he competent to judge what he saw? Are there verifying or corroborating witnesses? Sometimes the historian records a report with the frank judgment, "I don't believe this, but here is what he says." Strabo displayed such objectivity with the report about the island named "Thule" and inhabitants in the northern regions.[1] Sometimes the historian explains what he thinks the witness intended to say. But the historian has no right to distort the record or tamper with the evidence. Once he does that, he has destroyed whatever objectivity there may be, and future historians — or for that matter, all of us — are no longer able to make independent judgments.

In the last analysis, then, the historical method consists of witness and faith. The person who was there tells us what he saw and heard. We either believe him, or we refuse to believe him.

This is why a carefully trained scholar, who certainly knew what scientific methodology is, could write,

> Christianity is grounded in certain historical events, which faith interprets as acts of God. If these events never occurred, they were certainly not acts of God. What is most distinctive in Christian faith could not be true.[2]

This is why he could also say,

> It is my considered conclusion, however, that if one will go through any of the historic statements of Christian faith he will find nothing that has been or can be disproved by the Dead Sea Scrolls.[3]

---

[1] Strabo *Geography* 2.5.8. Strabo provides many examples of the principles we have been discussing, and his work is worth careful reading.

[2] Burrows, *More Light on the Dead Sea Scrolls*, p. 44.

[3] *Ibid.*, p. 39.

# BIBLIOGRAPHY

*Discoveries*

John C. Trever, *The Untold Story of Qumran* (Westwood, N.J.: Revell, 1965; 214 pp.). Trever's account of his part, told for the first time.

Mar Athanasius Yeshue Samuel, *Treasure of Qumran: My Story of the Dead Sea Scrolls* (Philadelphia: Westminster, 1966; 208 pp.). Mar Samuel's account of his part in the web of handling the Scrolls.

Yigael Yadin, *The Message of the Scrolls* (New York: Simon and Schuster, 1957; 192 pp.). Based on the author's work in Hebrew, this volume records the part played by Eleazar L. Sukenik (Yadin's father) in recognizing, bargaining for, and obtaining some of the Scrolls.

Roland de Vaux, *L'Archéologie et les manuscrits de la Mer Morte* (Schweich Lectures, 1959; London: Oxford University Press, 1961; 107 pp., XXXVIII Pl.). The definitive account of excavations and the finds.

J. T. Milik, *Ten Years of Discovery in the Wilderness of Judaea* (Studies in Biblical Theology, No. 26, London: SCM, 1959; 160 pp.). A careful account of the discoveries and their significance by one of the scholars on the international team who has worked on the Scrolls from the beginning.

Géza Vermès, *Discovery in the Judean Desert* (New York: Desclée, 1956; 237 pp.). Written by a scholar expert in Hebraic and Judaic studies. Some of the texts are translated for the reader.

J. van der Ploeg, *Excavations at Qumran* (London: Longmans-Green, 1958; 233 pp.). The translated work of a Dutch scholar, accurate in its presentation.

John M. Allegro, *The People of the Dead Sea Scrolls in Text and Pictures*. (Garden City, N.Y.: Doubleday, 1958; 192 pp. including 182 pl.) The plates and their captions are excellent. Unfortunately, I cannot give the same high recommendation to the text.

David Noel Freedman and Jonas C. Greenfield, eds., *New Directions in Biblical Archaeology* (Garden City, N.Y.: Doubleday, 1971; 211 pp.). We note particularly the chapters on Qumran by F. M. Cross, R. G. Boling, P. W. Skehan, J. A. Sanders (Cave 11Q discoveries), and Y. Yadin (the Temple Scroll). D. N. Freedman has a chapter on "The Old Testament at Qumran," and F. V. Filson on "The Dead Sea Scrolls and the New Testament," that should be considered under "Discussions and Interpretations."

*Discussions and Interpretations*

Millar Burrows, *The Dead Sea Scrolls* (New York: Viking, 1955; 435 pp.); *More Light on the Dead Sea Scrolls* (Viking, 1958; 434 pp.). I still consider these two works to be the best all-around presentation of the Scrolls in the English language. Further, the only completely reliable translations of the Scrolls in English (in my opinion) are included at the end of each volume.

Frank M. Cross, Jr., *The Ancient Library of Qumran and Modern Biblical Studies* (Garden City, N.Y.: Doubleday, 1958; 196 pp.; rev. ed. 1961 [*Anchor Books*]; 260 pp.). A careful work by one of the foremost authorities on the Scrolls. The chapter on "The Old Testament at Qumran" is most important.

Frederick F. Bruce, *Second Thoughts on the Dead Sea Scrolls* (Grand Rapids, Mich.: Eerdmans, 1956; 143 pp.; 2nd ed. 1961; 160 pp.). A reliable introductory presentation.

André Dupont-Sommer, *The Essene Writings from Qumran* (Oxford: Basil Blackwell, 1961; 428 pp.). The results of twelve years of scholarship by this dynamic French scholar, translated into English by Vermès. All the relevant texts of Philo, Josephus, and Pliny the Elder, and all the Qumran texts known at the time of publication, are included. My reactions to the extreme views of Dupont-Sommer are scattered throughout the foregoing pages.

Krister Stendahl, ed., *The Scrolls and the New Testament* (New York: Harper, 1957; 308 pp.). A number of outstanding scholars had published important works in English, French, German, and Latin, on various aspects of the subject covered by the title. Professor Stendahl has made these available in English, in some cases with extensive revision to bring them up to date.

Jerome Murphy-O'Connor, *Paul and Qumran: Studies in New Testament Exegesis* (Chicago: Priory, 1968; 254 pp.). Important articles by several outstanding scholars; unfortunately, some of them, which had been previously printed, are relatively old and have not been updated.

H. H. Rowley, *The Dead Sea Scrolls and the New Testament* (London: S.P.C.K., 1957; 32 pp.). Professor Rowley was able to say in a paragraph what most of us take a page to say. Moreover, his documentation provides us with a full bibliography on any subject he treats. This small monograph is "must" reading.

————, *The Qumran Sect and Christian Origins* (reprinted from the *Bulletin of the John Rylands Library* 44 [1961-62], pp. 119-156); *The Teacher of Righteousness and the Dead Sea Scrolls* (reprinted from *ibid.* 40 [1957-58], pp. 114-146); *The History of the Qumran Sect* (reprinted from *ibid.* 49 [1966-67], pp. 203-232). These monographs, like the preceding entry, deserve careful reading. Professor Rowley avoids the extremes that many other scholars adopt.

Geoffrey Graystone, *The Dead Sea Scrolls and the Originality of Christ* (London: Sheed & Ward, 1956; 117 pp.). A splendid treatment of the subject by a qualified Catholic writer.

G. R. Driver, *The Judaean Scrolls. The Problem and a Solution* (Oxford: Blackwell, 1965; 624 pp.). For evaluation cf. p. 42 n. 15 above. This work, however, is not to be dismissed lightly.

Gert Jeremias, *Der Lehrer der Gerechtigkeit* (Göttingen: Vandenhoeck & Ruprecht, 1963; 376 pp.). A thorough work on the subject, with which I am not always in agreement.

Helmer Ringgren, *The Faith of Qumran* (Philadelphia: Fortress, 1963; 310 pp.). A systematic approach to the theology of the Qumranians.

W. H. Brownlee, *The Meaning of the Qumran Scrolls for the Bible* (New York: Oxford, 1964; 309 pp.). A cautious approach by a careful scholar, who has worked on the Scrolls from the first day they were known to the English-speaking world.

William Sanford LaSor, *Amazing Dead Sea Scrolls* (Chicago: Moody Press, 1956, rev. 1959; 251 pp.; a new printing, unfortunately not revised, has been planned for 1972). I endeavored to provide a reliable work for the intelligent layman, with full documentation for those interested in further study, and which was comparatively complete and conservative in approach. I believe it still meets that need.

Lucetta Mowry, *The Dead Sea Scrolls and the Early Church* (Chicago: University of Chicago, 1962; 260 pp.). Stimulating discussion of the subject.

Edmund F. Sutcliffe, *The Monks of Qumran as Depicted in the Dead Sea Scrolls* (London: Burns & Oates, 1960; 272 pp.). A very fine study of the Qumran Community.

Roland E. Murphy, *The Dead Sea Scrolls and the Bible* (Westminster, Md.: Newman, 1956; 119 pp.). Brief and direct, and commendable.

*Texts*

D. Barthélemy and J. T. Milik, *Discoveries in the Judaean Desert* (later vols. add *of Jordan*) (Oxford: Clarendon Press, 1955ff., 5 vols. to date). The definitive work on the texts and fragments.

A. M. Habermann, *m*ᵉ*gillôt midbar y*ᵉ*hûdā* [*The Scrolls from the Judean Wilderness*] (Tel Aviv: Machbaroth Lesifrut, 1959; 175 pp. + 20 pl. + XIV pp. of English summary). The Hebrew text of 1QpHab, 1QS, 1QM, 1QH, and most of the important fragments known at that date, plus a concordance. The texts have been edited and vowel points added.

Eduard Lohse, *Die Texte aus Qumran, Hebräisch und Deutsch, mit Masoretischer Punktation, Übersetzung, Einführung und Anmerkungen* (München: Kösel, 1964; 294 pp.). Somewhat more complete than Habermann.

### Periodicals

*Revue de Qumrân* (Paris: Letouzey et Ané, edited by Abbé Jean Carmignac and published approximately quarterly). Devoted entirely to the Dead Sea Scrolls and containing a continuing, complete bibliography of works on the Scrolls. For about six years it was my privilege to edit the *Bibliographie*.

*The Biblical Archaeologist* (New Haven, later Cambridge, Mass.: American Schools of Oriental Research, published quarterly, currently edited by E. F. Campbell, Jr.). The issues from Volume 11 (1948) and the following years, and occasionally even to the present, contain original reports of the discoveries, explorations, and some fragments.

*Bulletin of the American Schools of Oriental Research* (published quarterly at the same address as the *Biblical Archaeologist*). Issues from 1948 and the following years contain more detailed reports and technical discussions bearing on the Scrolls' discoveries.

*Revue Biblique* (Paris: J. Gabalda et Cie., published quarterly). The organ of *L'École pratique d'études bibliques* (*L'École biblique*), in Jerusalem, contains many of the preliminary reports of the archeologists and textual scholars working on the Scrolls. Many of the shorter texts and fragments were first published, translated, and discussed in *Revue Biblique*.

### Bibliographies

Christoph Burchard, *Bibliographie zu den Handschriften vom Toten Meer* (Berlin: Töpelmann, Vol. 1, 1957, 118 pp.; Vol. 2, 1965, 359 pp.). An exhaustive bibliography of practically all works on the Scrolls to the end of 1962 (Burchard counts 1,713 authors, 4,420 works, in 30 languages), listed by authors.

William Sanford LaSor, *Bibliography of the Dead Sea Scrolls 1948-1957* (Pasadena, Calif.: Fuller Theological Seminary, 1958; 92 pp.).

An almost-complete listing of all writings on the Scrolls in the first ten years, listed by subject.

B. Jongeling, *A Classified Bibliography of the Finds in the Desert of Judah 1958-1969* (Leiden: Brill, 1971; xiv + 140 pp.).

It is obvious that the above bibliography is not intended as a complete guide. I have omitted many splendid works. The bibliography is intended to assist the reader to get started in the Scrolls. Each work consulted will lead in turn to others, as will the footnotes scattered throughout the preceding pages.

# INDEX OF SUBJECTS

# INDEX OF AUTHORS

# INDEX OF REFERENCES